Nothing but Love in God's Water

Volume

1

Nothing but Love in God's Water

BLACK SACRED MUSIC FROM THE CIVIL WAR TO THE CIVIL RIGHTS MOVEMENT

ROBERT DARDEN

The Pennsylvania State University Press, University Park, Pennsylvania

Library of Congress Cataloging-in-Publication Data

Darden, Bob, 1954– , author.
Nothing but love in God's water / Robert Darden.
        volumes   cm
Summary: "The first of two volumes chronicling
the history and role of music in the African-
American experience. Explains the historical
significance of song and illustrates how music
influenced the Civil Rights Movement"—Provided
by publisher, Volume I.
Includes bibliographical references and index.
Contents: Volume I. Black sacred music from the
Civil War to the Civil Rights Movement.
ISBN 978-0-271-05084-3 (Volume I, cloth : alk.
paper)
1. African Americans—Music—History and
criticism.
2. Spirituals (Songs)—History and criticism.
3. Gospel music—History and criticism.
4. African Americans—Civil rights—History.
I. Title.

ML3556.D33 2014
780.89'96073—dc23
2014018652

Published by
The Pennsylvania State University Press,
University Park, PA 16802–1003

The Pennsylvania State University Press is
a member of the Association of American
University Presses.

It is the policy of The Pennsylvania State
University Press to use acid-free paper.
Publications on uncoated stock satisfy the
minimum requirements of American National
Standard for Information Sciences—Permanence
of Paper for Printed Library Material,
ANSI Z39.48–1992.

This book is printed on paper that contains 30%
post-consumer waste.

Dedicated to

Rep. John Lewis,

warrior and hero.

Contents

Preface

Denied access to the political process, limited in what they could acquire in the schools and dehumanized in popular culture, black Southerners were compelled to find other ways to express their deepest feelings and to demonstrate their individual and collective integrity. What helped to sustain them through bondage and a tortured freedom had been a rich oral expressive tradition consisting of folk beliefs, proverbs, humor, sermons, spirituals, gospel songs, hollers, work songs, blues and jazz.

—LEON LITWACK

I really did like the way you started off this meeting with song. It reminded me that when I was a youngster working in the logging camps of Western Washington, I'd come to Seattle occasionally and go down Skid Road to the Wobbly Hall, and our meetings there were started with a song. Song was the great thing that cemented the IWW together.

—HARVEY O'CONNOR

Just as I was beginning to write this book, pro-democracy uprisings in Tunisia, Egypt, and Libya erupted and spread across the Middle East. At the time, I had no idea where those spontaneous heart-cries for freedom would lead, but it made for a compelling—and eerily familiar—background from which to write. In the midst of this, I reread Zora Neale Hurston's chapter on High John de Conquer in *The Sanctified Church*:

> High John de Conquer came to be a man, and a mighty man at that. But he was not a natural man in the beginning. First off, he was a whisper, a will to hope, a wish to find something worthy of laughter and song. Then the whisper put on flesh. His footsteps sounded across the world in a low but musical rhythm as if the world he walked on was a singing-drum. Black people had an irresistible impulse to laugh. High John de Conquer was a man in full, and had come to live and work on the plantations, and all of the slave folks knew him in the flesh.
>
> The sign of this man was a laugh, and his singing-symbol was a drum. No parading drum-shout like soldiers out for show. It did not call to the feet of those who were fixed to hear it. It was an inside thing to live by. It was sure to be heard when and where the work was hardest, and the

lot the most cruel. It helped the slaves endure. They knew that something better was coming. So they laughed in the face of things and sang, "I'm so glad! Trouble don't last always." And the white people who heard them were struck dumb that they could laugh. In an outside way, this was Old Massa's fun, so what was Old Cuffy laughing for?

Old Massa couldn't know, of course, but High John de Conquer was there walking his plantation like a natural man.[1]

You never know how or when the threads of your lives intertwine. I have written three books in recent years and, upon reflection, I see that they are interrelated: *People Get Ready!: A New History of Black Gospel Music*; *Reluctant Prophets and Clueless Disciples: Understanding the Bible by Telling Its Stories*; and *Jesus Laughed: The Redemptive Power of Humor*. And now with the first volume of *Nothing but Love in God's Water, Black Sacred Music from the Civil War to the Civil Rights Movement*, I see where they all connect. They've all helped prepare me for this moment.

I wrote *People Get Ready* because gospel music has been part of my life. I wanted to know more about it, about how it all fits together. I wrote *Reluctant Prophets*, in part, because story is at the heart of everything I write and teach, fiction and nonfiction. Story was at the heart of *People Get Ready*. I wrote *Jesus Laughed* in part because of the visits Mary and I had made to black churches in the course of writing *People Get Ready*. Black churches resound with laughter before, during, and after the services in a way that the white churches I've attended do not. Where did we lose that capacity to laugh? I've written *Nothing but Love in God's Water* in part because of the ways black sacred song—from the spirituals through the union movements through the civil rights movement—has continued to irrepressibly bubble up and envelop black people at their times of greatest need . . . as if this music is always there, always available, always waiting for a moment like this.

And now I stumble across Zora Neale Hurston's essay on High John de Conquer, a magical, mythic black figure who predates John Henry and Stagger (or Stack-o) Lee. High John's weapons are laughter and song. And speed. High John is fast, as Hurston writes, "Maybe he was in Texas when the lash fell on a slave in Alabama, but before the blood was dry on the back, he was there. A faint pulsing of a drum like a goat-skin stretched over a heart, that came nearer and closer, then somebody in the saddened quarters would feel like laughing and say, 'Now High John de Conquer, Old Massa couldn't get the best of him. That old John was a case!' Then everybody began to smile."[2]

Back in the present, I'm astounded as *New York Times* reporters and BBC commentators remark time and time again at the speed with which the message—the story—of the youthful protestors spreads within their countries and across the Middle East. The social media have added new wings to the feet of High John, it seems.

Armed with that image, I see now that *Nothing but Love in God's Water* is ultimately about *story*—a story that came from Africa that sustained the slaves and their descendants for generations. It's about *song*—songs that came from Africa and enveloped the best of the Christian faith and withstood the dogs and water cannons in Birmingham. And it's about *laughter*—the laughter that came from Africa and enabled blacks in the Jim Crow south to secretly laugh at those who spent most of their waking moments trying to figure out ways to crush High John and the millions like him. It is no accident, Hurston writes, that High John de Conquer has evaded the ears of white people. They were not *supposed* to know. You can't know what folks won't tell you.

And so it is with *Nothing but Love in God's Water*. I tried to tease out from the songs and singers *how* this music helped them get over . . . about *what* this music provided that enabled them to challenge the most powerful nation on the planet . . . armed only with love, justice, and song. It's all there in those old spirituals and those unstoppable, irresistible gospel songs—the stories, the laughter, the music. It's important. John Lovell, Jr., the greatest expert on the spiritual, writes that the African-American slaves were the "largest homogenous group in a melting pot America." And, as Lovell added in 1939, referring to the African-American, "He analyzed and synthesized his life in his songs and sayings. In hundreds of songs called spirituals, he produced an epic cycle; and, as in every such instance, he concealed there his deepest thoughts and ideas, his hard-finished plans and hopes and dreams. The exploration of these songs for their social truths presents a tremendous problem. It must be done, for, as in the kernel of the *Iliad* lies the genius of the Greeks, so in the kernel of the spiritual lies the genius of the American Negro."[3]

Two years after I began writing, and many years after I started researching this vast and endlessly wonderful topic, I'm still seeing (and hearing) through a glass darkly. I do know this: If the freedom rebellions in Egypt and beyond are to survive and flourish, they will have their own version of High John, their own stories, songs, laughter . . . and prayer. Fortified with this knowledge, once again, I prayed for strength every day that I sat at my computer to do justice to that song, that laughter, that story.

The good news was that I didn't have to do this alone. I had a lot of help. Gavin Weightman's *Industrial Revolutionaries: The Making of the Modern World, 1776–1914*, tells the story of Abraham Gesner, who perfected the creation of illuminating and lubricating oils, a significant technological advancement that led to a host of *other* technological advancements. Late in life, Gesner wrote his own book, *A Practical Treatise on Coal, Petroleum, and Other Distilled Oils*, and made this intriguing statement: "The progress of discovery in this age, as in others, has been slow and gradual. It has been carried on by the labors not of one mind, but of many, so as to render it difficult to discover to whom the greatest credit is due."[4]

Acknowledgments

Nothing but Love in God's Water would not have been possible without the contributions of a massive number people, all of whom paved the way for me, some without knowing they did so. Even if I could list everybody, nobody would want to read the whole thing. Thank you all. These are but a few of those people and institutions that made this possible.

In the beginning, historians Taylor Branch and David Garrow both graciously spent much time with me before I began the serious research into what would become this book. Both gave me invaluable tips, contacts, suggestions, advice, and—perhaps most important—encouragement to pursue this path.

I must also thank the following:

Dr. Elizabeth Davis, Provost, Baylor University
Dr. Lee Nordt, Dean of Arts and Sciences, Baylor University
Department of Journalism, Public Relations and New Media, Baylor
    University
Centennial Professor Committee, Baylor University
Moody Library, Baylor University
Interlibrary Loan, Moody Library, Baylor University
Institute for Oral History, Baylor University
Black Gospel Music Restoration Project, Baylor University
Seventh & James Baptist Church, Waco, Texas
Birmingham Public Library, Department of Archives and Manuscripts
Birmingham Civil Rights Institute
University of Memphis Library, Special Collections/Mississippi Valley
    Collection
Center for Black Music Research, Columbia College, Chicago
American Gospel Quartet Convention

Thanks to Jim Barcus, Doug Ferdon, Bob Friedman, Casey Graham, Terry Gross, Bill Hair, Carol Hobbs, Janet Jasek, Rev. Dr. Stanley Keeble, Margaret Kramer, Tim Logan, Jan Loosier, Billie Lugo-Peterson, Bob Marovich, Pattie Orr, Ella Pritchard, Denyse Rodgers, Charles Royce, Becky Shulda, George W. Stewart, Sara Stone,

Darryl Stuhr, Tony Tadey, and David Wallace, as well as to Horace Boyer, Ray Funk, Anthony Heilbut, John Lovell, Jr., and Jerry Zolten, and John Kutsko and Robert A. Ratcliff for the initial idea and early support.

Thanks to Rachel Payne, Katie Buchanan Spitaletto, Ryan Pierce, Zhang Fang-fang, Yan Shi, Yueqin Yang, Lian Qiu, and Kelsey Prenger.

To my late parents, Col. Robert F. Darden, Jr. (USAF Ret.), and JoAnn Darden, who were always so supportive of both me and this project; and to my family, Dan, Ashley, Rhett, Mark, Rachel, Asa, Eilan, and Van.

Special thanks to my preternaturally patient and loving wife, Dr. Mary Landon Darden, for her insight, laughter, editing skills, adventurous spirit, and critical eye.

INTRODUCTION

The Beginnings of a Singing Movement

It is important to recognize here at the very beginning that the Movement . . . was larger, more inclusive, more revolutionary than the misnamed and misinterpreted "civil rights movement." Contrary to the pablum we read in media and in textbooks, the Movement was a national phenomenon, which anticipated and paved the way for the millions of people singing "We Shall Overcome" in the freedom movements sweeping through Eastern Europe and Southern Africa. All Americans, in fact, are indebted to the men, women, and little children who broke into American history like beneficent burglars, bringing with them the gifts of vision, passion, and truth.

And a case can be made and ought to be made that the Movement freed more white people than Black people.

—LERONE BENNETT, JR.

Did the civil rights movement begin with the Montgomery bus boycott, the Emancipation Proclamation, or when the first slave said "no" or slowed down in the work assigned? And did it end with the death of Martin Luther King, Jr.? It is clear that beginnings and endings are determined by the critic's perceptions and ability to get others to agree to those perceptions.

—MALCOLM O. SILLARS

When does something become a movement? What if it always was a movement, long before there were words to name it? In fact, what if *movement* is not the best way to describe what has happened—and, in some cases, what is continuing to happen? In the case of the civil rights movement, perhaps it is better described as a "continuous, irresistible action," an action that began the moment Africans were enslaved, forcefully brought across the Middle Passage, and bludgeoned into a lifetime sentence of enslavement with only the barest possibility of manumission, a servitude nearly unparalleled in human history for its brutality and inhumanity.

From the very beginning, when the first Africans were torn from their native lands and brought in chains to the Americas, they desired freedom. The records show that the slaves did more than just desire freedom; they employed every means possible to achieve that end. On the slaving ships of the Atlantic Ocean, despairing Africans took their own lives, tried repeatedly to escape, rose in rebellion, and committed infanticide rather than face slavery. Once in the Americas, slaves continued their desperate efforts to be free, employing violence and nonviolence, stealth and brazen action, spoken and written pleas. Those who covertly learned to read and write wrote passionately, arguing the unholiness of their fate. They escaped. They escaped and were caught and then escaped again. They prayed, first to the African gods they left behind and ultimately to the God of Christianity. At great personal cost, they made the exploitation of their forced labor increasingly more expensive. That ongoing, never-ending action was an unrelenting fight for freedom.[1]

And they did one other thing. They sang. By every known account, the Africans of a dozen nations and people groups arrived in the Americas singing and continued to sing. They sang because they sang in Africa and singing was an inextricable, irreducible part of their lives and souls. While scholars say there were significant cultural differences among the Songhai, Akan, Yoruba, Ibo, Wolof, Oyo, Asante, and all the people groups taken into slavery, the music they sang bore remarkable similarities. And singing, like dancing, was central to their lives. The very best guess by the very best scholars in the field is that long before Africans knew of Christianity, even as they became African-American slaves, they sang.[2]

At the time of the slave trade, singing was virtually continual in Africa. The lyrics Africans sang concerned every facet of their lives, of events hundreds of years ago, of the mundane tasks of daily life, of the glories of their natural world.[3] The physical and spiritual worlds were interchangeable—all songs were sacred, all songs were profane, all were important.[4] And if the goal of African music "has always been to translate the experiences of life and of the spiritual worlds into sound, enhancing and celebrating life," as Samuel A. Floyd writes,[5] then how could the continually resisting African-American slave *not* sing of a loss as elemental as freedom?

Not surprisingly, with singing being such an integral part of their lives, the words African-American slaves sang, the concepts they expressed, were often complex, with multiple layers of meaning. Centuries later, Henry Louis Gates, Jr., would dub this "double-voicedness" as "signifyin'"—a special language to convey meaning available only to those listeners who knew the hidden contextual keys and language.[6] Other scholars have shown how this trait was apparent both in Africa at the time of the slave trade and continues on the continent to this day.[7] This "shadow language" would become an essential part of African-American life, a buffer between the worlds of whites and blacks, a weapon that plays its part in that ever-present, ongoing quest for freedom.

As a means of establishing what they believed was absolute control, slave owners in North America, especially in what would become the southern United States, successfully destroyed the shared heritage, religion, customs, and language of their slaves, systematically separating and dispersing new arrivals from various African tribal peoples to other plantations. Within a short generation or two, few memories of physical Africa remained.[8] Rarely has this much effort gone into obliterating a conquered people's social, spiritual, and cultural identity. Only their music remained: "Now, no slave ever has any rights: personal, family, property, time, privacy, freedom of motion, freedom of opinion nor freedom of the physical body. That is the symbolism of the chains. But the only thing that cannot be chained is human thought unexpressed. So if you do not want your slave to speak freely you should also forbid him to sing—even without words. The human voice in speech only releases the thought; in singing, the same voice gives it wings."[9]

The slaveholders did not destroy the slaves' music. It was too firmly entrenched in all of Africa's children, too potent, too much a part of their DNA to ever fully eradicate. Of course, the slaves made it difficult for the owners to forbid singing. Very early in their enslavement, African-American slaves convinced their overseers that they better accomplished their backbreaking work if they were allowed to sing their "nonsense" songs. Short of actual physical confrontation or escape, these songs may have been the first nonviolent protest of an enslaved people. The songs helped the myths and memories survive—the stories of the forebears of Monkey, Rabbit, High John de Conquer, Stagger (or Stack-O) Lee, John Henry, and the rest. Apparently the slave owners paid them little mind, for they flourished.

Another critical factor was the introduction of the white man's religion, Christianity, to a people who had, for the most part, been forcibly separated from their gods. The spread of the Christian faith among African-Americans was a slow and torturous process, one hindered by the absence of a faith among many of the plantation owners themselves. After all, the teachings of Jesus systematically eliminated distinctions among believers, and few slaveholders were willing to admit that the creatures they despised were also human. Christianity did eventually filter out to the slaves, particularly following the Second Great Awakening in the United States. While the slaveholders sought to minimize the damage by obsessively focusing on the Bible verses that emphasized unquestioning slave obedience,[10] slaves eventually cobbled together a very real version of the faith, one with remarkable similarities of first-century C.E. Christianity.[11]

And with the introduction of Christianity to the slaves, they added the heroic stories of Moses, Daniel, and Jesus, heroes who led their people from physical and spiritual bondage to freedom. It was to these iconic figures that later freedom fighters like Harriet Tubman (fig. 1) and Martin Luther King, Jr., looked to inspire and encourage an enslaved people to act.

If the spiritual is such a catalyst, what did it sound like? Scholars like Dena J. Epstein and John Lovell, Jr., spent decades meticulously combing through fragmentary antebellum records to answer that question (and many others). Stripping away the racist stereotyping, the comments by listeners without a background in music composition or theory, and the utter disinterest most southern slave owners held in the lives of their charges, Epstein and Lovell establish a sense of what the original spirituals must have sounded like.[12] When combined with the early recordings of isolated churches in the Deep South made by John and Alan Lomax for the Library of Congress, a fuller aural soundscape emerges.[13]

William Francis Allen, Charles Pickard Ware, and Lucy McKim Garrison also tried to describe the music in the days before recording devices in their seminal book *Slave Songs of the United States*. Allen and Garrison were both musicians and, even in the midst of the project, Ware admitted his difficulties in accurately capturing what the collectors had heard being sung, and said that he was driven to "despair" in trying to convey the "effect" of group-singing among the slaves. Other white writers of that era used words like "unearthly," "wild," and "weird" to describe slave song melodies. The authors cite a pre–Civil War article by W. H. Russell of the *London Times*, who described the music this way:

> The oarsmen, as they bent to their task, beguiled the way by singing in unison a real negro melody, which was unlike the works of the Ethiopian Serenaders as anything in song could be unlike another. It was a barbaric sort of madrigal, in which one singer beginning was followed by the others in unison, repeating the refrain in chorus, and full of quaint expression and melancholy:
> "Oh your soul! Oh my soul! I'm going to the churchyard
>   To lay this body down;
> Oh my soul! Oh your soul! We're going to the churchyard
>   To lay this nigger down."[14]

Russell's description does address, at least briefly, how the music was usually sung. Whether in a church, hidden brush arbor meeting, slave quarters on the edge of the plantation, or in a work-related setting (rowing, hoeing, harvesting, shucking), the spirituals were usually performed in a call-and-response interaction, the opening line or couplet shouted by someone in the group, the response sung in return.

The music itself, as compiled from the various sources, is described as being composed of rich, otherworldly melodies with notes that often did not fall within the western European pentatonic scale (the "blue notes," or flatted sevenths, gapped scales, and ambiguous thirds). The music and accompanying words appeared to have been improvised on the spot, changing constantly until there is today no definitive version of any spiritual—only what the (mostly white) compilers hastily captured as a snapshot of a single performance.

Other distinctive elements: The musical accompaniment to the words of the spirituals always left room for ample improvisation. There was frequent repetition of both the melody lines and the words, particularly in the first two phrases. There was the tendency, according to the accounts, for the spirituals to be accompanied by movement. And there was a constant, undying love of rhythm, poly-rhythm, and counter-rhythm, a powerful survival from Africa that molds and directs black music in the West even today.[15] One former slave once wrote of the sacred music experiences of his childhood:

> The colored people . . . have a peculiar music of their own, which is largely a process of rhythm, rather than written music. There is largely, or was . . . a sort of rhythmical chant. It had to do largely with religion and the words adopted to their quaint melodies were largely of a religious nature. The stories of the Bible were placed into words that would fit the music already used by the colored people. While singing these songs, the singers and the entire congregation kept time to the music by the swaying of their bodies or by the patting of the foot or hand. Practically all of the songs were accompanied by a motion of some kind . . . the weird and mysterious music of the religious ceremonies moved old and young alike in a frenzy of religious fervor.[16]

The pieces were all in place. We have a resourceful, courageous, freedom-loving people with a heritage of music and story. And we have a religion that united this people in their centuries-long quest to wrest freedom from their oppressors.

In short, at that moment, we have a *movement*.

Unlike all the other peoples that entered the New World, the Black man was forcibly brought there against his will, to serve other men's material needs. When, in 1619, John Rolfe, the tobacco king of Virginia, spoke of the ship that brought the first Blacks to the shores of America, he declared, "The ship brought not anything but 20 and odd negroes." Little did he know that inside the hold of that vessel were the dynamics that were to change the whole American panorama. In that ship were the seeds of the Spirituals, the Denmark Veseys, Nat Turners, the Frederick Douglasses, the Civil War, the Gettysburg Address, the seeds of the blues and jazz and the spirit of the Harlem Renaissance—in a word—"soul."

—LEONARD E. BARRETT

1

THE ORIGINS AND SETTINGS
OF THE SPIRITUALS

The songs are indeed the siftings of centuries; the music is far more ancient than the words, and in it we can trace here and there signs of development. My grandfather's grandmother was seized by an evil Dutch trader two centuries ago; and coming to the valleys of the Hudson and Housatonic, black, little, and lithe, she shivered and shrank in the harsh north winds, looked longingly at the hills, and often crooned a heathen melody to the child between her knees.

—W. E. B. DU BOIS

The old songs are in our collective consciousness, perhaps even in our genes. They are our spiritual chromosomes. They make us who we are as a people.

—GLORIA SCOTT

What percentage—if any—of the spirituals were related to the African-Americans' desire to shake off the bondage of slavery? This is one of several questions involving the spiritual that ignited wide-ranging academic debate. At one extreme were the writers from the 1930s and '40s who believed that African-Americans "borrowed" the music and lyrics of spirituals from white sources—implying, of course, that it would be unlikely that the lyrics contained sophisticated hidden messages.[1] At the other extreme, some scholars asserted that most spirituals were not actually concerned with religious matters, but were instead devoted almost exclusively to freedom—most specifically, freedom in Canada or Africa.[2]

Modern scholarship now decisively attributes the composition of the spirituals to the unnamed slave composers (and, later, freed slaves), who primarily based their creations on African melody forms, and supports the notion that many of the spirituals—perhaps more than we will ever know—contained coded messages designed for an audience eager to find a way out of slavery.[3] In fact, Bernice Johnson Reagon cautions that so "powerful are the metaphorical and connotative interpretations" of the spirituals that separating them from those messages "castrates the songs."[4]

Epstein's research meticulously details every known printed reference to black sacred music in hundreds of newspapers, journals, books, and official records in the years leading up to the Civil War. There are tantalizing hints scattered throughout the record as to what might have been the first mention of spirituals or "sperichils," as the authors of *Slave Songs of the United States* and others called them.[5] Because the widespread opposition to introducing Christianity to slaves continued into the 1800s, it is not surprising that only a few dismissive mentions of original religious music among the slaves survives, when there is any mention at all. Some, but not all, of the more sympathetic observers of the day were careful to differentiate between "hymns" (religious songs the white listener knew) and the "extravagant and nonsensical chants" of the slaves' own devising. A critic in 1818 bemoaned the presence of "hymns . . . most frequently composed and first sung by the illiterate blacks of the society," and Epstein writes that this could be the first known reference ("short scraps of disjointed affirmations . . . with long repetition choruses") to what would become known as "Negro spirituals."[6] Whatever the name, something like the spiritual was clearly spreading throughout the United States by that time. And while the name "spiritual" would not be widely known (or accepted) until the early days of the American Civil War, forces that heightened its ultimate impact in both the black and white communities were gathering strength in the first half of the nineteenth century.

Obviously, for a spiritual to be a spiritual and not a work song, it must have a religious foundation. The slow spread and rise of Christianity among slaves finally picked up momentum in the early years of the nineteenth century. The hidden brush arbor services continued out of necessity on some plantations, while on others, the rudimentary services were conducted by white preachers of the slave owners' own choosing and attendance was compulsory. But at night, those slaves would often reconvene and testify to a Jesus who did not endorse slavery, and sing to a Moses who led his people to freedom.[7]

Whether through a clandestine operation fueled by the slave "grapevine" or through an officially sanctioned denomination, the Christian faith came, in time, to permeate the lives of the slaves. Christianity gave solace and hope to the slaves; their surviving writings and diaries are filled with praise for their faith and their God: "The old meeting house caught on fire. The spirit was there. Every heart was beating in unison as we turned our minds to God to tell Him of our sorrows here below. God saw our need and came to us. I used to wonder what made people shout but now I don't. There is a joy on the inside and it wells up so strong that we can't keep still. It is fire in the bones. Any time that fire touches a man, he will jump."[8]

And because their faith was so important, the study of the impact of the spirituals on the freedom movement is a difficult undertaking. How can you quantify something that cannot be explained in rational terms? It is much easier to focus on the politics or the economics or the sociology of the slave system than to unravel the mysteries of faith. Still, as many of the spirituals quite explicitly proclaim, belief was one of the few joyful aspects in the otherwise short, brutal life of a slave: "O walk Jordan long road, And religion so sweet / O religion is good for anyt'ing, And religion so sweet / Religion make you happy, And religion so sweet."[9]

But the presence of common religion gave the slaves more than just happiness and patience and the promise of heaven. Regardless of the original religious denomination, a common slave religion (what Raboteau calls the "invisible institution") spread throughout the antebellum South in the late eighteenth and early nineteenth centuries. The advent of Christianity and the concurrent rise of the spiritual had to result in the same outcome, for the "fundamental theme" of both is the same—"the need for a change in the existing order." Virtually all forms of creative expression, save singing, were forbidden of slaves. Once Christianity became tolerated on the plantations, religious singing became "the chief field of their expression"—not just religious expression, not just creative expression, but all expression. The fundamental theme of change that "pervades" the spiritual, Lovell says, is equally fundamental to biblical Christianity. Only now the slave had a means to voice it.[10]

Now connected by a common form of expression, something as radical as "change to the existing order" could thus be shared from slave to slave, plantation to plantation, town to town, state to state. And it could be accomplished by the "slave poets" (Lovell's term) within earshot of the cruelest overseer, using the "undercurrent symbolism" of Christianity. Symbolism, of course, is essential for all kinds of poetry, and it provides both a creative outlet and a protective covering for poets who need to express unpopular truths. In short, when a common religious term like "heaven" can mean both the ultimate destination of believers and the free lands north of the Ohio River, and can be sung with impunity in front of a slave owner, then "the Christian religion was made to order for the slave poet."[11]

Another "gift" in the widespread adoption of Christianity was the repeated message of the New Testament concerning the worth and value of all humans, including slaves. No matter how many times "ministers" paid by the plantation owners preached the same verse over and over ("Servant obey your master"), it was passages from the Book of Luke that resonated most with the slave: "He has sent me to proclaim release to the captives and recovery of sight to the blind, to let the oppressed go free" (4:17–19). The battle between the two versions of the same Gospel was an unequal contest—slaves had learned from their first days in the

Americas not to trust their masters. James H. Cone quotes from a writer who openly despairs at the way slave owners had turned their slaves against the "white man's" version of Christianity: "I have seen colored men at the church door, scoffing at the ministers, while they were preaching and saying, you had better go home, and set your slaves free. A few nights ago . . . a runaway slave came to the house where I live for safety and succor. I asked him if he were a Christian; 'no sir,' said he, 'white men treat us so bad in Mississippi that we can't be Christians.'"[12]

Even so, the slave religion eventually found almost universal acceptance in the South. It just was not the same Christianity practiced (or *not* practiced) by their owners. By the early 1800s, most slaves in the United States were native born, with no direct memories or experiences of Africa or their African religions, which meant that even the opposition to Christianity among slaves was nearly gone. Not that Christianity ever wholly eradicated the many gifts of Africa, of course: "Nevertheless, even as the gods of Africa gave way to the God of Christianity, the African heritage of singing, dancing, spirit possession, and magic continued to influence Afro-American spirituals, ring shouts and folk beliefs. That this was so is evidence of the slaves' ability not only to adapt to new contexts but to do so creatively."[13]

This new slave religion took the best of what the Christian faith offered and discarded the rest. This is an important step, however long it took and wherever it took place. Throughout the history of Christianity, the God of the rich, the powerful, the oppressor, is not the same as the God of the poor, the weak, the oppressed. The slave quickly saw through this dichotomy, noting the presence "by definition" of "two different religions and . . . two different gods." To Jeremiah Wright, "the God of Africans in diaspora is consistent with the God of the Bible who enters into history on the side of the oppressed . . . fighting the cause of the slaves and the descendants of slaves."[14]

As mentioned earlier, the belief expressed repeatedly in the teachings of Jesus Christ that every human mattered, that every human being was precious in God's eyes, was crucial to the slave: "Consider the ravens: they neither sow nor reap, they have neither storehouse nor barn, and yet God feeds them. Of how much more value are you than the birds!" (Lk. 12:24). Slaves found potent ammunition in sacred texts proclaiming that "there is no longer slave or free, there is no longer male and female" (Gal. 3:28 [NIV]).

If the slave is taught and comes to believe that he is a human being, someone worthy of love, despite all his master's teachings and beatings to the contrary, then that slave has the potential to be an agent of change. Lovell's argument to that effect is built, in part, on the texts of the surviving spirituals themselves. Consider, he writes, the following verses: "All my troubles will soon be over with / Soon be over with, soon be over with / All my troubles will soon be over with / All over this world." Thus, if the slave poet genuinely believes those words, they really only offer him one of two choices: either he will die and go to a glorious, joy-filled heaven where Jesus will be waiting for him, or the current world will change. Since death is never mentioned in the spiritual, then the slave must believe in a coming transformation of the existing order, something that is echoed in both the Mosaic and Messianic texts in the Bible.[15] For someone living in intolerable conditions, it is a short step from believing for the first time that the world will change to becoming an active participant in effecting that change.

Lovell takes the argument a step further by citing a second spiritual, "I'm so glad trouble don't last always / Hallelujah, I'm so glad trouble don't last always." Here the words indicate that not only is the unnamed poet self-aware enough to *know* that slavery is not the natural order of things, but that the "hallelujah" indicates that the poet believes that change *is* coming—and soon.[16] Slavery, in fact, in Christian parlance, was a "sin" to many slaves—a grievous error in the natural order and not pleasing in God's sight. After examining many, many slave narratives, Stephen Butterfield concludes that the great majority of slaves did indeed believe slavery to be a sin and something to be resisted.[17] Or, as a fugitive slave wrote before the Civil War, "We believe slavery to be a sin—always, everywhere, and only sin."[18]

In 1850, Frederick Douglass, himself a former slave, wrote unequivocally that "slavery is alike the sin and the shame of the American people."[19] Once slaves embraced Christianity, their "aggressive and subversive behaviors" against slavery were "justifiable retaliatory actions as long as they were directed against the masters," because slavery itself was a sin and an affront to God. They were "justified in fighting the evil system" and would thus help pave the way for a "deliverer–hero."[20]

Knowing another human is sinning against God (and the natural order of things) places the one who has that knowledge in a much different position than before, a position of moral authority—even if one is a virtually powerless slave amid yet another senseless whipping. It is yet another justification for resistance against that sin, however, and whatever form that resistance takes. That knowledge is, in many ways, empowering: "The religion practiced in the quarters gave the slaves the one thing they absolutely had to have if they were to resist being transformed into the Sambos they had been programmed to become. It fired them with a sense of their own worth before God and man. It enabled them to prove to themselves, and to a world that never ceased to need reminding, that no man's will can become that of another unless he himself wills it—that the ideal of slavery cannot be realized, no matter how badly the body is broken and the spirit tormented."[21]

Another component in the slaves' multifront war on slavery was also being created and assembled in the years before the Civil War. The use of satiric songs was well established in the original American colonies. Before they became citizens of the United States of America, colonists made fun of their absentee British landlords with songs like "Yankee Doodle" and others often adapted from familiar (and sometimes religious) English airs and songs.[22]

But the use of religious music for a transformative purpose was less common, at least until the rise of the abolitionist movement. The country's first issue-oriented popular singing group, the Hutchinson Family Singers, became something of a sensation in the 1840s. Ardent abolitionists, the Hutchinsons were greeted by large crowds wherever they toured, particularly in New England.[23] Originally comprising four brothers (one brother was later replaced by their sister, Abby), the group sang popular songs, arranged hymns, original compositions, and spirituals (including "Reign Oh Reign, Massa Jesus Reign!") in their intricate four-part harmonies.[24] The Hutchinsons eventually supported the temperance movement and women's suffrage as well. In later years, Abby Hutchinson Patton even traveled to Florida to collect spirituals for a book.[25] The popularity of the Hutchinson Family Singers may have helped, at least in some small part, to raise the public's awareness of the possibility of sacred music with a secular message and thus pave the way for the publication and acceptance of African-American spirituals in the early 1860s. The publication of the Hutchinson Family sheet music and, later, the publication of the spirituals, spread this message throughout the United States, enabling parts of the country where slavery was illegal and spirituals virtually nonexistent to hear it.

This occurred at a time when there was a growing acceptance of religious music being used for purposes other than evangelical. It could be used in a transformative way, a change that was made possible by the perception that there could be a shift in the existing order. The Hutchinson Family Singers were part of a larger circle of influential writers, religious leaders, artists, poets, and politicians, including Frederick Douglass, John Greenleaf Whittier, William Lloyd Garrison, Thomas Wentworth Higginson, Lowell Mason, and others who supported the abolitionist cause. Some (Higginson and Garrison) were members of the new Unitarian–Transcendentalist movement, a "theosophy" that very early embraced the African-American spirituals as legitimate sacred musical expression. Jon Cruz argues that a unique set of historical, cultural, and religious forces converged in the decades just before the Civil War to give the spiritual its greatest exposure and potency as a transformative agent. In fact, black and white abolitionists joined together to not just bring the spiritual into the (white) public's view for the first time, but also to "set into motion a form of cultural interpretation that was contextually unique and also symptomatically modern. This orientation hinged on interpreters comprehending and making use of black song while bringing a new focus upon the cultural and racial margins within American society."[26]

The spirituals had always been there, challenging and encouraging African-American slaves. When they were finally made public, those songs had the potential to transform white listeners as well. This was an important sea change in sensibilities, especially since—to most Americans—if they knew the term "spiritual" at all, they associated it with the grossly sentimental and often racist religious ditties usually written by white composers (including Stephen Foster) and sung at the end of "blackface" minstrel shows, the dominant form of popular entertainment of the era.[27] Or, as Du Bois notes, in the estimation of the most rabidly racist Americans of the day, "Nothing—nothing that black folk did or said or thought or sang was sacred."[28]

The War Between the States commenced with the assault on Fort Sumter in South Carolina on April 14, 1861. Within weeks, fugitive slaves sought asylum with Union forces, particularly at Fort Monroe, overlooking the entrance to Chesapeake

Bay. Immediately, indignant slave owners demanded the return of their slaves. But General Benjamin Butler, who commanded the fort, denied their request, terming the slaves "contraband of war." The term was adopted by the northern abolitionist movement and became a national catchphrase.[29] It also swept through the South, but via what Booker T. Washington called the slave "grape-vine," whereby all news was passed quickly from plantation to plantation, often at such a speed that slaves knew of Union victories on the field before southern newspapers did.[30] As a result, the trickle of slaves seeking refuge at Fort Monroe and elsewhere soon turned into a flood. Before long, the contrabands were visited by relief workers, teachers, missionaries, writers, and musicians, the next crucial step in the evolution of black sacred music as a means of effecting political change.

Among the initial civilian visitors to Fort Monroe was the Reverend Lewis C. Lockwood, a young employee of the YMCA who was sent by the American Missionary Association to "investigate" conditions among the contrabands. Lockwood arrived on September 3, 1861, and heard spirituals sung on his very first day at a prayer meeting where a lay preacher delivered an impassioned prayer asking that the God who "brought Israel out of Egypt, Jonah out of the mouth of the whale, and Daniel out of the den of lions" would deliver the slaves "spiritually and temporally." Lockwood then told those gathered of his mission and the audience of freed slaves responded with "deep, half-uttered expressions of gladness and gratitude." Then they sang, and Lockwood jotted down the words, "Go down to Egypt—tell Pharaoh / Thus saith my servant, Moses / Let my people go." Lockwood noted that the singers sang with an "accent on the last syllable, with repetition of the chorus." To Lockwood, the style of singing caused the words "every hour to ring like a warning note in the ear of despotism." His account of what he saw and heard that night was printed in the *National Anti-Slavery Standard* on October 12, 1861. Epstein believes that this was the first published report of "Go Down, Moses,"[31] one of the most significant spirituals of all time.

Newspaper dispatches like those written by Lockwood and other reporters and observers soon became a popular feature in virtually all northern newspapers and magazines and served to further the cause of the abolitionists. Lockwood sent the full text of the spiritual to the secretary of the sponsoring YMCA in New York, who then forwarded it to a reporter at the *New York Tribune*. The words were reprinted again in the *National Anti-Slavery Standard* on December 21, 1861. Epstein notes that only three of the twenty stanzas in Lockwood's original account were published, and an editor at one of the two publications apparently reworked the words into standard English. Nonetheless, the power of the lines is undeniable, even in their "sanitized" form:

> *When Israel was in Egypt's land,*
> *O let my people go!*
> *Oppressed so hard they could not stand,*
> *O let my people go!*

O go down, Moses,
Away down to Egypt's land,
And tell King Pharaoh
To let my people go!

Thus saith the Lord, bold Moses said
O let my people go!
If not I'll smite your first-born dead
O let my people go!

No more shall they in bondage toil,
O let my people go!
Let them come out with Egypt's spoil,
O let my people go![32]

The popularity of the spiritual was such that a publisher quickly scrambled to provide sheet music, although the music bore little resemblance to an actual spiritual. For Epstein, the "social forces unleashed by the war led directly to the emergence of the Negro spiritual."[33] Other print versions of spirituals followed, but given the power of "Go Down, Moses" over the next century, it would be appropriate that this was the first to see print.

Recognition of the possible "double-voicedness" of the spirituals was slow in coming, however. A perceptive newspaper reporter with the *New York Evening Post* wrote a dispatch from the Port Royal schools on March 25, 1863, and it was published a little more than a month later in the *National Anti-Slavery Standard*:

One song, sung with peculiar force and unction, had for refrain an aspiration for liberty which not even the masters, probably, ventured to check. I remember but two lines:
   I'll follow Jesus's way, No man can hinder me!
   I'll do what Jesus says, No man can hinder me![34]

Another pivotal event in the dissemination of the spiritual was a letter by Lucy McKim (later Garrison) published in the influential *Dwight's Journal of Music* on November 1, 1863. McKim was a remarkable young woman, a Harvard graduate at a time when that was a novelty, and one of the few trained musicians among the many collectors of spirituals in the Civil War era. She came from a family of well-known abolitionists and possessed a rare sensitivity to the music of the contrabands. She joined her father, James Miller McKim, at the contraband settlement on Port Royal Island in June 1862. (Shortly after the war, she married Wendell Phillips Garrison, third son of the noted abolitionist and writer William Lloyd Garrison.) It was at Port Royal that she heard the spirituals sung. Though Garrison was only nineteen at the time, her letter was the first to contain a truly accurate depiction of spirituals. Shortly thereafter, she oversaw the publication of two of those spirituals as sheet music—"Poor Rosy, Poor Gal" and "Roll Jordan, Roll." Epstein believes that this may well be the first genuine attempt to capture in standard western European notation the music itself and to make that music available to the general public.[35]

While Garrison's sympathetic treatment apparently generated only a modest amount of conversation at the time, an article in the influential *Continental Monthly* in August 1863 did attract widespread attention. "Under the Palmetto" was written by Unitarian minister Henry George Spaulding, another visitor to Port Royal in early 1863. Spaulding's article included the melodies (which he may have transcribed himself) and at least partial texts to five songs: "O Lord, Remember Me," "Hold Your Light," "Dar's a Meetin' Here To-night," "Done wid Dribers Dribin'," and "O Brudder William, You Want to Get Religion." Spaulding's descriptions of the music and aspirations of the contrabands were both accurate and sympathetic to the slaves' plight.[36]

Perhaps the most compelling article of all, "Negro Spirituals," was published in the *Atlantic Monthly* on June 7, 1867, written by Col. Thomas Wentworth Higginson, another fascinating individual. He fought to overturn and undermine the Fugitive Slave Act in 1850 (including at least one attempt to free a runaway slave being held in a Boston jail, awaiting return to the South). As a leader of the World's Temperance Conference, he admonished leaders who refused to include women in the leadership or speaking schedules. He traveled to Kansas in 1856 to fight the expansion of slavery into the state and financially supported John Brown in 1859. And during the Civil War, he commanded the first all-volunteer, all-black regiment. A graduate of Harvard Divinity School, he was, as noted above, a Unitarian and a supporter of Transcendentalism (although more politically active than most Transcendentalists) as well as an early advocate of the Hampton Institute. Higginson was much lauded in his lifetime (one of his most vocal admirers was W. E. B. Du Bois), and both the article and a later book-length expanded version, *Army Life in a Black Regiment, and Other Writings*, published in 1870, reached an unprecedented audience.[37]

Higginson's affection for the men of the 1st Regiment, South Carolina Volunteers is obvious. He notes that the volunteers from South Carolina, Georgia, and Florida each arrived with different spirituals, which "have nothing but the generic character in common, until all were mingled in the united stock of campmelodies." Sitting or standing in the darkness outside the campfires each evening, Higginson would discreetly jot down the words of the spirituals as best he could. He states that the most popular song among the Volunteers—sung twice as often as any other—was always accompanied by "the clatter of many feet" and rhythmic hand clapping:

> *Hold your light, Brudder Robert,*
>   *Hold your light,*
>   *Hold your light on Canaan's shore.*

What makes ole Satan for to follow me so?
Satan ain't got notin' for do wid me.
    Hold your light,
    Hold your light,
    Hold your light on Canaan's shore.

With each new chorus, the name of one of the former slaves present would be inserted.[38] Many of the lyrics that Higginson lists are notable for the implied (and sometimes overt) allusions to escaping to freedom, as these examples from the article illustrate:

"BOUND TO GO"
    Jordan River, I'm bound to go,
    Bound to go, bound to go,
    Jordan River, I'm bound to go,
    And bid 'em fare ye well.

    O, my mudder is gone! My mudder is gone!
    My mudder is gone into heaven, my Lord!
    I can't stay behind!

"ROOM IN THERE"
    Dere's room in dar, room in dar,
    Room in dar, in de heaven, my Lord!
    I can't stay behind.

"HAIL MARY"
    One more valiant soldier here
    O help me bear de cross.

On "Hail Mary," Higginson speculates that prior to arriving in camp as free men, the singers may have wisely substituted "soul" for "soldier" during their time in slavery. Higginson's reconstruction of the lyrics is accompanied by sensitive commentary as he presents spiritual after spiritual in the context of the camp. He also makes clear distinctions between what he believes are "original" spirituals and the three songs he believes were based on "an old camp-meeting melody," although he admits that he "cannot find them in the Methodist hymn-books."[39]

The article contains an unprecedented (for the time) listing of hitherto unknown spirituals and their words, and Higginson unequivocally writes that the spirituals had more than more one function:

Some of the songs had played an historic part during the war. For singing the next song, for instance, the negroes had been put in jail in

Georgetown, S.C., at the outbreak of the Rebellion. "We'll soon be free," was too dangerous an assertion; and though the chant was an old one, it was no doubt sung with redoubled emphasis during the new events. "De Lord will call us home," was evidently thought to be a symbolic verse; for, as a little drummer-boy explained to me . . . "Dey tink de *Lord* mean for say *de Yankees.*"

> *We'll soon be free,*
> *We'll soon be free,*
> *We'll soon be free,*
> *When de Lord will call us home.*[40]

Equally inflammatory, at least in the mind of the slave owners, was "Many Thousand Go," which Higginson believed was composed *after* the start of the Civil War. His book notes that a "peck of corn and a pint of salt" were the rations of the average slave:

> *No more peck o' corn for me,*
>   *No more, no more,*
> *No more peck o' corn for me,*
>   *Many t'ousand go.*
>
> *No more driver's lash for me . . .*
> *No more pint o' salt for me . . .*
> *No more hundred lash for me . . .* [41]

Higginson closed his extraordinary article by stating that while the Volunteers would sing the "long and short metres of the hymnbooks" on Sunday, they would do so "reluctantly," saving their "potent excitement" for their spirituals:

> By these they could sing themselves, as had their fathers before them, out of the contemplation of their own estate, into the sublime scenery of the Apocalypse. I remember that this minor-key pathos used to seem to me almost too sad to dwell upon, while slavery seemed destined to last for generations; but now that their patience has had its perfect work, history cannot afford to lose this portion of its record. There is no parallel instance of an oppressed race thus sustained by the religious sentiment alone. These songs are but the vocal expression of the simplicity of their faith and the sublimity of their long resignation.[42]

In the 1860s, there were no musicologists, there was no academic discipline of folklore, and—according to Epstein—what passed for anthropology then would not be acceptable today. The term "white man's burden" was already in the language and even the most enlightened, educated Quaker said things that would sound shockingly racist today. In Europe, the collection of folk songs had barely begun. And yet, three people assembled a book of "permanent historical value." Allen, Ware, and Garrison, along with their invaluable collector friends—most notably Higginson—may not have understood the spirituals, but they recognized those spirituals as being "valuable, attractive and eminently worth preserving."[43]

Like Garrison, Allen came from a progressive, academic New England family. He graduated from Harvard in 1851 as a trained historian, and was also a fine amateur musician. Allen and his wife, Mary, who had read Spaulding's "Under the Palmetto" and written about it, heard the requests for teachers in the Georgia Sea Islands by the Educational Commission for Freedmen. The couple volunteered and traveled there in November 1863. Once there, Allen met his cousins Harriet and Charles Ware, who had already been working on the islands for a year. Within days of arriving on the Sea Islands, Allen heard his first spirituals.[44]

The third author listed on the cover of *Slave Songs of the United States*, Charles Pickard Ware, another Harvard man, had been placed in charge of five abandoned plantations. Like his cousin Allen, Ware was struck by the music of the contrabands. Almost upon his arrival, he quickly began copying and collecting as many spirituals as possible. According to the authors of *Slave Songs*, Ware ultimately contributed the "largest and most accurate single collection in existence" to the book.[45]

First published in 1867, *Slave Songs of the United States* remains a valuable tool, although few of its spirituals are familiar today, in part because the book was received with critical indifference upon its release by all save the abolitionist press and soon went out of print. Subsequent reprintings have since reinforced its position as an invaluable resource and historical document. Other important collections would soon follow.[46]

The next important publication in the preservation and dissemination of spirituals is *The Jubilee Singers of Fisk University, and Their Campaign for Twenty Thousand Dollars* by Gustavus D. Pike in 1872. The Fisk Jubilee Singers emerged from the desperate financial straits facing Fisk University, a small African-American college founded near Nashville by the Freedmen's Bureau (fig. 2). The Fisk Singers originally performed standard western European–styled classical music, including arias, before turning (reluctantly at first) to the spirituals. When they began singing arranged versions of the old spirituals, their popularity soared, both in the United States and in Europe. Once "jubilee" was added to their name, it eventually became the name of an entire genre of sacred part-singing and spawned numerous competitors.[47] The collection of spirituals was assembled by Pike, with the help of a former Fisk professor, and includes invaluable interviews with the singers, including several recently freed slaves. Unlike *Slave Songs of the United States*, these sixty songs include many that would remain both familiar and popular a century later. As Harold Courlander wrote in a twentieth-century reissue, "The publication of *Slave Songs of the United States* in 1867 was, in its own way, something like our

FIGURE 2

The Fisk Jubilee Singers were
initially reluctant to turn to spirituals, but their popularity soared
in the United States and Europe
once they did. The group's success
spawned an entire genre of sacred
part-singing.

first orbital lunar flight. It was not the end but a beginning that helped set a course from which, thereafter, there would be no turning back."[48]

However, as many musicologists have been quick to point out, these are not "true" spirituals. The rough, improvisatory nature of the spirituals has been smoothed out, the verses and choruses harmonized and made more regular, and the language standardized. While the words are apparently intact, only the basic melody line would have been recognizable to a former slave—although some spirituals were sung to several melodies through the centuries.[49]

In the years that followed, a number of significant collections were published, some of which enjoyed many years of popularity and brisk sales. The following list of prominent collections of spirituals is by no means complete, but it shows the sustained interest in the spiritual for more than a century.

1873 Gustavus D. Pike, *The Jubilee Singers of Fisk University, and Their Campaign for Twenty Thousand Dollars* (Boston: Lee and Shepard)

1881 J. B. T. Marsh, *The Story of the Jubilee Singers: With Their Songs* (Boston: Houghton, Mifflin; repr., New York: Negro Universities Press, 1969)

1887 *Jubilee and Plantation Songs: Characteristic Favorites, as Sung by the Hampton Students, Jubilee Singers, Fisk University Students, and Other Concert Companies; Also, a Number of New and Pleasing Selections* (Boston: Oliver Ditson)

1899 William E. Barton, *Old Plantation Hymns: A Collection of Hitherto Unpublished Melodies of the Slave and the Freedman, with Historical and Descriptive Notes* (Boston: Lamson, Wolffe; repr., New York: AMS Press, 1972)

1901 Thomas P. Fenner, Frederic G. Rathbun, and Bessie Cleveland, arr., *Cabin and Plantation Songs as Sung by the Hampton Students* (New York: G. P. Putnam's Sons)

1918 Natalie Curtis Burlin, *Negro Folk-Songs*, book 2, *Spirituals* (New York: G. Schirmer)

1925 James Weldon Johnson, ed., with J. Rosamond Johnson, arr., *The Book of American Negro Spirituals*, 2 vols. (New York: Viking)

1925 Dorothy Scarborough, *On the Trail of Negro Folk-Songs* (Cambridge: Harvard University Press)

1926 William Arms Fisher, ed., *Seventy Negro Spirituals* (Bryn Mawr, PA: Oliver Ditson)

1927 R. Nathaniel Dett, ed., *Religious Folk-Songs of the Negro as Sung at Hampton Institute* (Hampton, VA: Hampton Institute Press)

1927 Eva A. Jessye, *My Spirituals* (New York: Robbins-Engel)

1930 Mary Allen Grissom, *The Negro Sings a New Heaven* (Chapel Hill: University of North Carolina Press)

1933 E. A. McIlhenny, *Befo' de War Spirituals* (Boston: Christopher)

1940 *American Negro Songs and Spirituals: A Comprehensive Collection of 230 Folk Songs, Religious and Secular, with a Foreword by John W. Work* (New York: Bonanza Books)

1942 Lydia Parrish, *Slave Songs of the Georgia Sea Islands* (New York: Farrar, Straus; repr., Hatboro, PA: Folklore Associates, 1965)

1948 Roland Hayes, *My Songs: Aframerican Religious Folk Songs Arranged and Interpreted by Roland Hayes* (Boston: Little, Brown)

Some additional collections, including those by well-known African-American composers Harry T. Burleigh and Hall Johnson, were primarily classically arranged versions of spirituals and contain few previously unknown (at least to the white audience) pieces. In 1972, Lovell noted that since the release of *Slave Songs of the United States*, more than five hundred "collections" (a term he uses to denote any book, or magazine or newspaper article, that features one or more spiritual texts) of spirituals had been published and "about six thousand independent spirituals" had been cataloged—and that he believed that the list would continue to grow.[50] It is safe to assume that many, many more spirituals were lost, or never written down, or fell out of favor among slaves before the first collectors showed up at Port Royal, St. Helena, in the Georgia Sea Islands, or elsewhere.

Slave Songs of the United States contains 136 spirituals, along with the authors' invaluable commentary, written during and immediately after the war. Consequently, to scholars seeking to establish a direct connection between the spirituals of the Civil War and the gospel songs, freedom songs, and revamped spirituals of the civil rights movement, it is to the one-of-a-kind collection by Allen, Garrison, and Ware that researchers return time and time again.[51] Because of the authors' connections with some of the most powerful abolitionists in the country, Ronald Radano called the book's publication a "watershed moment in the documentation of American slave music" that "tacitly challenged European musical superiority together with its associations with the American national character."[52]

2

THE SPIRITUALS AS PROTEST SONGS

The most potential and beneficial gifts given to our "Grandparents" were the "Spiritual Songs." For the songs guided and protected them from many dangerous toils and snares. Suppose those poor creatures didn't have that secret weapon. If they couldn't have laid one of their soothing-salve spirituals, "You Can Have All This World—Just Give Us Jesus" upon the other fellow, which appealed to his ego to solve some of their downhearted problems, perhaps they might've been extinguished just like the belligerent Indians.

—PERRY BRADFORD

A great song arose, the loveliest thing born this side of the seas. It was a new song. It did not come from Africa, though the dark throb and beat of that Ancient of Days was in it and through it. It did not come from white America—never from so pale and hard and thin a thing, however deep these vulgar and surrounding tones had driven. Not the Indies nor the hot South, the cold East or heavy West made this music. It was a new song and its deep and plaintive beauty, its great cadences and wild appeal wailed, throbbed and thundered on the world's ear with a message seldom voiced by man. It swelled and blossomed like incense, improvised and born anew out of an age long past, and weaving into its texture the old and new melodies in word and in thought.

—W. E. B. DU BOIS

The idea of a revolution in the conditions of the whites and blacks, is the corner-stone of the religion of the latter.

—CHARLES BALL

O nce the African origin of the melodies of most spirituals was established and widely accepted, the scholarly conversation, naturally, turned to the words. It is possible, even at this great distance from the advent of the spirituals, to parse their apparently hidden meanings. Certain spirituals, such as "Go Down, Moses," "Didn't My Lord Deliver Daniel?," and a few others, along with the quasi-spiritual "John Brown's Body," possibly contain clues as to messages contained in spirituals that may—or may not—have been deliberately hidden from outsiders. What is clear is that since the 1940s, academics have plumbed the slave narratives, diaries, and letters of observers (and even some slave owners) from the antebellum era and come to a general consensus: Charles Ball (in the epigraph above) has it exactly right. Slaves desperately wanted to be free. And the primary universal expression of that sentiment available to slaves was song: "Song making, after all, was central to the slaves' abilities to produce a discursive grasp of slavery, despite the fact that such collective activity and communal expression, such cultural work, operated within the context of surveillance, and, in many cases, perpetual repression."[1]

Cruz convincingly argues that virtually all southern slaves knew the "deep meanings" of the spirituals and the "larger stakes involved" because they alone were the insiders privy to the secret meanings of the words. Otherwise, why would they have invested so much time and energy into creating the "elaborate codes underneath ostensibly restricted codes if they did not know the meanings of their own songs?" His conclusion is that since history has shown that slaves were "capable of revolting and rebelling," then logic and human nature suggest that they were capable of "singing about the meaning of things and of the world they wished to change or leave."[2] Since these "elaborate codes" were known only to those creating and carefully disseminating them, the meaning of some spirituals is lost and may never be known. It may be that some spirituals were apparently wholly religious in nature, with no hidden meaning. But other spirituals may have had their "second" meanings interpreted by former slaves. Other spirituals have been long identified with abolitionism and the slaves' search for freedom. And from the vantage point (or disadvantage point) of history, still other spirituals appear to be espousing a liberation theology or expressing an overt protest against an unjust system. I propose to draw from this "deep pool" of spirituals to examine those messages.

"Go Down, Moses"

In addition to being what researchers believe to be the first spiritual to see print in the United States (see chapter 1), "Go Down, Moses" has had a long and influential history. It is the only spiritual in *The Jubilee Singers, and Their Campaign for Twenty Thousand Dollars* that contains a full second page of verses, twenty-five in all. The lyrics in this version vary only slightly from Lucy McKim Garrison's, as well as subsequent versions, except that, as was common in all the Fisk spirituals, the dialect has been made to conform to the standard English of the day. But the words retain their sense of implied power, especially when coupled with the urgent, insistent chorus. A sampling of the better-known verses:

> When Israel was in Egypt's land:
>   Let my people go:
> Oppress'd so hard they could not stand:
>   Let my people go.

> Go down, Moses, Way down in Egypt land
> Tell old Pharaoh, Let my people go.

> Thus saith the Lord, bold Moses said,
>   Let my people go:
> If not I'll smite your first-born dead,
>   Let my people go.

> The Devil he thought he had me fast,
>   Let my people go:
> But I thought I'd break his chains at last,
>   Let my people go.[3]

"Go Down, Moses" appears in *The Jubilee Singers, and Their Campaign for Twenty Thousand Dollars* (1873), *The Story of the Jubilee Singers: With Their Songs* (1881), *The Book of American Negro Spirituals* (1925), *Religious Folk-Songs of the Negro as Sung at Hampton Institute* (1927), and *American Negro Songs and Spirituals* (1940), among others, including most modern collections.

One of the most poignant instances of the spiritual being sung was at the signing of the Emancipation Proclamation by President Abraham Lincoln at the White House on January 1, 1863. Immediately following the reception, a number of freed slaves sang, including an "aged woman" who performed "Go Down, Moses."[4] Among the many dignitaries who heard the Fisk Jubilee Singers sing "Go Down, Moses" were both President Ulysses S. Grant, who wished them "a glorious success" on their tour in 1872, and Queen Victoria in England, who requested the spiritual and listened "with manifest pleasure." The group also sang "Steal Away" and "John Brown's Body" for the queen.[5]

However, no spiritual is more closely identified with an individual than "Go Down, Moses" is with Harriet Tubman. Tubman, a heroic freedom fighter who, despite a host of serious physical ailments and a $40,000 bounty on her head, gained fame as a "conductor" as she led hundreds of slaves to freedom during the Civil War.[6] One of the earliest references to Tubman as "Moses" appeared in "The Commonwealth" of July 17, 1863, where she is dubbed "Moses the deliverer."[7] However, Tubman may have been known as "Moses" as early as 1855.[8] The story of Moses, who led the Hebrew people from Egyptian slavery into freedom, is of course one of the most popular themes in the spirituals, and just the mention of Moses's name carried powerful, direct symbolism for the slaves.[9] Some of that power derives from the slaves' sense of time and place—the stories of the Bible were happening in "the eternal now" and the events in the Holy Land were taking place in the present day just across the county or state line. The awe and reverence slaves held for President Lincoln was reflected in their title for him, "Father Abraham," and calling Tubman "Moses" had the same effect.[10] Likewise, the first book on Tubman from 1869 is subtitled "The Moses of Her People." Author Sarah H. Bradford knew Tubman and wrote the small book in an effort to raise money for "Moses," who was virtually penniless in her later years. Bradford included a breathless account of Tubman leading a "starving party" of slaves through dark woods and singing "Go Down, Moses." Bradford said she personally heard Tubman sing this spiritual and includes two verses and the chorus:

> *Oh Pharaoh said he would go cross,*
> *Let my people go,*
> *And don't get lost in de wilderness.*
> *Let my people go.*
>
> *You may hinder me here, but you can't up dere,*
> *Let my people go,*
> *He sits in de Hebben and answers prayer,*
> *Let my people go.*[11]

Again, some of Tubman's almost mystic power to escape detection and lead slaves to safety comes from the appellation "Moses." One Union chaplain, upon visiting former slaves in Alabama in 1865, declared, "Moses is their *ideal* of all that is high, and noble, and perfect, in man."[12] Those same slaves believed that Moses was much, much more than just another figure in the Bible. He was the embodiment of a godly leader of what Feiler calls the "emerging black nation within the nation," a "blueprint for the famed living metaphor of nineteenth century America, the Underground Railroad."[13]

And while not the only spiritual that focuses on Moses, "Go Down, Moses" is the one most identified with him. Isabella Beecher Hooker, half sister of Harriet Beecher Stowe (the author of *Uncle Tom's Cabin*), called it "the Negro Marseillaise."[14] Other spirituals featuring Moses, particularly the stories involving Pharaoh, the parting of the Red Sea, and the loss of Pharaoh's army when the waters come crashing down again, include "Didn't Ole Pharaoh Get Lost," "Turn Back Pharaoh's Army," "Mary, Don't You Weep," "I Am Bound for the Promised Land," "Brother Moses Gone," "Come Along, Moses," "When Moses Smote the Water," "Ride On, Moses," "W'en Israel Was in Egypt's Lan'," and "I Wish I Had Died in Egypt Land."

Lovell believes it is in the stories of Abraham, Moses, Joshua, Samson, Daniel, and others that the slaves' "commitment to freedom in spirituals begins . . .

with songs about Old Testament heroes and devils." The greatest of these heroes is Moses, and virtually "every song about Moses is intended to chide Americans, South and North, about permitting slavery and to issue a solemn warning that slavery will not be indefinitely tolerated."[15] For Dixon, the combination of the spiritual and political in a single spiritual is "not mutually exclusive." In fact, it is part of a "peculiarly American" understanding of scripture: "['Go Down, Moses'] includes the central idea of the Exodus—that because God acted mightily and miraculously in the past, believers may be assured of his mighty hand today to free them from unjust political oppression."[16]

In time, as the storm clouds of secession and war gathered, some southerners began to sense that certain spirituals were not actually harmless and banned their singing in several states. It is not insignificant that "Go Down, Moses" has been both identified with and sometimes attributed to Nat Turner, the Baptist preacher who in 1831 led the bloodiest of all the hundreds of slave revolts of the eighteenth and nineteenth centuries.[17] Denmark Vesey, who led the failed slave revolt in Charleston, also used "Go Down, Moses" as a powerful weapon to rally support. In both cases, it was what the slave owners feared most—charismatic religious leaders attached to a revolutionary religious song.[18]

And therein may lie one of the keys to this particular spiritual, and all the great spirituals—it is dangerous. Like all great music it has the power to affect the singer as well as the listener; it is dangerous because it has the power to influence both events in the present and those still to come. For Jon Michael Spencer, the force of the spiritual is tied to an implicit understanding among slaves that Moses killing the Egyptian who was savagely beating his Hebrew slaves initiated the quest for liberation. At the same time, not every slave "had to be a Moses in order to initiate the process of liberation." However, with "the first blows of liberation dealt, it was God's time to compel the oppressors by a mighty hand."[19] If there had been a successful violent revolution (extremely unlikely both in the days of Moses and in the era of slavery in the American South), then a human could have taken credit for the victory. Thus it appears that the Exodus was accomplished *only* through the miraculous intervention of God, and the slaves gave God full credit in the words "Thus saith the Lord, bold Moses said / Let my people go / If not I'll smite your first-born dead / Let my people go." When Cornel West writes about the transformative nature of the spirituals in this regard, it is this spiritual that he cites. To West, "Go Down, Moses" presents a "political message of freedom and a hope for endurance in the face of death and despair": "In short, the spirituals challenge any Enlightenment notion of human autonomy. They force us to confront the paradox of human freedom: we must be strong enough to resist the prevailing forms of bondage yet honest enough to acknowledge our weaknesses in the face of death and disappointment. This honesty about our weakness is itself a supreme form of strength that precludes paralysis and impotence."[20]

"Go Down, Moses" held a special place in the heart of gifted composer/arranger James Weldon Johnson. In *The Book of American Negro Spirituals* (1925), he calls the spirituals "noble music" and argues that their survival and continued influence are due, in part, to the "dignity" of the words and music, especially "Go Down, Moses," where "there is not a nobler theme in the whole musical literature of the world. If the Negro had voiced himself in only that one song, it would have been evidence of his nobility of soul. Add to this 'Deep River,' 'Stand Still Jordan,' 'Walk Together Children,' 'Roll Jordan Roll,' 'Ride on King Jesus,' and you catch a spirit that is a little more than mere nobility; it is something akin to majestic grandeur."[21]

All the spirituals mentioned by Johnson have that dignity, and yet "Go Down, Moses" possesses an uncommon intensity as well, one derived in part due to the direct nature of the chorus, "Let my people go!" This is the voice of righteous anger, emphatic and implacable, hindered not by the sometimes limited vocabularies of the unknown slave poets, but instead given additional force and weight because these words are directed specifically *at* the slave owners. To the slave, these words are not sung in their voices—they are sung in the voice of Yahweh/Jehovah, the God of Abraham, Moses, Jacob, Isaac, and Daniel. Great Jehovah is on the side of the oppressed slave. Great Jehovah demands justice.

The chorus of "Go Down, Moses" is "thunderous" because it boldly states, like few other spirituals, that Moses's power to free the slaves comes directly from God. This is a righteous demand, one that God will hear because slavery is a sin, an abomination before the Almighty. As a result, Lovell calls it "unquestionably the best" of the spirituals that address freedom:

> No more passionate songs have ever been written to proclaim the concept of freedom. Perhaps the American slave knew more about freedom than anyone who has ever lived. Whether or not this is true, his songs declare freedom as well as or better than it has ever been declared: "No more peck o' corn for me, No more, no more," "And why not every man?" "Tell ol' Pharaoh, let my people go," "If I had my way . . . I'd tear this building down," "Before I'd be a slave I'd be buried in my grave," "Done wid driber's dribin'," "No second class aboard dis train"—for the concept of freedom, where can you find their superiors?[22]

As for Tubman, she spent her final years in Auburn, New York, active in her church and still fighting for women's suffrage, despite declining health. And, according to one author, "She never ceased to sing those roaring songs with the religious words and revolutionary meaning, like 'The John Brown Song' and 'Go Down, Moses.'" Tubman died at home, surrounded by friends, on March 10, 1913. The Auburn newspaper recorded that she led those at her bedside in singing "Swing Low, Sweet Chariot" with her final breath.[23]

"Go Down, Moses," like the spirituals about Daniel and Jesus, was/is adaptable to a host of settings. The Bible provides precious few physical or psychological details about any of these heroes, save that Moses stuttered and was prone to anger (on multiple occasions) and that Jesus grew angry with the Pharisees and scribes and during the cleansing of the Temple.[24] This very lack of detail enables all readers, not just African-American slaves in the eighteenth and nineteenth centuries, but also Christians, Jews, and Muslims, to claim these figures—as needed. In addition to the "divine connection," it is this "blank canvas" that allows them to be so adaptable. Feiler quotes the Reverend Petra Heldt as saying that Abraham is not identified with any particular group, nation, or people: "You can put everything into that vessel you would like. He's open enough. He's broad enough. . . . He's planted in that space of the world, so he precedes all of us, he's therefore with all of us."[25]

The Moses in "Go Down, Moses" and a dozen other spirituals (and doubtless many more long-lost spirituals) is a particularly potent symbol. He was born of slaves, challenged and overcame a world power, and led his people to freedom, even if he himself did not live to see that freedom. Despite or perhaps because of this lack of personal detail, the Moses narratives provide the ultimate hero's journey to the slave poets, representative of a "very good hero" who is ageless and timeless: "That's why everyone loves them."[26]

This sheer malleability enables the Moses of the Old Testament to assume the wider mantle of a mythic folk hero, one particularly attractive to African-American slaves because of the "trickster" motif—someone who is able to outwit much stronger foes through his quickness and cleverness. This, John W. Roberts says, allows for the many spirituals on Moses and other biblical figures based on "speculative retrospection." Moses rarely directly confronted the powerful Egyptians, preferring instead to trust in God and utilize God-inspired trickery. Yahweh sends the waters crashing down on the Pharaoh's army, not Moses. This trickster avatar, after all, is a common motif in the many traditions of the Africans who were brought to the United States during slavery and would probably be familiar to many slaves, even several generations removed from Africa.[27]

To overcome an institution as heinous as perpetual slavery, enforced by the armed might of a powerful nation, calls for equally powerful, spiritually compelling heroes. The Moses narratives from the Old Testament provide such a hero. In the course of leading his people out of slavery into the Promised Land, the reluctant hero Moses endured many trials and hardships, ordeals that gave him the "spiritual knowledge and power" necessary to confront the Pharaoh and his vast armies. At the same time, the "empowerment of Moses" represented for African-American slaves the "rewards" of maintaining a relationship with God: "Inasmuch as converted Africans believed that 'de God that lived in Moses' time jus' de same today,' they also believed that He would answer their prayers and empower a deliverer hero from one among their number."[28]

While initially making a case for Joseph (he of the coat of many colors who is sold into slavery in Gen. 37–50) as the best model for African-Americans, both during slavery and later, Albert Murray writes emphatically that "no one can deny to Moses, great emancipator that he was, the position as epic hero of anti-slavery movements."[29] The songs and stories of Moses sustained the slaves through the hundreds of known revolts, large and small. Their God-ordained deliverance eventually came at the hands of Union armies directed by Abraham (Lincoln)—a marvelous bit of cosmic synchronicity! The constant singing of "Go Down, Moses" surely provided slaves with physical, spiritual, and emotional comfort during the long nightmare of American slavery.

According to James Weldon Johnson and J. Rosamond Johnson, two influential African-American composers and writers from the early years of the twentieth century, both of whom knew former slaves, the stories of the Old Testament—and the spirituals derived from them—did indeed sustain the slaves: "This story at once caught and fired the imaginations of the Negro bards, and they sang, sang their hungry listeners into a firm faith that as God saved Daniel in the Lion's den, so would He save them; as God preserved the Hebrew children in the fiery furnace, so would He preserve them; as God delivered Israel out of bondage in Egypt, so would He deliver them. How much this firm faith had to do with the Negro's physical and spiritual survival of two and a half centuries of slavery cannot be known."[30]

By the 1930s, "Go Down, Moses" was ubiquitous enough in popular American culture, and its use by slaves as a not-so-covert freedom song was well known enough, that Margaret Mitchell has one of the slave characters, Big Sam, defiantly sing it (albeit in a torturous, phonetically rendered version of the slave dialect that would be virtually impossible to read if the spiritual were not so familiar) in *Gone with the Wind*:

> *Go do-ow, Mos-es! Waa-ay, do-own,*
> *in Eee-jup laa-an!*
> *An' te-el O-le Faa-ro-o*
> *Ter let mah—pee-pul go!*[31]

In the years following World War II, the great African-American lyric tenor Roland Hayes noted that "there is a grave simplicity in the lines of this noble song that has stamped it indelibly with universal human appeal." When Hayes sang it a century after the Civil War, the spiritual still held a power for African-Americans living in a country where Jim Crow yet ruled: "Not daring to speak openly of freedom, my people, enslaved, found through song a means to give this utterance incredible strength."[32] The story of Moses and the spiritual "Go Down, Moses" have continued to serve as a rich and compelling force through the civil rights movement and beyond, ultimately achieving a cross-cultural position of power enjoyed by few songs of *any* kind. And, according to Jerry Silverman, it has achieved an extraordinary full circle in American life: "Nowhere in the entire literature of slave spirituals is the identification between the black slave and the biblical Israelite more direct than in 'Go Down, Moses.' To complete the historical circle, today's Jews often sing this stirring slave song during the Passover seder, the meal that celebrates the Hebrews' escape from slavery in Egypt."[33]

"Didn't My Lord Deliver Daniel?"

"Didn't My Lord Deliver Daniel?" is another powerful spiritual, one that, hundreds of years later, still amazes the reader/audience in its direct, confrontational nature. It was the brave slave who sang these words in front of an overseer. "Didn't My Lord Deliver Daniel?" appears in most of the major collections, although the version in *Slave Songs of the United States* (1867) is called "O Daniel" and varies both lyrically and musically, and may be a pastiche of different original songs: "O my Lord delivered Daniel, O Daniel, O Daniel / O my Lord delivered Daniel, O why not deliver me too?"[34] Another variant is found in *Befo' de War Spirituals* (1933), titled "Why Don't You 'Liver Me?" and was collected on Avery Island, in extreme southern Louisiana: "Oh ma Lord 'liver Daniel, Daniel, Daniel / Ma Lord 'liver Daniel / Why don't You 'liver me too?"[35] The most familiar version appears in *The Jubilee Singers, and Their Campaign for Twenty Thousand Dollars* (1872) and most subsequent collections:

> *Didn't my Lord deliver Daniel, D'liver Daniel, d'liver Daniel*
> *Didn't my Lord deliver Daniel, And why not every man?*
>
> *I set my foot on the Gospel ship,*
> *And the ship it begin to sail,*
> *It landed me over on Canaan's shore,*
> *And I'll never come back any more.*[36]

This is a rich, multifaceted piece of art, rife with allusions—and rebellion. Daniel, of course, is a significant figure in the Old Testament to the slaves. The story of the righteous Daniel, who stands firm in his religious beliefs before the all-powerful king and is thus thrown first into the fiery furnace and later into the lion's den—only to be delivered both times by the Lord's angel and restored to a place of honor—has obvious appeal for an oppressed people.

"Didn't My Lord Deliver Daniel?" may well be "the most politically radical of all the spirituals." The key is in the line "And why not every man?" which "expands the idea of deliverance to encompass all the downtrodden" by raising what Richard Newman terms a "revolutionary" question.[37] The slaves believed that a joyful Day of Judgment was coming, when all would be put right. Henry Mitchell calls it a "liberationist desire to know" the answer to the question because, in their belief system, when they sang of heaven it was actually a "social-protest shorthand" for what should be true on earth. "These were not distant ideas," he writes. "They were sung with zest and sincere enthusiasm, born of specific certainty and personal identification."[38]

The dramatic nature of the two miracles, the furnace and the lion's den, required miraculous, supernatural interventions on behalf of Daniel (and his friends Shadrach, Meshach, and Abednego). For the African-American slave in the years before the Civil War, the descendant of slaves with no hope of manumission, living in a country that permitted slavery in its legal code and in the southern states where the rape, violent abuse, and murder of human beings was tolerated and sometimes encouraged, it would take nothing less than such a divine intervention to set him or her free. And, to be sure, many slaves did despair at the sheer hopelessness of it all. But Lovell suggests that is precisely why the Daniel stories in general and this spiritual in particular are so potent: "The Lord had proved He was equal to the occasion; and the slave had proved he was deserving. Thus the miraculous deliverance was inevitable."[39]

"Daniel and the Lion's Den" and "Didn't My Lord Deliver Daniel?" (and the other spirituals featuring, or at least mentioning, Daniel) may have had "identical" themes even though the evidence indicates that they were created generations apart. Both before and after the Civil War, the stories of Daniel and the clear, forceful nature of spirituals like this one, Wyatt Tee Walker believes, confirmed to the slaves that God was aware of their plight. That this spiritual would continue into the civil rights era and beyond is proof of its moral and spiritual authority: "It is not difficult to fathom the reason for both the antebellum believers and those after the Civil War to grasp the hopefulness in Daniel's spectacular deliverance when one considers the hopelessness of their sociology. In both instances the faith-response was that God delivered Daniel from the lions' den, so would he deliver his children of darker hue from the lions' den of slavery and twentieth century racism."[40]

Daniel is a particularly attractive figure because he is not depicted as having any particular power or insight or even special access to Jehovah. Daniel is simply a normal man who believes. It is his faith that ensures his deliverance from the lions and the furnace. He typifies, like Joseph, Moses, Noah, Joshua, and the other popular subjects of spirituals drawn from the Old Testament, an enduring faith in God when faced with temptation and torture. The spirituals continually reassured beleaguered African-American believers that God would, in time, prevail and that the suffering would be redeemed. The spirituals presented believers and unbelievers alike "dramatic evidence" that their continued faithfulness, Roberts maintains, "outweighed the temporary costs that they paid."[41]

It is for these reasons that Lovell considers "Didn't My Lord Deliver Daniel?" as "the best song of freedom," even more so than "Go Down, Moses," because it "makes no reservations or allowances" for slavery under any condition. Slavery will not stand because Almighty God is against it. The Bible has shown repeatedly that, at God's command, supernatural deliverances from mighty foes occurred. So why should God *not* continue to do so now? The slaves clearly believed God would intervene. Just as Daniel stood strong in his faith against absolute tyranny, so would the slaves in a thousand ways continually seek to overthrow the unjust, sinful reign of slavery. And why not *every* man? As Lovell wryly adds, as "bold and explicit" as "Didn't My Lord Deliver Daniel?" is, "the white people who heard it sung and permitted it, must have been trusting souls indeed!"[42] This is not just insurrection; this spiritual is a declaration of war.

"John Brown's Body"

While many spirituals retained their popularity for a century or more, others were gradually sung less and less until they became forgotten, save for the work of scholars and collectors. "John Brown's Body," in its various guises, has been popular almost from the second it emerged from its murky beginnings. The spiritual surfaced shortly after the radical abolitionist Brown's quick trial and execution on December 2, 1859. From there, the song enjoyed nearly unparalleled popularity among abolitionists and, during the Civil War, among slaves and Union soldiers, who also relished its jaunty, martial beat.

But "John Brown's Body," though adopted by slaves and freed slaves alike, is not a true spiritual. In fact, its authorship (both the music and the words) has been something of a Gordian knot for scholars to unravel. There was, apparently, *another* John Brown, a sergeant assigned to the 2nd Battalion of the Massachusetts Infantry and then later to the 12th Massachusetts in Boston. The original lyrics poked fun at the sergeant's quirks and foibles. Even the melody was based on a familiar camp-meeting tune, "Say Brother, Will You Meet Us?" (which, itself, was apparently based on an English folk song). Assuming that account is true, the stirring tale of the John Brown of Osawatomie and Harpers Ferry soon replaced the humorous story of the original, now forgotten, sergeant, and the lyrics were quickly altered:

> *John Brown's body lies a mouldering in the grave,*
> *His soul's marching on!*
> *He's gone to be a soldier in the army of the Lord,*
> > *His soul's marching on!*
> *Glory, glory, hallelujah,*
> *His soul's marching on.*[43]

Kenneth Bernard writes that the song "gave the North the piece which, above all others, became the *musical symbol* of the slave set free."[44] Douglass, one of Brown's many financial supporters, had been forced to flee the United States following Harpers Ferry. In the following six months, Douglass traveled first to Canada, then England. He returned home after hearing of the death of his beloved daughter Annie. During that time, Douglass wrote that "great changes had now taken place in the public mind." The country, which to him had seemed to be acceding to all the demands of the southern, slaveholding states, had responded with revulsion to the kangaroo-court execution of the mortally wounded Brown in December: "All over the North men were singing the John Brown song. His body was in the dust, but his soul was marching on."[45]

During the Civil War, "John Brown's Body" was very early in the repertoire of community and military bands. The popular band 79th New York Regiment (the "Highlanders," who specialized in Scots-related songs and performed in full

Highlander regalia, including kilts) sang the song (as well as other instrumental numbers) outside the White House in October 1861. A month later, Julia Ward Howe, who after hearing the original and agreeing with another listener that perhaps the lines, especially "John Brown's body lies a-mould'ring in the grave," were somehow not "fitting and worthy," rewrote the words. Howe kept the same melody, retitled it "The Battle Hymn of the Republic," and, beginning with the stirring line "Mine eyes have seen the glory of the coming of the Lord," created the most popular song among Union soldiers and civilians alike. The original song (with its original words) would remain popular as well, especially among former slaves.[46] In the years ahead, both "John Brown's Body" and "Glory Hallelujah" were repeatedly sung (sometimes with band accompaniment) by numerous groups performing for Lincoln.

The "original" version of the song spread back to contraband camps and became adopted as a spiritual. A report from the May 31, 1862, issue of the *National Anti-Slavery Standard* from St. Helena Island (probably written by Laura Towne, another early collector/reporter on the spiritual) mentions that the author heard the contrabands singing "John Brown's Body" during a "rude kind of drill."[47] Another teacher among the Port Royal contrabands was Charlotte Forten, who, at about the same time, taught the song to the children: "I felt to the full the significance of that song being sung here in S.C. by little negro children, by those whom he—the glorious old man—died to save."[48]

So it is clear that from the early days of the Civil War, "John Brown's Body" was a song with a transformative power. (However, perhaps because it was not a "true" spiritual, the song is not included in *Slave Songs of the United States*. Both Towne and Forten are thanked as contributors, so it was doubtless known to the volume's three collaborators.)[49] Nor is it included in most of the early collections of spirituals, save for *The Story of the Jubilee Singers: With Their Songs* (1881), which adds these verses, while retaining the "Glory, glory, Hallelujah" chorus:

> John Brown died that the slave might be free,
> But his soul's marching on.
> Now has come the glorious jubilee,
> When all mankind are free.[50]

The fall of Petersburg effectively marked the fall of the Confederacy, although a few more bloody battles would ensue before the rebellion formally ended at Appomattox Court House. As Union troops entered Richmond, the southern capital, Union soldiers and bands, black and white, sang and performed "John Brown's Body," along with "Yankee Doodle," "Kingdom Coming," "Year of Jubilo," "Rally 'Round the Flag, Boys," "The Star-Spangled Banner," and others.[51] In Booker T. Washington's autobiography, he writes that the slaves had been "expecting" the end of the war through the slave grapevine. He writes that "freedom was in the air" and adds the intriguing detail that as the Union victory neared, songs filled the slave quarters with greater and greater frequency: "It was bolder, had more ring, and lasted later into the night. Most of the verses of the plantation songs had some reference to freedom. True, they had sung those same verses before, but they had been careful to explain that the 'freedom' in these songs referred to the next world, and had no connections with life in this world. Now they gradually threw off the mask, and were not afraid to let it be known that the 'freedom' in their songs meant freedom of the body in this world."[52] Washington does not record whether those songs actually included "Go Down, Moses," "John Brown's Body," or any of the other well-established spirituals of the day, but it would have been strange had they not.

Another freedom fighter of the era, Sojourner Truth, also wrote new lyrics to the tune of "John Brown's Body," which she titled "The Valiant Soldiers" in honor of the Colored Regiment from Michigan. In addition to the now-familiar "Glory, glory, Hallelujah" chorus, Truth wrote a number of powerful, convicting verses, including:

> They will have to pay us wages
> The wages of their sins
> They will have to bow their forehead
> To their colored kith and kin
> They will have to give us house room
> Or the roofs will tumble in
> As we go marching on.
> Now Abraham has spoken
> And the message has been sent
> The prison doors are opened
> And out the prisoners went
> To join the Sable Army
> Of African descent
> As we go marching on.[53]

In light of the earlier discussion on the use of the Christian concept of the "sin" of slavery as a justification for resistance against the institution and their masters (see chapter 1), Truth's line "They will have to pay us wages, / The wages of their sins" is particularly telling. More than a century later, Bernice Johnson Reagon, a civil rights activist, would perform "The Valiant Soldiers" with her group, Sweet Honey in the Rock.[54]

Brown's significance to African-Americans was such that Du Bois, one of the cofounders of the Niagara Movement that advocated equal rights for all, traveled with the other founders to Harpers Ferry, the site of Brown's raid, and read their declarations calling for justice for blacks and tied Brown's "martyrdom" to that other popular sacred song of the Civil War, "The Battle Hymn of the Republic," ending with the words, "And here on the scene of John Brown's martyrdom, we reconsecrate ourselves, our honor, our property to the final emancipation of the race which John Brown died to make free." Incidentally, Du Bois also wrote a biography of Brown, published in 1909, which he called "one the best written of my books."[55]

"John Brown's Body" does not disappear after Appomattox, however. "Glory Hallelujah" remained popular in white circles, and African-Americans for many years continued to sing it as a spiritual. Much of the credit goes to the Fisk Jubilee Singers (and some of their collegiate counterparts/competitors). Following their successful performance before Queen Victoria in July 1873, the Jubilees' performance of "John Brown's Body" at the annual meeting of the Freedmen's Aid Society shortly thereafter received a "thunderous ovation" and the crowd threw "handkerchiefs and hats into the air." Another performance of the song, this one before the Prince and Princess of Wales and other members of the royal family at the home of Prime Minister William Gladstone, met with an equally frenzied response. Until the Fisk Jubilee Singers' tour, the British audiences had previously considered the song "comical."[56]

It is also difficult to overestimate the influence of the Hutchinsons in the preservation and popularization of the song. The singing family ultimately performed for seven American presidents. Audience reaction to this song ranged from cheers to boos, depending on where they sang: "It may well be that the Hutchinsons altered the course of American history, that their music hastened the confrontations and conflicts that led inexorably to the Civil War, that their songs fanned passions and created the sense of togetherness and resolve necessary to convert ideas and ideals into action, that their singing of 'John Browns' Body' converted more people to the antislavery cause than all the speeches and sermons of their time."[57]

In the century to come, both "John Brown's Body" and "The Battle Hymn of the Republic" (or "Glory Hallelujah") would be resurrected as needed by singers searching for a stirring, emotional marching song in times of crisis during the ongoing struggle for civil rights for all people. Artists as varied as Paul Robeson (fig. 3), Joan Baez, Pete Seeger, and, later, Van Morrison have recorded "John Brown's Body."[58] As for "The Battle Hymn of the Republic," President John F. Kennedy invited Mahalia Jackson to sing it on September 22, 1963, on the steps of the Lincoln Memorial as part of centennial ceremonies honoring the Emancipation Proclamation. Despite the presence of Thurgood Marshall, Nelson Rockefeller, Archibald MacLeish, Robert F. Kennedy, and Adlai E. Stevenson, Jackson was the "undisputed star" of the event. At its conclusion, she led the large crowd in a "stirring, unscheduled" rendition of "The Battle Hymn of the Republic."[59] Lisa Brevard writes that by "gospelizing" what had become known as a political song, "Jackson showed the power of African-American gospel music spirituality in straddling the line between the sacred and the political."[60] But perhaps its most poignant use was as the final line of the final sermon/speech delivered by the Reverend Martin Luther King, Jr., at the sanitation strike in Memphis, just before his death: "Mine eyes have seen the glory of the coming of the Lord."[61]

FIGURE 3

Paul Robeson was one of many artists to have
recorded "John Brown's Body." The song—
whose popularity was heightened by the Fisk
Jubilee Singers after the Civil War—influenced
many to convert to the antislavery cause.

The Jesus Spirituals

A host of spirituals prominently feature Jesus, including many of the spirituals relating to the birth of Jesus (most notably "Sweet Little Jesus Boy," "What Month Was Jesus Born In?" and "Go Tell It on the Mountain"), although there is virtually nothing in the literature concerning hidden messages in Nativity spirituals. It is easy to see why the spirituals about Jesus enjoyed such an enduring popularity and variety. The stories of Jesus of Nazareth in the New Testament books of Matthew and Luke tell of a baby born of poor parents in an occupied land. Like Moses, his life is constantly in danger and yet he regularly outwits the authorities (sometimes through supernatural intervention). In the end, Jesus is crucified on a wooden cross—a symbol that surely resonated with southern slaves, who constantly lived with the possibility of lynching on a nearby tree—but confounded his enemies by rising again on the third day. Some of the most notable "Jesus"-related spirituals found in the early collections include the following.

From *Slave Songs of the United States*	"Tell My Jesus 'Morning'"; "Jesus on the Waterside"; "Jesus Won't You Come By-and-By?"; "No Man Can Hinder Me"; "Nobody Knows the Trouble I've Had"
From *The Story of the Jubilee Singers: With Their Songs*	"Steal Away"; "Ride On, King Jesus"; "I'm Troubled in Mind"; "I'm Going to Live with Jesus"; "A Little More Faith in Jesus"; "Run to Jesus"; "Give Me Jesus"
From *The Jubilee Singers, and Their Campaign for Twenty Thousand Dollars*	"Nobody Knows the Trouble I See"; "Give Me Jesus"; "Ride On, King Jesus"; "I'm Troubled in Mind"; "I'm Going to Live with Jesus"; "A Little More Faith in Jesus"
From *Cabin and Plantation Songs*	"Did You Hear My Jesus?"; "Ef Ye Want to See Jesus"; "He Raise a Poor Lazarus"; "Jesus Ain't Comin' Here t' Die No Mo'"; "Tell Jesus"
From *Befo' de War Spirituals*	"Give-er Me Jesus"; "Give-er Me Jesus When I Die"; "I Want to See Jesus in the Mornin'"; "Jesus Rollin' In-er His Arms"; "King Jesus Sittin' on de Water Side"; "Rollin' in Jesus' Arms"
From *Jubilee and Plantation Songs*	"A Little More Faith in Jesus"; "Give Me Jesus"; "I'm Going to Live with Jesus"; "Judgment Day Is Rolling 'Round"; "Little More Faith in Jesus"; "Nobody Knows the Trouble I've Seen"; "Reign, Master Jesus"; "Run to Jesus"
From *The Book of American Negro Spirituals*	"Give Me Jesus"; "Steal Away to Jesus"
From *My Songs: Aframerican Religious Folk Songs Arranged and Interpreted by Roland Hayes*	"I'm Troubled"; "Steal Away"; "Sister Mary Had-a But One Child"; "Lit'l Boy"; "Live a-Humble"; "Hear de Lambs a-Cryin'?"; "The Last Supper"; "They Led My Lord Away"; "He Never Said a Mumberlin' Word"; "Did You Heard When Jesus Rose?"; "Were You There?"

As mentioned above, during the Second Great Awakening, evangelical denominations such as Baptists and Methodists began to systematically take the Christian message to African-Americans in both the North and South. Unlike the more formal liturgy and ritual of the Roman Catholic, Anglican/Episcopal, or even the Presbyterian or Lutheran churches, Methodists and Baptists espoused a more emotional form of worship, one centered on a personal relationship with Jesus Christ. It was a much more palatable style of worship for the slaves, many of whom embraced it—and the implied equality that came with Jesus's message. This style of worship would have also been more familiar to the older slaves who remembered their African religions.[62] Consequently, the sheer number of spirituals about Jesus and their more intimate tone are not surprising. Of the many "Jesus spirituals," "Steal Away" (or "Steal Away to Jesus") is perhaps the best known and most associated with the double-voicedness of the slaves:

> Steal away, steal away, steal away to Jesus! Steal away, steal away home.
>   I hain't got long to stay here.
> My Lord calls me, He calls me by the thunder; The trumpet sounds it in
>   my soul: I hain't got long to stay here.
> Tombstones are bursting—poor sinners stand trembling; The trumpet
>   sounds it in my soul: I hain't got long to stay here.[63]

"Steal Away" was in the repertoire of the Fisk Jubilee Singers and is sometimes linked to Harriet Tubman, as is "Go Down, Moses" and "Wade in the Water," although none of the major biographies makes that claim.[64] "Steal Away" is also attributed to minister–insurrectionist Nat Turner, most notably by Fisher, who devotes a pivotal chapter in *Negro Slave Songs of the United States* (1953) to the spiritual and others that he dates from 1800 to 1831.[65] In referencing the spirituals, Du Bois called "Steal Away" the "song of songs" and one of the "ten master songs . . . one may pluck from the forest of melody-songs of undoubted Negro origin and wide popular currency, and songs peculiarly characteristic of the slave."[66]

John W. Work, who also directed the Fisk Jubilee Singers, recounts the story of a group of slaves on a plantation on the Red River in the early 1800s who crossed the river each Sunday to worship at a nearby mission in the Indian Territory. In time, the slave owner heard that the missionary was from the North and, fearing that the man put ideas of freedom in their heads, ended the practice. But the slaves began sneaking away at nights to attend the services, singing "Steal Away to Jesus" as their cue. When the missionary heard the soft singing, he would go to the river's edge to help the slaves ashore. Work believed that the spiritual originated at this very plantation, and that the closing words, "I ain't got long to stay here," were a "sharp reminder" to the slaves not to delay too long on the opposite shore, because the slave owner exacted harsh penalties on those who defied him.[67]

Dorothy Scarborough quotes a story from Reverend Dr. R. H. Boyd, then eighty years old and head of the National Baptist Convention Publishing Board for the National Baptist Convention of America in Nashville. Boyd, who had published his own collection of spirituals, *Plantation Melody Songs*, said that "Steal Away" was sung on "a few plantations" in "slavery times" as a signal to other believers that a forbidden religious service would be held. In his account of his childhood, he often saw slaves invert a large "iron wash pot," place a stick beneath it, and sing "in such way that the sound would be muffled under the pot."[68]

Unlike some spirituals, where there is some question whether there is a secret, or at least covert, message about freedom, "Steal Away" appears to be straightforward and direct, particularly in the chorus. Blues/jazz singer/promoter Perry Bradford quotes "Grandma Betsy," herself a former slave, who flatly declared that the words always meant "steal away from their bosses and beat it up north to the promised land."[69]

To establish what he calls the "revolutionary principle" or "revolutionary spirit" of the spirituals, Lovell chooses "Steal Away" as his primary example. In a country where their permanent servitude was mandated by law and attempted escape was brutally (sometimes fatally) punished, and in the face of endless "religious" sermons demanding that the slave obey his master, running away itself was, of course, a revolutionary act. Regardless, slaves continued to sing about freedom in the spirituals—hence the words "steal away." But even the most thickheaded overseer might have recognized the intent of a statement as bold as "steal away." So, to lull the owner's suspicions and give the song a superficial veneer of piety, the words "to Jesus" would be added: "Now, [the slave poet] is in the clear. From now on, he can say whatever he pleases. The oppressor, always close by, is satisfied that this is a purely religious enterprise; his suspicion, aroused by the first 'Steal away' is fully allayed. But the slave poet goes on: Steal away, steal away home, I ain't got long to stay here."[70]

The slave owner presumably would not know until it was too late that the slave singing this spiritual was perhaps planning to escape or had already made contact with someone connected with the Underground Railroad. But the other slaves knew, of course, what the words meant.[71] Dixon also cites "Steal Away" as one of the most powerful spirituals, in part because it is "a religious song which gained a political meaning, yet without losing its spiritual dimension," and because of its direct reference to the visions in the apocalyptic Book of Revelation. With such dramatic imagery, it is no wonder that "Steal Away" retained its popularity among African-Americans long after the Emancipation Proclamation and the end of the Civil War, and continued to sustain singers and listeners through the great crises of American life. Dixon also recalls a conference on black literature she once attended where a concentration camp survivor—a Jewish woman from the Netherlands—spoke. According to the speaker, "The humming of 'Steal Away' was the code which helped 200 women in the barracks of a German concentration camp preserve their 'soul' while their bodies were submitted to a brutal process ending in annihilation."[72]

Nearly as well known, and equally obvious (at least from the vantage point of nearly 150 years later), is "Run to Jesus":

Run to Jesus, shun the danger, I don't expect to stay much longer here.
He will be our dearest friend, And will help us in the end. I don't expect to
stay much longer here.
Oh, I thought I heard them say, There were lions in the way, I don't expect
to stay much longer here.[73]

A passage in Douglass's autobiography (1855) about his plans to escape from yet another abusive, sadistic master cites this spiritual, which he writes had "a double meaning." He calls it "a favorite air" and said the slaves conspiring to flee sang it often, sometimes in front of their master. Some sang it as a paean to heaven, but for Douglass "it simply meant a speedy pilgrimage toward a free state, and deliverance from all of the evils and dangers of slavery."[74] In *The Story of the Jubilee Singers: With Their Songs* (1881), J. B. T. Marsh adds a note at the top of the page containing the words and music to "Run to Jesus," reporting that the song was presented to the Jubilee Singers in Washington, D.C., by Douglass himself, "with the interesting statement that it first suggested to him the thought of escaping from slavery."[75]

Many of the spirituals featuring Jesus have a different tone than their counterparts about Old Testament heroes, such as Moses, Daniel, or Abraham. Both "Steal Away" and "Run to Jesus" have an element of protectiveness about them. Jesus is a comforting, nurturing presence where safety can be found. There is an intensely personal nature to them. It is then not difficult to understand the slaves' attraction to the Nativity spirituals, where the helpless infant and the refugee parents in an occupied land find shelter in a cave or barn, surrounded by animals. The infant Jesus is tenderly, lovingly presented in these spirituals: "Sister Mary had-a but one child, Born in Bethlehem / And every time-a the-a baby cried, She'd-a rocked Him in the weary land."[76] But there is sometimes a note of defiance even amid the most tender depiction of Jesus as a baby. The "sentimental image of a baby in a manger" in a spiritual like "Sweet Little Jesus Boy," Mitchell suggests, should not "be confused with a faith without teeth":

Sweet little Jesus boy, they made you be born in a manger.
Sweet little Jesus boy, they didn't know who you was.
They treat you mean, Lawd; treat me mean, too,
But that's how things is down here; they don't know who you is.[77]

At the other end of his life, the death of Jesus is likewise presented in an intensely personal manner, often with the singer present at the time of Jesus's death on a Roman cross: "Wasn't it a pity an' a shame! An' He never said a mumberlin' word, Oh, not a word, not a word! / Dey nailed Him to de tree! An' He never said a mumberlin' word, Oh not a word, not word!" One of the most beautiful and haunting of all the spirituals, "Were You There?" also deals with the crucifixion. Like other spirituals set in "the eternal now," its lyrics place the listener at the scene itself: "Were you there when they crucified my Lord? Were you there when they crucified my Lord? / Oh, sometimes it causes me to tremble, tremble, tremble."[78]

Between the birth and crucifixion of Jesus, there is a fascinating body of spirituals that are quietly revolutionary, each in its own way. Even as they emphasize the nurturing, succoring side of Jesus, some of them also display a hint of defiance. If they did nothing else, these spirituals disprove the persistent lie that has resurfaced in some revisionist histories that the slaves were happy and content in their servitude. Included in the seminal *Slave Songs of the United States*, "Nobody Knows the Trouble I've Had" (alternately, "Nobody Knows the Trouble I See" or "Nobody Knows the Trouble I've Seen") has remained in the repertoire of many modern singers. The lyrics are full of surprising twists and turns, as befitting a spiritual that (like many others) had numerous unknown contributors through the centuries:

> *Nobody knows de trouble I've had, Nobody knows but Jesus.*
> *Nobody knows de trouble I've had, Glory hallelu!*
> *Sometimes I'm up, sometimes I'm down, Sometimes I'm almost on de groun'.*
> *What makes ole Satan hate me so? Because he got me once and he let me go.*[79]

At the bottom of the page containing the music and lyrics for this spiritual, the authors of *Slave Songs* include a fascinating note concerning an impromptu performance of "Nobody Knows" at the "colored schools" in Charleston in 1865 and an appearance by the Union commander, General Oliver O. Howard. Howard arrived at the schools when the former slaves were troubled over the prospect that the "confiscated lands" of the Sea Islands would not be awarded to them, as originally promised, but instead returned to the landowners. Saddened by the injustice of the situation, Howard asked those in attendance to sing before he spoke: "Immediately an old woman on the outskirts of the meeting began 'Nobody Knows the Trouble I've Had,' and the whole audience joined in. The General was so affected by the plaintive words and melody, that he found himself melting into tears and quite unable to maintain his official sternness."[80]

Of the "Glory hallelu!" (sometimes written as "hallelujah" in other collections) in the chorus to "Nobody Knows," Howard Thurman writes that the "triumph in God rings out trumpet-tongued!" Further, he believes that "there is something bold, audacious, unconquerable" in this spiritual.[81] Rather than simply a mournful paean to stoicism, as it appears on the surface, West also believes that the triumphant "Glory hallelujah!" is a "dialectical reversal" in the sense that "Nobody Knows the Trouble I've Seen" is not about patience, but about *change*.[82] In that light, spirituals like "Nobody Knows," "Trouble in Mind," and "Sometimes I Feel Like a Motherless Child" are not about the singer seeking pity—although doubtless some did. Instead, the singer has experienced pain and pity but is using the knowledge of that pain in a transformative way.[83] The overseer can whip the slave mercilessly, but privately the slave believes that Jesus will provide solace—and someday, deliverance.

In 1933, Jennie Hill, ninety-six, was interviewed about her life as a slave in Missouri. Her vivid memories of the violence done to helpless slaves are still disturbing to read, decades later. While her masters considered her little better than an animal, Hill knew better: "The slaves loved their families even as the Negroes love their own today and the happiest time of their lives was when they could sit at their cabin doors when the day's work was done and sing the old slave songs, 'Swing Low, Sweet Chariot,' 'Massa's in the Cold, Cold Ground' and 'Nobody Knows What Trouble I've Seen.' Children learned these songs and sang them only as a Negro child could. That was the slaves' only happiness, a happiness that for many of them did not last."[84]

"Swing Low, Sweet Chariot" is cited in several sources as a song with a hidden message relating to the Underground Railroad, and is another spiritual sometimes associated with Harriet Tubman. "Massa's in the Cold, Cold Ground," however, is a Stephen Foster song, written in the style of a spiritual.[85] So, when Hill lumps "Nobody Knows" with "Swing Low," this spiritual has a meaning beyond the surface request for Jesus to ease the singer's suffering.

Frederick Herzog draws an analogy with how a mother forgets the pain of childbirth when she sees her child: "so also liberated man rejoices when he finds himself freed through audacious suffering."[86] The pain and anguish the slaves suffered and sang about is "audacious" in that through their "unquestioning faith," Spencer suggests that they knew it was for a purpose—their freedom—and cites the chorus to "Nobody Knows the Trouble I've Seen" as proof.[87]

But then, simply surviving can also be a victory. In the late 1950s and early '60s, songwriters and civil rights activists Guy and Candie Carawan spent time on the isolated Johns Island off the coast of South Carolina. Even in the decades after the Civil War, certain spirituals provided the psychic relief necessary to keep going. Among the longtime inhabitants the Carawans interviewed was Esau Jenkins, a Johns Island native who served as an advocate for the island's many poor. Jenkins recalled "an old woman" he helped move from the plantation where she had lived her entire life:

> The only thing keep [sic] her going was some days she would look up at the sun and sing "Nobody Knows the Trouble I've Seen, Nobody Knows but Jesus." Other days she would sing "I Been in the Storm So Long." And when older folks sang those songs, it helped them realize they're trusting in God and reaching for a better day. . . .
>
> Now if we hide those sweet songs and try to get away from what we came from, what will we tell our children about the achievement we have made and the distance we have come?[88]

With that in mind, Floyd reminds us that the spirituals are songs of "longing and aspiration as well as chronicles of the black slave experience" in the United

States. And a spiritual like "Nobody Knows the Trouble I've Seen," in particular, records "the transition of the slave from African to African American, from slave to freedman, and the experiences that the African underwent in transition."[89] That unbreakable, unquestioning trust in Jesus permeates these spirituals not as a lament but as an expression of faith. From the beginning, we have known that we will get over. We will overcome someday.

In a similar vein is the spiritual "I'm Troubled in Mind" (alternately "Trouble in Mind"): "I'm troubled, I'm troubled, I'm troubled in mind / If Jesus don't help me, I surely will die." This spiritual, too, has a short preface written by Marsh, which says that the Jubilee Singers received it from a former slave, a "Mrs. Brown of Nashville" who first heard it sung by her father when she was a child: "After he had been whipped he always went and sat upon a certain log near his cabin, and with the tears streaming down his cheeks, sang this song with so much pathos that few could listen without weeping from sympathy: and even his cruel oppressors were not wholly unmoved."[90]

Once again, it is to an intimate, personal Jesus that the singer goes for relief. The slave in the story would slip away and pour out his pain and hurt in song, like a prayer. In this respect, these spirituals (and others like them) are more like the Psalms of the Old Testament—they may be laments, they may contain wisdom, they may be praise, they may be hopeful expectations of deliverance, sometimes all in the same piece! As Cheryl Ann Kirk-Duggan suggests, while they may "either implicitly or explicitly focus on the enemies," they are *not* statements of hopelessness or despair.[91]

There is still another aspect of Jesus depicted in the spirituals—not the nurturing Jesus of "Steal Away," not the tender Jesus of the Nativity, not even the Jesus of the intensely personal grief/triumph songs. These spirituals celebrate an altogether different Jesus Christ, the conquering redeemer of a fallen world: "Ride On, King Jesus," "King Jesus Sittin' on de Water Side," "Reign, Master Jesus" and others. "Ride On, King Jesus," with its allusions to the Book of Revelation, is especially intriguing: "Ride on King Jesus, no man can hinder him."[92] The spiritual refers to Revelation 19:11–16; a more militant, triumphant end-times image an embattled slave could hardly have hoped and prayed for, a deliverer, riding a white horse, leading the armies of heaven, who will "tread the wine press of the fury of the wrath of God the Almighty." It is interesting to compare the dramatic "Ride On, King Jesus" and this passage from the Revelation of John with this verse from "The Battle Hymn of the Republic":

> *Mine eyes have seen the glory of the coming of the Lord:*
> *He is trampling out the vintage where the grapes of wrath are stored;*
> *He hath loosed the fateful lightning of His terrible swift sword:*
> *His truth is marching on.*[93]

"Ride On, King Jesus" is clearly, at least from the disadvantage point of examining it 150 years after the fact, another spiritual of overt protest and rebellion. It is more stridently militaristic than most. The spiritual poet is confidently proclaiming a future victory over slavery, one that will come to those who are steadfast in their faith. When the time is right, Jesus, riding the white horse, will free the slaves: "The functions of Jesus as a deliverer are far-reaching. He is, first of all, an indomitable ruling king who does not hesitate a second in favoring his subjects, 'Ride on King Jesus! No man can hinder him,' or 'Ride on King Jesus, I want to go to heav'n in the mornin.'"[94]

A similar spiritual, found by Lydia Parrish in the Georgia Sea Islands in the early years of the twentieth century, is even more explicit, for the singer states, "I'm a ridin' my horse in the battlefield." The title, "Ride On, Conquering King," makes the context plain.[95] These related spirituals are an incisive example of what William Banfield calls "codes of insurrection, messages of spiritual freedom or political liberty" that are part of African-American music's "long-standing tradition as an art form of rebellion and cultural creation." Once a slave heard "Ride On, King Jesus," he or she experienced "a reverberation of meaning, a duality that reveals there is always more than what the word says on the surface." This "reverberation" is something that an outsider, not privy to the "coded private yet communal rituals," will ever truly understand.[96]

There are, of course, many, many other spirituals that various scholars and writers and even former slaves have, at different times, identified with the slaves' desperate yearning for freedom: "Swing Low, Sweet Chariot," "Oh Freedom," "Most Done Ling'rin' Here," "Wade in the Water," "Good News, de Chariot's Comin,'" "Hold the Wind," "Joshua Fit the Battle of Jericho," "Oh, Wasn't That a Wide Riber" (also "One More Riber to Cross"), "Many Thousand Gone," and "Heaven" (alternately, "Heav'n, Heav'n," "Goin' to Shout All Over God's Heaven," or "All God's Children Got Shoes"):

> *Oh, heaven, heaven*
> *Everybody talkin' about heaven ain't goin' there,*
> *Heaven, heaven,*
> *I'm going to shout all over heaven.*
> *Ah, you got shoes, I got shoes,*
> *All God's children got shoes.*
> *And when I get to heaven, goin' try on my shoes,*
> *I'm goin' to shout all over heaven.*[97]

There is a sharp comic/satiric edge to this spiritual, with the implication that once the slaves (or former slaves) get to heaven, they will either "take over" or at the very least be on the same level as their former masters. Additionally, while the singers themselves may not have owned shoes, their offspring will own shoes in heaven.[98] Many slave owners prohibited, upon pain of severe punishment, the owning of shoes in a vain attempt to keep their slaves from running away. How galling the line "*All* God's children got shoes" must have been to them. Likewise, the line "Everybody talkin' about heaven ain't going there" has a barbed point aimed directly at the hired white (and sometimes black) preachers who only preached obedience, the pious slave owners who whipped their slaves for attending a brush-arbor church, or even the white religious denominations that refused to condemn slavery. As another equally dangerous, almost subversive spiritual claims, "I'm going to tell God how you treat me." And, as in so many spirituals, "heaven" is a code word for "freedom," even as the slave poet also meant a literal "universe beyond the grave."[99]

"I Got Shoes" is also an excellent example of how the slaves used spirituals to create both a community and "esprit de corps" in the face of the owners' attempts to isolate and dehumanize them. Since spirituals were usually sung communally, Sanger posits that singing "I" and "you" created a "conversation" among the slaves. The singing of the lines "I got a shoe, you got a shoe" "affirmed the initial claim made by the others." And the final line, "*All* God's children got shoes," then "explicitly identified themselves as a community."[100]

For Howard Thurman, writing in 1945, few spirituals—and his writings reveal a man who clearly loved the spirituals—had the power of "Heaven." In *"Deep River,"* he imagines a slave, chopping cotton in sun, singing these words, then looking pointedly at the "big house," where the master lived in comfort off of the slave's misery:

> This is one of the authentic songs of protest. It was sung in anticipation of a time that even yet has not fully come—a time when there shall be no slave row in the church, no gallery set aside for the slave, no special place, no segregation, no badge of racial and social stigma, but complete freedom of movement. Even at that far-off moment in the past, these early singers put their fingers on the most vulnerable spot in Christianity and democracy. The wide, free range of his spirit sent him in his song beyond all barriers. In God's presence at least there would be freedom; slavery is no part of the purpose or the plan of God. Man, therefore, is the great enemy of man. This is the mood of that song.[101]

The persistent and pervasive nature of the "protest spirituals" indicates, as so many writers have suggested, that these songs provided slaves with both comfort and passion, kindling and rekindling hopes of deliverance from bondage. Their double-voicedness enabled them to convey multiple layers of meaning—educational, devotional, revolutionary. The effectiveness of the protest spirituals is only one of the reasons that they would survive beyond the Civil War to aid freedom fighters yet unborn in the difficult century ahead.

INTERLUDE

The Post–Civil War Era Through the Great Migration

I would argue . . . that music is the highest expression of the culture of freedom created by the most unfree people in the United States. . . . Not just the struggle for freedom but also the struggle of how you preserve your humanity at the existential level, not go crazy, not go insane, not lose your dignity, not lose your sense of being a human being as opposed to just a commodity or a piece of cattle or a piece of property.

—CORNEL WEST

Through fugitive slaves and irrepressible discussion this desire for freedom seized the black millions still in bondage, and became their one ideal of life. The black bards caught new notes, and sometimes even dared to sing,—

"O Freedom, O Freedom, O Freedom
   over me!
Before I'll be a slave
I'll be buried in my grave,
And go home to my Lord
And be free."

For fifty years Negro religion thus transformed itself and identified itself with the dream of Abolition, until that which was a radical fad in the white North and an anarchistic plot in the white South had become a religion to the black world.

—W. E. B. DU BOIS

How do you survive leaving everything you know to try to reconstruct your life and future in a new way? What do you carry with you on your journey to the new place? . . . I look at the place and function of our sacred music tradition as a source of strength that helped us to survive spiritually and emotionally in our new places within and without. When studied carefully, our music culture documents a lot about how we saw ourselves in our movings.

—BERNICE JOHNSON REAGON

For the slaves in the South, the end of the Civil War meant that as they had believed and sung all along, God had intervened on their behalf. Through their unwavering faith, their spirituals, and their prayers, they had played an active part in their own deliverance. As Du Bois writes, "To most of the four million black folk emancipated by civil war, God was real. They knew Him. . . . His plan for them was clear; they were to suffer and be degraded, and then afterwards by Divine edict, raised to manhood and power; and so on January 1, 1863, He made them free."[1]

Still, if a great many of the spirituals had been about physical freedom on earth as well eternal freedom in heaven, what use would they be in this new world? Their most compelling raison d'être was gone. Soon, a number of observers agreed, all the old plantation songs and hymns would be forgotten and eventually lost. In fact, every few years, a number of writers would bemoan the disappearance of the spirituals.[2] But after the too-short spring of Reconstruction, life in the South quickly became a harsh winter for the newly freed slaves. A series of broken promises gave way to the nightmarish world of Jim Crow laws, state-sanctioned murder, rape, intimidation, lawlessness, and virtual serfdom that differed from slavery only in degree.[3]

But the spirituals *did* survive through a variety of both expected and unexpected sources. While many of the former slaves eventually fled North (see below), those left behind turned again to the only institution left to them, the African-American church, which became not just an "extension of the family," but also "a school, a lecture hall, and recreational center." The church provided a safe place to gather and share information.[4] Established (sometimes covertly) during the Civil War, southern black churches provided a haven for beleaguered, abused African-Americans, providing everything from insurance to banking. Just as important, they created a place to replicate the "African extended-family society" necessary for survival in a hostile land.[5]

Tempered by the fire of adversity, the leaders of these African-American churches were well equipped to provide leadership during Reconstruction and beyond. These pastors were neither the "products of white paternalism" nor possessed of a "concentration camp system" mentality. Instead, Vincent Harding suggests, they "felt ready to walk directly out of slavery into the dangerous and necessary freedom of self-government." They were, he says, "their own best signs of the new times."[6]

The first task, of course, was survival. But beyond survival, from its earliest origins, "the Black Church has been set on freedom." Consequently, the African-American church seamlessly made the transition from slavery to the "new" America with its focus and integrity intact, though its activism sometimes followed a "meandering course." Mary Sawyer argues, however, that even when "survival was the task of the day, freedom was the longing of the heart, and in that longing were nourished the seeds of black political action."[7] And in the case of the post-Reconstruction black church, the singing of spirituals was a logical extension of that "activism," as author and civil rights activist Wyatt Tee Walker asserts. The African-American church was the "chief reservoir of Black sacred music," which held a "vast potential for a ministry of social change at both the personal and collective levels." This is due in part, he believes, to the fact that the sacred music of the African-American has always been "geared" to "liberation themes":

> The music of Euro-American churches was not created in the social context of resistance to racism and oppression. It is patently clear that people at worship should be singing the music that relates directly to their social context. The social context of Black people is the need for liberation from racism and oppression.
>
> If Black people are to pursue the most direct route to liberation via religion, there is a need for them to embrace the music which in large measure has demonstrated its relevance and usefulness in resisting racism and oppression.[8]

With this in mind, and Walker's wry note that "you can't organize Black folks for anything without music,"[9] the rapid expansion of African-American affiliated denominations, such as the African Methodist Episcopal, African Methodist Episcopal Zion, Colored (later Christian) Methodist Episcopal, the various "free" Baptist churches, and other smaller denominations during and after Reconstruction, is hardly surprising. Most of these groups began in the larger southern cities and gradually worked their way to the smaller towns in the early 1800s until virtually every village had one or both, followed, at the turn of the following century, by the founding of the Holiness/Pentecostal churches.[10]

The spirituals continued to be sung, particularly in those smaller, rural southern churches where resources for hymnals were often scarce. But the spirituals gradually made their way into some northern black churches as well, including those founded by Richard Allen and Absalom Jones in Philadelphia in the 1790s, which were among the first independent African-American churches in the United States. Allen's "Mother Bethel" was successful enough that he commissioned and edited hymnals for the church that included spirituals.[11]

However, in many of the black churches in the industrial North, where labor employment opportunities meant that there was something approaching an African-American middle class, the leaders often stressed "education and restraint" over "emotional religion" (and singing). The music in these churches differed little from the music sung and performed in white churches across town.[12]

John W. Work writes in 1915 that with Emancipation, some African-Americans, especially in the "first generation" after slavery, simply chose to leave the spirituals behind. The songs were painful reminders of slavery, something to be ignored with "silent contempt" or regarded with "positive apathy." This post-slavery generation, he suggests, often "laugh[ed] them to scorn."[13] But other African-Americans refused to discard the spirituals. Langston Hughes paints a vivid picture in 1926 of the split that emerged with the advent of the better-educated, middle-class African-Americans who attended sedate "high church" denominations, and the recently arrived "low-down folks, the so-called common element" who are "the majority." That group, he writes, did not aspire to be white, nor to emulate the religious practices of most whites: "Their joy runs, bang! into ecstasy. Their religion soars to a shout." They were not, he adds, "afraid" of spirituals, as are "their more intellectual brethren."[14] Those storefront churches on Chicago's State Street, as Hughes notes earlier, and many, many more beside them not only ensured the survival of the spiritual, but also provided the fertile ground from whence the gospel music of Thomas Dorsey and Mahalia Jackson would later spring.

A more unlikely source for the continued survival of the spirituals, blackface minstrelsy retained its place as the dominant popular music form late into the nineteenth century, when it was replaced by what would become Tin Pan Alley.[15] Minstrel shows evolved into elaborate confections, sometimes with nearly a hundred musicians, singers, comics, and dancers, complete with dramatic interludes, and usually ending with a "sacred" concert, with a quartet (and sometimes the entire company) singing both mock spirituals and, occasionally, the real thing. The minstrel shows eventually included more and more African-American performers and some, like the Georgia Minstrels, were booked into America's most prestigious venues, both North and South. The racism that marked the minstrel format was still present, even into the twentieth century, but the presence of black songwriters and singers provided yet another opportunity for the use of "double-voicedness" in the lyrics and soliloquies.[16]

The autobiography of W. C. Handy, the "Father of the Blues," provides one of the few detailed personal accounts of the evolution of American music from minstrelsy to the rise of Tin Pan Alley. During his short tenure as a band director at an all-black college, Handy once delivered a stirring defense of the financial opportunities it provided African-Americans, even in this most racist of popular music formats, at the turn of the twentieth century. "If morning stars sing together," he once said, "who shall say that minstrel men may not lead parades through pearly gates and up streets of gold?"[17]

The best-known, most popular minstrel show, the all-black Callender's Georgia Minstrels, began adding spirituals (and pseudo-spirituals) and "jubilee quartettes" in 1876, which remained a popular feature with the troupe for many years.[18] One intriguing bit of cross-fertilization: in his survey of all major African-American musicians during that time, James Trotter writes that "a year or two ago" (ca. 1879), the jubilee quartet from the Georgia Minstrels was invited to sing at "one of the most fashionable churches" in an unnamed "Western" city, where "these fine singers did full justice to the proprieties of the occasion."[19]

Eventually, the minstrel shows declined in popularity in the waning years of the nineteenth century, even as the jubilee groups from African-American colleges flourished well into the twentieth century. For white audiences, tastes in popular music shifted first to the English dance hall tradition of song, then to the catchy melodies cranked out by the songwriters of the various small music publishing houses on East 14th Street in New York's Union Square theater district, which morphed the minstrel shows into variety shows, popularly called *vaudeville*.[20]

Another significant factor in the survival of the spirituals was the success of the Fisk Jubilee Singers (see the previous chapter) and the various other similar collegiate organizations, such as those from the Hampton Institute, Atlanta University, Talladega College, and Tuskegee Institute, which not only kept the old spirituals alive in the second half of the nineteenth century, but actively sought out and published previously unheard or undocumented spirituals.[21] Some of these college jubilee groups even took the spirituals to new audiences abroad, including virulently racist South Africa, where their legacy is still evident today.[22] Still, it is significant that the founder of the troupe was initially forced to add "Jubilee" to the group's name to differentiate it from the overwhelmingly popular minstrel shows, which performed in the same venues and towns.[23]

The Fisk influence was felt in other areas as well. Two early directors of the Fisk Jubilee Singers were John Wesley Work II and his son, John Wesley Work III, both mentioned above. Both men collected, arranged, and published additional spirituals. John W. Work III's book *American Negro Songs and Spirituals: A Comprehensive Collection of 230 Folk Songs, Religious and Secular* (1940) includes a scholarly analysis of the musical composition of spirituals as well as the words and music to both familiar and newly uncovered spirituals from "more than half a century of collecting."[24]

Work was joined by an extraordinary collection of African-American composers, arrangers, and performers whose diligent efforts kept the "arranged spiritual" alive in the latter half of the nineteenth century and the first half of the twentieth. It should be noted that "arranged spirituals" are considered "adaptations" of the originals, arranged, edited, and performed in classically formalized settings, akin to what a white college choral group of the time might sing. By our earlier definition, they are not *true* spirituals, which are always improvised and sung without accompaniment and generally for multiple purposes, only some of which were religious in nature. Consequently, concert singers could only present an "approximation" of how the spirituals had originally been sung by slaves.[25]

Most important, the basic texts and melodies survived, which enabled them to remain available when African-Americans needed them again in the decades to come. Consequently, the work of composers or singers like Roland Hayes, Jules Bledsoe, Marian Anderson, Paul Robeson, Harry Thacker Burleigh, Samuel Coleridge-Taylor, R. Nathaniel Dett, Hall Johnson, J. Rosamond Johnson, Clarence Cameron White, William Grant Still, Jester Hairston, Leontyne Price, and Jessye Norman, among others, in identifying, cataloging, arranging, and performing the spirituals was vitally important.[26] Some of these artists, and many more, are referenced in Trotter's *Music and Some Highly Musical People* (1878). Trotter's book is an exhaustive survey of the many "serious" African-American artists of his day. He is obviously partial to musicians and singers who perform the classical repertoire of western Europe, but black singers who incorporate carefully notated arrangements of spirituals do draw his praise as well. Like Handy, Trotter cites the high-quality musicianship of the Georgia Minstrels, even as he decries the "malicious caricaturing" of African-Americans.[27]

The spiritual continued in yet another incarnation—jubilee. Jubilee is the spiritual sung in the style of a barbershop quartet. Barbershop—generally an all-male form of a cappella part-singing—originated in the African-American barbershops of North America, perhaps as early as the Reconstruction era. Whites generally did not cut hair until the beginning of the twentieth century, and black barbershops became popular meeting places for African-American men.[28] Not surprisingly, given the popularity of the Fisk Jubilee Singers and the minstrel shows featuring close-harmony spirituals (or at least mock spirituals), many of the singers adapted the old spirituals into this new singing form. Writing in 1915, when the larger jubilee groups were beginning to fall out of favor, Fisk Jubilee Singers director John W. Work II cites this style of singing spirituals for rejuvenating the university jubilee singing movement.[29] According to Abbott, barbershop, which "precipitated a shift from mixed-voice choral groups to male quartets," was clearly the most popular venue in which to spread the message.[30]

In 1925, James Weldon Johnson wrote that barbershop-styled singing began even earlier still. He notes that he heard African-American barbershop quartets as a young boy in Jacksonville: "Indeed, it may be said that all male Negro youth of the United States is divided into quartets."[31] Both Jelly Roll Morton and Louis Armstrong sang in jubilee groups in New Orleans in the 1890s. Morton's group sang "Steal Away to Jesus" and other spirituals at wakes—for the plentiful food and beer that followed.[32] And jubilee groups were among the first to be recorded by Thomas Edison and others in the early days of cylinders and recorded sound.[33]

One last phenomenon aided in the widespread survival of the spiritual when other musical forms—from hokum to ragtime—eventually faded from the public's consciousness. For many years, religious singers would not sing secular songs—a point of view maintained by Mahalia Jackson throughout her career and continued by some gospel singers even today. But at some point, apparently during the hard economic times of the 1890s or somewhat later, a new breed of musicians appeared, singing religious songs, including spirituals, on busy street corners and at train stations in both the North and South. Usually accompanying themselves only on a battered guitar, these "songsters" (to use Paul Oliver's term) were different from the itinerant bluesmen (and occasional blueswomen) who sometimes could be found busking on the same corners in the same rough-hewn style.[34]

The rise of the songsters is little understood and virtually no paper trail follows them. The (now) best-known songster of them all, Blind Willie Johnson (fig. 4), has a recorded legacy of just thirty known songs, which features several spirituals (or songs that came to be performed as spirituals), including "If I Had My Way I'd Tear This Building Down" (also known as "Samson and Delilah"), "John the Revelator," "Jesus Make Up My Dying Bed," and "Nobody's Fault but Mine." His

FIGURE 4

Despite the scarcity of his recordings and the fact that virtually nothing is known about him, Blind Willie Johnson's singing and slide-guitar playing have been deeply influential on modern musicians.

singing and slide-guitar playing are profoundly influential on modern musicians, yet virtually nothing is known about the man.[35] These singer/guitarist/composer songsters combined the lyrics and melodies of the spirituals, along with some self-penned topical songs (usually a recent well-known disaster, such as a Mississippi Delta flood or the sinking of the *Titanic*), but sang them with the pronounced beat of the blues.[36]

For all these reasons, the spiritual endured. The various collections of spirituals released around the turn of the twentieth century through the 1950s generally make no distinction between ancient spirituals (that only recently had been heard and notated) and recently created spirituals—if, indeed, that distinction is even possible to make. In cases where there is a topical reference or a mention of a recent technological advance (the airplane or radio, to name two) in a song, it is possible to guess the date of composition. However, in "true" spirituals, the "airplane" or "radio" reference could just as likely be part of a recently composed wandering couplet inserted by an enthusiastic singer on the night a collector was present!

For instance, *Old Plantation Hymns* is subtitled *A Collection of Hitherto Unpublished Melodies of the Slave and the Freedman, with Historical and Descriptive Notes* and comprises spirituals William E. Barton collected between 1880 and 1887 in "the South." It includes only a small handful of spirituals found in earlier collections. *Old Plantation Hymns* also contains a number of spirituals referencing railroads, which would (apparently) place their time of composition/compilation after the advent of the steam engine in the South.[37] Likewise, the collection by singer Eva Jessye (printed in 1927, when she was in her early thirties) is drawn from her memories of rural Coffeyville, on the Kansas–Oklahoma border, and of the songs of former slaves, and it contains a number of spirituals not found in other collections. None of these spirituals has any topical references and their "composition" could just as easily predate the Civil War.[38]

The spiritual (and its later permutation, gospel) continued to spread with the advent of the twentieth century and beyond, fueled in part by one of the greatest mass population shifts in world history, the Great Migration.[39] Despite grim economic conditions and worsening racism, including systemic violence in the South, an estimated 200,000 blacks migrated to the North between 1890 and 1910. However, one source estimated that 330,000 blacks moved northward in 1915 alone.[40] Another key catalyst for the move was the Supreme Court's infamous *Plessy v. Ferguson* decision in 1896, which codified existing racial segregation. While blacks in both the North and South responded by painstakingly building their own institutions, many whites in the Jim Crow South used *Plessy* to seize what few rights remained to African-Americans.[41]

The differences in the living conditions between the North and much of the South widened dramatically in 1915. Once war was declared and more nations were drawn into hostilities, the waves of European immigration into the United States slowed dramatically, just as U.S. industries were ramping up to supply war material to the nations that would soon become America's allies. For the first time, tens of thousands of jobs were available to African-Americans. Conditions in the South were such that blacks had certainly been ready to leave. It took a "precipitating event"—World War I—to get many of them to do so. It also took optimistic, encouraging letters from those who had gone before and the constant urging of respected publications such as the *Chicago Defender* to prompt African-Americans to make the arduous, often dangerous journey northward.[42]

They left behind grinding poverty and the worst of Jim Crow, the "violently enforced codes of the southern caste system," which survived from 1880s into the early 1970s. In time, this migration would be larger than either the California Gold Rush of the 1850s or the various Dust Bowl migrations. "But more remarkably," writes Isabel Wilkerson, "it was the first mass act of independence by a people who were in bondage in this country for far longer than they have been free."[43]

The Great Migration was a complicated, moving tapestry, a series of continual smaller migrations for various reasons to various locations. African-Americans moved to the industrial cities of the South (Birmingham, Norfolk, Memphis) and great Midwestern cities like St. Louis, Kansas City, Toledo, and Akron, as well the fabled destinations of Chicago and Detroit. Sometimes they moved to three or more of the cities mentioned above, then moved back again.[44]

Regardless, it was an act of protest, one reflected in every aspect of the immigrants' lives, including their music. It changed the United States. To cite one example, Chicago's black population at the beginning of the Great Migration was about forty-four thousand. By 2000, it was more than a million. More African-Americans now lived in Chicago, the eventual incubator of gospel music, than in the entire state of Mississippi.[45] This migration may have had little effect on the South (save for some labor shortages), but it had a profound effect on whites and blacks in the North:

> In the realm of politics, too, the migration that took black southerners out of the South and brought them within reach of the ballot box had revolutionary consequences. Disfranchised in the South, African-Americans were able to exercise their citizens' rights and pursue their political interests in only the most constricted and indirect manner. Without black constituents, southern politicians had little reason to embrace issues of importance to those who were the victims of racial and economic oppression. Only when large numbers of blacks were voters—which meant only when large numbers of blacks had left the South—did the Federal Government begin to support black civil rights.[46]

The African-Americans (and, to a somewhat lesser degree, the whites) who were part of this diaspora arrived with their culture, including their music and religion, intact. More than half of all churchgoers in the South were Baptists and three-quarters of black Christians were Baptists. It was, as one writer puts it, "a migration of Baptists, millions of Baptists." This is significant because, as we will see below, those Baptists brought with them their deep-rooted beliefs about singing and the power of song.[47]

Recent studies have also shown that these migrants were often better educated than those who remained behind in the South and soon were making—on average—better incomes than the African-Americans already established in the North, despite being relegated to the worst-paying jobs.[48] For those who actually arrived from rural villages on the Mississippi Delta, Chicago's Bronzeville on the South Side and other African-American enclaves must have seemed magical indeed. To mention one area—music—black audiences, at least in the larger northern cities, had access to the classical music of Beethoven and Bach, marching bands to match those of John Philip Sousa, as well as popular music sung by African-Americans in their own venues. Just as significantly, they had access to the music originating in their own neighborhoods. This was music drawn from the original African-American work songs and spirituals—barbershop, hokum, reels, barrelhouse-styled piano, swing, ragtime, and especially jass (later written as "jazz") and the blues. This was music that would later be wholeheartedly embraced by white listeners as well.[49] The Harlem Renaissance and its Chicago counterpart featured equally extraordinary opportunities in theater, film, dance, literature, and all the other arts.[50] Richard Wright spoke for many transplanted Mississippians when he had a black worker respond to a white's dismissive view of the North as follows: "We'd rather be a lamppost in Chicago than the president of Dixie!"[51]

And, most important, these potential immigrants were told that there were jobs for the taking up North. Good jobs. Jobs that paid a decent wage that would enable them to get out of debt, put their kids through school, give something to their church, and maybe even enjoy the fruits of the Harlem Renaissance. But the industrial cities of the North were *not* Shangri-la. Blacks who arrived looking for employment were herded into small, overcrowded areas, usually in the inner city, with tightly regulated (officially or otherwise) boundaries. As for the jobs themselves, the great majority were backbreaking, low-paying, manual positions with no chance at advancement: construction workers, janitors, elevator operators, trash collectors, servants, maids, or waiters. Most of the labor unions, corporations, local government, and even the federal government used every means to keep African-Americans out.

Nevertheless, through the work and sacrifice of thousands, times changed, at least in some of the unions. The story of African-Americans and labor is extraordinarily complex and, like the Great Migration, not something that lends itself to a linear narrative. Even blacks who had long lived in the North and who had been members of unions for many years felt both implicit and overt racism.[52] In the beginning, only a few labor unions allowed blacks, reluctantly, including the International Longshoremen's Association and the International Ladies' Garment Workers' Union, but even those relegated African-Americans to the most physically demanding, unskilled positions for the lowest wages.[53]

Not surprisingly, not all African-American leaders supported the unions. At a time when labor unions were weak in the North and virtually nonexistent in the South, and rarely supported the admission of black workers, Booker T. Washington was against both labor unionism and "labor solidarity between white and Negro workers." In 1918, Du Bois wrote in *The Crisis* that despite his longtime support of unions, harsh personal experience led him to believe that there was "absolutely no hope of justice" for African-Americans within the American Federation of Labor—a situation he found "peculiarly disheartening."[54] According to Gunnar Myrdal, "until after the First World War labor unions were looked upon as the natural enemies of Negroes."[55]

By the mid-1940s, however, following the New Deal and the Roosevelt reforms, Ralph Bunche would write that the "main hope" of African-Americans lies with "white labor," noting that "redemption" would never occur in southern politics "until labor, farm and industrial, black and white, has become so strongly organized and so bold as to present a forceful challenge to the authority of the entrenched interests." Myrdal quotes Bunche as predicting that it would take "a new agrarian and industrial revolution" before "significant changes in the fundamental relationships—political, economic or racial"—could take place.[56] Redemption and change did come, of course, just not in the way that Bunche—or virtually any other commentator at the time—predicted.

3

UNION SONGS, PROTEST SONGS, AND THE SPIRITUALS

Remember, this is the only American working-class movement which sings. Tremble then at the IWW, for a singing movement is not to be beaten. . . . They love and revere their singers, too, in the IWW. . . . I have met men carrying next to their hearts, in the pocket of their working clothes, little bottles with some of Joe Hill's ashes in them. I know no other group of Americans which honors its singers.

—JOHN REED

A singing army is a winning army, and a singing labor movement cannot be defeated. Songs can express sorrow as well as triumph, but the fact that a man sings shows that his spirit is still free and searching. When hundreds of men and women in a labor union sing together, their individual longing for dignity and freedom are bound into an irrepressible force. Workers who hesitate are swept into the movement, and before all these determined marchers, united by their purpose and their singing, the citadels of oppression crumble and surrender.

—JOHN L. LEWIS

I never danced 'til the Union came in.

—AUNT MOLLY JACKSON

The link between labor union songs and protest spirituals provides a connection between past and present in the civil rights movement. A number of Martin Luther King, Jr.'s advisers came from the labor movement, some of whom had strong connections to the use of black sacred music in a labor context. At a time when the mainstream media rarely reported on the lives and music of African-Americans, the socialist and communist press, along with various labor-oriented publications, chronicled the assimilation of spirituals into the union. Though labor's initial reluctance to become involved in the civil rights of African-Americans is well documented, the importance of the images and connections made when black and white workers joined together in song on the picket lines and in the union halls is a significant part of the larger narrative. The connection between the spirituals of the Civil War and the freedom songs of the civil rights movement is, in many ways, the spiritual-turned-labor-song of the 1930s.

History

The idea of singing as a recruiting tool and as a way to unite and fortify union members during labor actions had been well established from the early days of unions in the United States.[1] Many of those labor songs were based on popular, well-known hymns and gospel songs. One writer estimates that a quarter "of all song-poems from the period 1865–1895 borrowed melodies of religious hymns." This is understandable, as the late nineteenth century was a period of deep-rooted religious activity among most Americans.[2] The first major American union, the Noble and Holy Order of the Knights of Labor, was founded in secrecy in 1869, and by 1886 was said to number seven hundred thousand members after a series of successful strikes. The Knights of Labor encouraged singing and frequently sang songs based on popular secular and religious songs of the day, including "Modern Missionary Zeal" (based on "Onward, Christian Soldiers"), "Storm the Fort, Ye Knights," and "Spread the Light" (both based on "Hold the Fort," a popular gospel hymn).[3]

However, with their grand, inclusive vision of "one big union" uniting *all* workers, the Industrial Workers of the World (IWW) distinguished itself from competing labor organizations by recruiting unskilled laborers and accepting both recent immigrants and African-Americans. During their brief heyday (from 1905 until America's involvement in World War I, although the organization continues in a truncated form even today), the "Wobblies" firmly established the concept of a "singing" union and none "aroused more passions, stirred more controversy, nor sang more loudly." The Wobblies drew their greatest strength from the ranks of the poorly paid, often uneducated, and most abused workers in the "woolen and silk factories, the mining and lumber industry, the cotton and produce fields," as well as the industrial assembly line workers of the Midwest.[4] One of the Wobblies' slogans was "Sing and fight," and the following statement was regularly repeated to IWW members: "Right was the tyrant king who once said, 'Beware of a movement that sings.' . . . Whenever and wherever the oppressed challenge the old order, songs are on their lips."[5]

The Wobblies are still known as the union of the legendary labor organizer (and songwriter) Joe Hill and for the songs "Solidarity Forever," "There Is Power in the Union," "Commonwealth of Toil," "Casey Jones," "The Preacher and the Slave," and most importantly, *The Little Red Songbook*, published in 1909 with the distinctive subtitle *IWW Songs—To Fan the Flames of Discontent*.[6] Longtime folk singer and activist Pete Seeger said the Wobblies were the "singingest union America ever had."[7]

The Little Red Songbook was not the first collection of labor songs. James and Emily Tallmadge published the influential *Labor Songs Dedicated to the Knights of Labor* in the 1880s.[8] Also predating the first IWW songbook was *Socialist Songs* (1900) and the larger *Socialist Songs with Music*, both released by Charles H. Kerr and primarily composed of songs from *Chants of Labor*, a well-known British labor publication first published in 1888.[9] But all were soon eclipsed by *The Little Red Songbook*.

Richard Brazier joined the Wobblies in 1907 after hearing about them from Canadian miners. Brazier was attracted by their songs and "the gusto with which its members sang them." Such singing, he believed, was both "good propaganda" and "held the crowd for Wobbly speakers who followed." Organizer J. H. Walsh promoted the creation of an IWW songbook to assemble the songs the group was already singing, replacing an informal collection of loose-leaf pamphlets and lyric sheets. Walsh and other Wobblies pointed to the use by workingmen and -women in other countries of "songs of discontent," including the "Marseillaise," the "Internationale," "The Red Flag," and "Hold the Fort." Songs, he said, were "easily remembered" even as "dull prose is soon forgotten." The "aims and principles can be recorded in songs as well as in leaflets and pamphlets—in some cases even better," since workers were more likely to remember a song than "a dry-as-dust polemic."[10]

From the beginning, many labor-related songs set new lyrics to the melodies of the popular tunes and religious hymns of the day.[11] The first Wobbly songbook, with its vivid red cover and IWW slogans ("An Injury to One Is An Injury to All" and "Labor Is Entitled to All It Produces"), included new words set to the music regularly performed by the Salvation Army bands, who often occupied the same street corners as Wobbly recruiters. Brazier notes that these bands would sometimes try to drown out IWW orators, who would respond by singing the new lyrics over the hymns.[12]

Despite the many editions of *Songs of the Workers: To Fan the Flames of Discontent* (sometimes titled *IWW Songs: To Fan the Flames of Discontent*), copies are relatively scarce and all instances of the second edition, published in 1910, are apparently lost.[13] The nineteenth edition (published in 1923, reprinted by Charles H. Kerr in 1989), titled *IWW Songs: To Fan the Flames of Discontent*, covers fifty-one songs and "Joe Hill's Last Will," written on the eve of Hill's execution. The pocket-sized booklet, just 4 by 5 ¾ inches, has no musical notation with the lyrics. Instead, various popular melodies are indicated under the titles. Many of the songs were based on religious source material.[14] Fifty years later, the thirty-fourth edition (1973) is larger in format, but has relatively few changes from the 1923 version. It covers fifty-two songs (a few with musical notation), along with several poems, parables, and tributes. Of those fifty-two, thirteen are based on religious source material.[15]

One of the most popular of those songs, "Hallelujah, on the Bum" (or "Halle-lujah, I'm a Bum"), was transcribed by American poet Carl Sandburg and included in his book *The American Songbag* in 1927. This version has remained remarkably resilient through the decades.[16] As a newspaper reporter, Sandburg was sympa-thetic to the plight of African-Americans in the United States and wrote at length about racism and segregation. When he toured the country reading his poems and singing the old songs he had collected, he included a number of songs that had their origins in the black community, including spirituals provided by Isa-dora Bennett Reed, DuBose Heyward, Julia Peterkin, "and other Southern friends." Sandburg also sang "prison and jail songs and labor anthems" provided by "IWW leaders and labor organizers."[17] Sandburg's immense popularity helped both causes, but was particularly helpful in exposing the power and the beauty of the spiritual to a further—that is to say, *white*—audience. From the standpoint of the continuity of the spiritual, *American Songbag*'s collection included sixteen African-American sacred songs, all but a few genuine spirituals.[18]

One particularly intriguing song featured in *American Songbag* is "God's Goin' to Set This World on Fire," which includes two different sets of lyrics. As his intro-duction to the spiritual suggests, Sandburg clearly admired the Wobblies: "They were outlaws, gypsies, vags. Several times they wrecked jails, tore the doors off hinges, twisted the bars, spoiled the plumbing, and defied all law and government. While in jail they often made the walls ring with a negro spiritual given here. Their favorite verse was 'God's Goin' to Set This World on Fire.' It suggests Fire wrecking the world as the I.W.W. wrecked jails."[19]

Version A reads more like a standard spiritual, although it does not take much imagination to substitute "scabs" or "bosses" for "sinners":

> *God's goin' to set this world on fire,*
> *One o' these days!*
> *All you sinners gonna turn up missing,*
> *One o' these days!*[20]

Sandburg writes that he received version B from Arthur Billings of Brooklyn, "who heard it from a group of negroes in a Virginia farm house five years ago." The lyric is accompanied by a small drawing of a town in the aftermath of a fire, with the church steeple leaning precariously. Where the lyrics read "valiant hearted soldiers," the allusion to versions of "John Brown's Body" long beloved by African-Americans is unmistakable:

> *God don't want no coward soldiers,*
> *Some o' these days.*
> *He wants valiant hearted soldiers*
> *Some of these days.*[21]

Evangelist Ira Sankey initially took "Hold the Fort" to England, where the British Transport and General Workers Union borrowed it from Sankey's revival meetings and rewrote the lyrics as a union song. The song then traveled back to the United States where the Knights of Labor used it as well. But it is *The Little Red Songbook* version that has remained in the repertoire of American labor.[22] When sixteen IWW men on the steamer *Verona* were assassinated in Everett, Washington, in November 1916, witnesses said the Wobblies died while singing "Hold the Fort."[23]

Legendary IWW member Joe Hill, who would later be hastily executed by Utah authorities under questionable circumstances in 1915, wrote a number of the best-known union songs, including "The Preacher and the Slave," which was included in the third edition of *The Little Red Songbook*. Sandburg recorded it on one of the 78-rpm records drawn from the music in *The American Songbag*.[24] Hill is also responsible for "There Is Power in the Union," based on a well-known camp-meeting hymn: "There is pow'r, there is pow'r / In the band of working-men."[25] But Hill's most lasting legacy may be as a larger-than-life symbol to the labor movement. His short life has served as both an inspiration to union members and a cautionary tale—after all, if Utah could frame and assassinate Joe Hill with impunity, they "could frame any honest worker." In 1930, writer Alfred Hayes wrote a poem titled "I Dreamed I Saw Joe Hill Last Night." Six years later, Earl Robinson set the poem to music. "I Dreamed I Saw Joe Hill Last Night" was reprinted in the *Daily Worker* and eventually recorded numerous times by artists ranging from Pete Seeger to Paul Robeson, and most famously by Joan Baez at Woodstock in 1969.[26] "Without question, today's Joe Hill belongs to workers both in and out of the IWW ranks and beyond national borders," writes labor historian and folklorist Archie Green.[27]

In 2007, Green and others compiled all 192 songs printed in the known copies of *The Little Red Songbook*, along with various essays and discographies on the Wobblies, in *The Big Red Songbook*. Again, a significant number of the songs (where the melodies are indicated) are based on religious source material, including some spirituals.[28] Green attributes one Wobbly song as definitively having been set to the music of an African-American spiritual, "The Bosses in Slavery Hold You," which another IWW historian suggests may have been set to the melody from the spiritual "Some of These Days": "The bosses will in slavery hold you / If you don't join the union one of these days."[29]

In the end, the IWW attained almost mythic status and is still celebrated for its principles—and its emphasis on singing, which inspired other protest organizations in the decades that followed. In 1951, James Jones's novel on pre–World War II army life, *From Here to Eternity*, featured this powerful monologue by the mysterious soldier Jack Malloy. Malloy recalls Wobblies singing Joe Hill–penned songs and Ralph Chaplin's "Solidarity Forever" in their prison cells, "a singing that swelled through the town until nobody could escape it": "There has never been anything like them, before or since. They called themselves materialist-economists, but what they really were was a religion. There were workstiffs and bindlebums like you and me, but they were welded together by a vision we don't possess. It was their vision that made them great. And it was their belief in it that made them powerful. And sing! You never heard anybody sing the way those guys sang! Nobody sings like they did unless it's for a religion."[30]

Lawrence, Massachusetts

The most famous of the IWW strikes took place in Lawrence, Massachusetts, in 1912. Lawrence was a massive complex of textile factories employing forty thousand people, more than half of them children. Conditions at the factories were appalling, with fifty-four-hour workweeks for women and children, and children dying at rate of 169 per 1,000 annually. "Lawrence" would eventually become a byword for legalized slavery: annual salaries were in the $300–$400 range, rents in Lawrence were higher than in New York City, and the company had a history of treating its workers brutally.[31] Despite heavy-handed actions by state authorities, strikers eventually won many of their demands, only to see them slowly lost in the following years.[32] During the long days of the strike, the Wobblies provided relief to the strikers and did what they knew best, according to observer Ray Stannard Baker: "This movement in Lawrence was strongly a singing movement. It is the first strike I ever saw which sang! I shall not soon forget the curious lift, the strange sudden fire of the mingled nationalities at the strike meetings when they broke into the universal language of song. And not only at the meetings did they sing, but in the soup houses and in the streets."[33]

For many union members, the best-loved song was "Solidarity Forever," the U.S. labor movement's "unofficial anthem" for many years. Set to the tune of "John Brown's Body"/"Glory Hallelujah," "Solidarity Forever" was another contribution featured in *Songs of the Workers*: "Yet what force on earth is weaker than the feeble strength of one / For the union makes us strong."[34] One of the legacies of Lawrence was the Joe Hill rewrite of "A Little Talk with Jesus," which existed as an African-American spiritual before it was used as a "rescue-mission song." Hill's version, "John Golden and the Lawrence Strike," deftly outlines the differences between the worker-oriented IWW and the American Federation of Labor (AFL), which represented only craft unions.[35]

Songs of the Workers inspired other groups. The short-lived Composers' Collective, a loose-knit organization of left-wing performing artists that included a number of well-known composers (including Charles Seeger, Carl Sands, and Earl Robinson), released *Workers Song Book*, vols. 1 and 2 (1934 and 1935), which included two African-American protest songs selected by collector Lawrence Gellert.[36] The widely traveled Gellert wrote several articles for *New Masses* on the topic, including one in January 1931 repeating a song he had heard in Travellers Rest,

NEGRO SONGS
OF
PROTEST

• Collected by LAWRENCE GELLERT
Arranged for Voice and Piano by ELIE SIEGMEISTER
Foreword by WALLINGFORD RIEGGER
Illustration by HUGO GELLERT

AMERICAN MUSIC LEAGUE

156 Fifth Avenue, New York, N. Y.

FIGURE 5

Many of the songs that Lawrence Gellert encountered on the road and wrote about for *New Masses* were collected and published in *Negro Songs of Protest* (1936).

South Carolina. Gellert wrote that the music "alternated in mood between that of a spiritual and a Scottish War Chant." In the same article, Gellert included a song that he believed was of Civil War origin. It, too, has all the earmarks of a spiritual: "Do you want to be a soldier / For the year of the Jubilee."[37]

In a different article, this one from April 1931 titled "Negro Songs of Protest," Gellert writes that a song he collected in Bethune, South Carolina, "The Preacher's Belly," may have been based on "an early spiritual."[38] Another African-American protest song collected by Gellert and published in the book *Negro Songs of Protest* (fig. 5) in 1936, "Let's Go to de Buryin'," is strongly evocative of several spirituals, most notably the melody and phrasing of "(Let's Go) Down to the River to Pray": "Cap'n kill my buddy, let's go to de buryin' / Heah a mighty rumblin', let's go to de buryin'."[39] Gellert, a self-taught collector and "independent researcher," was a fierce advocate of African-Americans from 1930s through the civil rights era. "I wasn't interested in just music for its own sake," he once wrote, "but rather music as a weapon" and as "propaganda."[40] The work of Gellert and others exhibits the continued use of the spiritual as a transformative agent, outside as well as inside the unions.

Congress of Industrial Organizations

The American Federation of Labor, founded in 1886 and led from the beginning by Samuel Gompers, eventually became the most powerful union in the United States, available only to skilled trades and craftsmen.[41] Like the Knights of Labor, the AFL did not initially discriminate by race, though that changed within a few decades. "By the 1930s," writes Nelson Lichtenstein, "AFL unionism was tainted by a patriarchal, racist odor that kept it at odds with so many of the new immigrants and the nation's African American population."[42] Nor was the AFL ever known as a "singing" union.

However, the members of the competing Congress of Industrial Organizations (CIO), founded in 1935 and led by John L. Lewis,[43] promoted singing in a wide variety of settings from the start. R. Serge Denisoff writes that it was the inclusion of members of the American Communist Party in some CIO leadership and organizing capacities, coupled with CIO miners, that "injected or reintroduced the propaganda song" into the organization's DNA.[44] (After the merger of the AFL and CIO in 1955, a veteran CIO staffer suggested a new union songbook. President George Meany's longtime secretary Virginia Tehas said, "What are you trying to do, make fools of us? . . . They don't sing at union meetings." When the CIO staffer replied that their unions built morale by singing on the picket lines, she snorted, "Well, I've never heard of anything so ridiculous in my life.")[45]

"The Age of the CIO," as Denning terms the period from 1929 to 1947, included a series of impressive progressive legislative and labor accomplishments achieved despite—or perhaps because of—the Great Depression and the onset of World War II.[46] The CIO's work toward eliminating discrimination was such that by the "end of World War II a half a million black workers had joined unions affiliated with the CIO."[47] It is during the 1930s, with African-Americans finally being accepted into the CIO and other unions (as well as forming the mostly black Brotherhood of Sleeping Car Porters under the direction of A. Philip Randolph in the mid-1930s), that the first instances of the widespread use of spirituals and labor songs based on spirituals are reported. According to Robin D. G. Kelley, the combination of the CIO's racially inclusive unionism and the place of religion among African-Americans was both inevitable and mutually advantageous. A number of unions, including the Food, Tobacco, Agricultural, and Allied Workers, the Steel Workers Organizing Committee, and the International Union of Mine, Mill, and Smelter Workers, all met regularly in black churches, and labor leaders actively courted African-American pastors. The "religious groundings of the Southern labor movement" is one of the foundational connections of the civil rights movement that began in earnest in the late 1950s. The uneasy marriage "gave its members a reason for interracial unity beyond basic utilitarianism," where black and white workers were all "children of God together in a collective struggle."[48]

Mining

One of the earliest adaptations of a spiritual is recorded at the Marion, North Carolina, strike in 1929, where strikers took the tune of the spiritual "We Are Climbing Jacob's Ladder" and created "We Are Building a Strong Union": "We are building a strong union / Workers in the mill! / We shall rise and gain our freedom / Workers in the mill!" Another spiritual that would be employed time and time again by union members across the country would endure into the 1960s and the civil rights era, "We Shall Not Be Moved." Edith Fowke and Joe Glazer call it "the best known and most widely sung labor song in the United States and Canada" other than "Solidarity Forever." They trace its origins to the West Virginia Miner's Union in 1931, led by Frank Keeney, who is named in the original first verse: "Frank Keeney is our captain, we shall not be moved." A staff member at Brookwood Labor College (see below) was present when the miners struck that year and recalled the first time she heard the old spiritual, sung in front of an African-American schoolhouse, the only place the racially mixed strikers could meet. Under a brutal summer sun and the watchful eyes of state police and mine guards with "their guns conspicuously displayed," the group of miners and their wives began "singing out their glory and their hopes." Though the strike was ultimately lost, organizers spread "We Shall Not Be Moved" widely. As the author added, "I even saw one version put out by the Communists for tenant farmers which ran, 'Lenin is our leader, we shall not be moved.'" The song endures in part because the format is such that it is easily adapted to local conditions and strikes. Fowke and Glazer tell of a 1945 strike in Biddeford, Maine, where "several thousand textile workers roared it out, adding new verses continuously for a solid half hour."[49] Even today the lyrics and music retain a powerful sense of dignity and strength:

We're fighting for our freedom; we shall not be moved.
Just like a tree that's planted by the water,
We shall not be moved.
We'll build a mighty union; we shall not be moved.
Just like a tree that's planted by the water,
We shall not be moved.

Into the Age of the CIO, the recorded examples of unions adapting spirituals become more and more common, particularly as the bulk of the mining shifted from Pennsylvania, Ohio, Indiana, and Illinois to Appalachia and as African-Americans began to work as miners. When afforded the opportunity, blacks became some of the fiercest supporters of the mining unions. George Korson's seminal *Coal Dust on the Fiddle* (1943) reports that many of their union songs are based on spirituals and that the word "union" itself—a carryover from Civil War when the forces of the "Union" freed them from the Confederacy—"was a traditional part of their lingo and so offered a convenient bridge by which to cross over from spirituals to mining ballads." This meant that, just as in the days of slavery, an African-American union organizer could sing a spiritual "under a boss's nose without suspicion." The enthusiasm for all things union among blacks certainly makes sense when, as late as 1932, some coal companies in Harlan County still had "whipping posts" and a "whipping boss" who was empowered to discipline African-American miners.[50] Songs like "Dis What de Union Done" appeared soon thereafter. The spiritual, based on "Honey in the Rock," was recorded by Korson in 1940:

In nineteen hundred an' thirty-three,
When Mr. Roosevelt took his seat,
He said to President John L. Lewis
"In union we must be.
Come let us work togedder,
Ask God to lead de plan,
By dis time anudder year
We'll have de union back again."

Some spirituals and gospel songs fit the format so well that their titles were little changed in the transition from spiritual to labor union song, including "I Can Tell the World About This," which became "I Can Tell de World." This version by the United Four Quartet of Barrackville, West Virginia, was recorded on April 3, 1940: "Tell 'em what John Lewis has done / Tell 'em dat de union has come / And it brought joy, great joy, unto my soul." Also recorded by Korson that day is a version of "It's Far Down Yonder," retitled as "No Unions Down Yonder" by the United Four Quartet: "Ain't no unions down yonder, Lord / Ah don't want to go, Lord." Other verses read, "Oh, it's scabs down yonder" and "Lord, it's hell down yonder."[51]

In 1965, Korson released a well-received vinyl recording based on the music he had collected, *Songs and Ballads of the Bituminous Miners*.[52] Astute reviewers and critics noted the pervasive African-American influence in the music, even among white miners.[53] Several of the seventeen songs on the LP feature African-American artists singing spirituals. In addition to Uncle George Jones's "This What the Union Done," Korson's recording, made over two decades, features the Evening Breezes Sextet of Vivian, West Virginia, harmonizing "in gospel style" on "The Coal Loading Machine" and Sam Johnson of Pursglove, West Virginia, singing "We Done Quit" to the tune of the spiritual "I Can Tell the World."[54]

The April 2, 1932, issue of *Daily Worker* reported that the "Kentucky Strike Executive Committee in Tazewell (Kentucky) Jail" sang what the unnamed reporter dubbed the "Kentucky Mining Song" during a union action there. The lyrics were reported to have been sung to an unspecified "Holiness Hymn," but the cadence and reoccurring lines appear more likely to have been taken from a spiritual: "Your daddy's gone to jail / For the NMU / And it just suits me" ("NMU" stands for "National Miner's Union").[55] Also in the 1930s, Alan Lomax recorded miners singing a song with a similar title, "Song of the West Virginia Miners," based on the spiritual "We Are Climbing Jacob's Ladder." The subversive nature of the original lyric shines through this version: "Company holds us all in slavery / Workers in the mine / But we'll rise up and gain our freedom / Workers in the mine."[56]

The horrific conditions in the mines—coupled with the antiunion actions of many of the mine owners—spawned generations of labor actions and labor songs. One of the most famous is a rewritten Baptist hymn, "Lay the Lily Low." The wife of a miner and union organizer in Harlan County, Florence Reece, was active in union activities in the early 1930s. When the local sheriff terrorized her family and threatened her husband, she wrote the haunting "Which Side Are You On?" For miners and their families in "Bloody Harlan," singing was essential rather than optional. The songs served to both "help form a union and to lift the spirits of the miners in their struggle." At the time, a biographer notes, their "faith in the union was as powerful as their belief in God."[57]

Harlan County also produced Aunt Molly Jackson, who would continue as a well-known folk singer performing old mountain and union songs for several decades to come.[58] Jackson, whose father was a Baptist preacher and whose mother was a singer, said it was her father who taught her "uniting" at an early age. Upon her death in 1960, she was said to have known "hundreds of traditional pieces and was one of the Library of Congress's best informants." Jackson's "I Am a Union Woman" was set to the tune of Reece's "Which Side Are You On?" although in later years she changed "NMU" to "CIO": "If you want to get your freedom / Also your liberty / Join the dear old CIO / Also the ILD" ("ILD" is an acronym for "International Labor Defense").[59]

Equally notable was Jim Garland (half brother to Aunt Molly), whose writings detail the importance to miners, loggers, and railroad workers of "lining out" songs, a practice borrowed from the Christian churches. As was practiced in early

African-American churches, a leader would sing a line of song, only to have it repeated back by those listening. According to Garland, a good "liner," who could improvise according to the needs of the moment with a spiritual such as "The Old Ship of Zion," would be paid more than the average worker. Railway workers frequently sang at least one version of "The Old Ship of Zion." According to Garland, songs like these and "Hold the Fort" passed through the IWW, the National Miners Union, and then the United Mine Workers in succession as these workers continued their age-old struggle with the mining companies.[60]

The old spirituals were continually resurrected, especially in the South and in border states like Kentucky, Tennessee, and West Virginia, as the template for protest songs. While northern organizers originally relied more on popular songs, the influx of southern workers—black and white—introduced more spirituals and camp-meeting songs into labor's repertoire.[61] In one of his collections, Seeger writes about a pre–Civil War spiritual called "Oh Freedom," which he says, "like most great works of art, contains contradictions." After a "triumphant opening line," the verse ends on a much darker note: "And before I'd be a slave, I'd be buried in my grave / And go home to my Lord and be free." Seeger adds that an unnamed black sharecropper in 1935 rewrote the last line to read, "I'll fight for the right to be free." The revised spiritual spread rapidly through the CIO unions in the years that followed. "Oh Freedom" would be resurrected yet again during the civil rights movement of the 1960s.[62] In his long career, Seeger encountered a number of rewritten spirituals among African-Americans, citing their "fine traditions of church singing," which "provided some of the best songs picked up throughout the country."[63] Finally, there's "It's Me, O Lord," another spiritual-turned-union song often sung by miners was recorded by Alan Lomax in the 1930s: "It's me, it's me, it's me, O Lord / Standing in the need of a home."[64]

Birmingham, Alabama

A very early use of spirituals and gospel songs was recorded at a district convention of the United Mine Workers (UMW) in Birmingham, held on June 30, 1900. The article in the *Birmingham Labor Advocate* is notable for the matter-of-fact way black and white miners are mentioned as working and singing together. At the convention, one of the "colored brethren" sang "We Are Marching to Canaan," which featured an "old-time camp-meeting lilt." The African-American delegates sang the chorus, "Who is there among us / The true and the tried / Who'll stand by his fellows / Who's on the Lord's side." Following a few more (apparently white) singers, "J. T. Allen, a colored delegate, sang in a powerful voice 'I Am a Child of the King.'"[65]

Even as the country reeled from the Great Depression, the need for memorable union songs to bolster labor's sagging fortunes never waned. In 1933, an African-American woman in Birmingham was credited with rewriting the lyrics to the spiritual "My Mother Got a Stone That Was Hewn Out of the Mountain." According to the *Daily Worker*, the new song "is gaining widespread popularity" and "has caught like wildfire since the recent Birmingham Anti-Lynch Conference where it was first sung":

> *The I.L.D. is the stone*
> *That was hewn out of history*
> *Come a'rollin' thru Dixie*
> *A tearin' down the kingdom of the boss.*[66]

For many decades, Birmingham was unique among southern cities, with an economy based not on agriculture but mining and the manufacture of iron and steel. It was one of the few places where unions were eventually established and open to African-Americans. Birmingham was also home to a small but active branch of the Communist Party, which published the *New South*. The March 1938 edition praised the folk music of the region and noted that "the throbbing note of protest" is "found even in the spirituals." While African-Americans were denied "the most elementary civil rights," the spirituals were "living prophecies of deliverance." The author states that "Joshua Fit the Battle of Jericho" is really a "camouflaged call to battle against the plantation owners." Another song, which the author said was "found" by Alan Lomax among African-Americans in Florida, is "an ominous prediction of the Civil War" and features these startling lines: "Fire in de East / Fire in de West / Fire in the de North / Gonna burn up all de rest." The article also summarizes the contributions of songwriters Aunt Molly Jackson and Ella May Wiggins and the rewritten spirituals of sharecroppers. The concluding statement, that "many" songs were still being created in the South, is eerily prophetic, especially from a writer for a Birmingham-based publication: "Who can doubt but that this traditional gift of song will result in the great folk epics which always precede revolutionary change? Who can doubt that the musicians of future generations will find much of their thematic material in the creative efforts of a people who knew dismal poverty but whose unremitting struggle reflected itself heroically in their music?"[67]

Birmingham was also the home of a long-standing tradition of jubilee and, later, gospel singing. The combination, according to McCallum, was responsible for the transformation of "religious songs [into] union songs which commemorated and canonized labor leaders, sanctified labor organizations and praised the gospel of black unionism." Some of the steel manufacturers initially instituted a relatively progressive (if tightly controlled) social welfare system that encouraged the formation of African-American cultural organizations, including jubilee quartets affiliated with the various companies, company towns, mine sites, and unions, but the Great Depression ended most of the initiatives. From that point forward, black workers in Birmingham faced the twin perils of deep-rooted racism and a "surplus labor pool" as desperate African-Americans looked frantically for employment. In times of economic and social uncertainty, music "was a resource of their faith" for many African-American workers. As before, it became a vehicle for self-expression, including protest. While gospel songs rarely "overtly protested or criticized" their present circumstances, the "mines and the mills of the Birmingham district were invisible yet ever-present backdrops."[68]

Mine companies and steel mills successfully stymied efforts by unions until the advent of the National Recovery Administration (NRA) Act in 1933, though full compliance did not occur until 1942, and only then due to ceaseless organizing efforts by the CIO.[69] The arrival of New Deal–era unionization "served as a legally and culturally sanctioned basis for social action and reform and provided relatively safe and noncombative strategies and modes of protest." Labor organizations such as the UMW became a secular version of the miners' and steel workers' home churches, and the gospel quartets took note. According to one former coal miner and gospel singer, the miners were "little horses" in the days before unions, "grazing on what was left." But the unions "opened up the way" for the workers—and that sentiment is reflected in at least one of the spirituals popular during the era, "Tell Old Man Pharaoh to Let My People Go."[70]

Korson, who had been hired by the UMW to identify and record promising union singers in coal mining regions, traveled widely in search of the best, most authentic singers and songs. Among the miners Korson recorded was Uncle George Jones, an African-American "bard and folk minstrel" who devoted his life to the union and sang church hymns, spirituals, and union songs commissioned by the UMW, including "What the Union Has Done." In 1940, Korson recorded Cleveland Perry, who had been hired by his company to sing spirituals at union meetings. Perry sang a song dedicated to the UMW titled "Got My Name on De Record": "Do you belong to dis union? / I'm a thoroughbred union [man]."[71] Perry also sang "We Got on Our Travelin' Shoes," one of many spirituals adapted to tout the union in general and CIO President John L. Lewis in particular:

> Well, we got on our travelin' shoes.
> John L. Lewis is our leader
> He's a mighty man,
> He made the NRA contract,
> Union people goin' to let it stand.[72]

Another Birmingham-area gospel group was the Sterling Jubilee Singers of Bessemer, organized in 1929 and drawn from employees of U.S. Pipe and Foundry. Renamed as the CIO Singers, they appeared on a local radio station for many years.[73] As late as 1952, the Sterling Jubilees recorded two "topical gospel–union ballads," "The Spirit of Phil Murray" and "Satisfied." A former member of the CIO Singers noted what McCallum calls "the strong sacred foundation" of the songs. "'Satisfied,'" she writes, "makes an extended statement on the origins of unionism in Biblical scripture and on salvation through union solidarity." The lyrics are straightforward and to the point: "He told his disciples / Stay in union / Together you stand / Divided you fall / Stay in union / I'll save you all / Ever since that wonderful day my soul's been satisfied."[74]

McCallum's splendid research supports her thesis that black sacred music, particularly gospel music, served to "negotiate a balance between continuity with the past, the discontinuities of the present, and prospects for the future." The gospel–union songs, both those few that were recorded and the great majority which have been sustained through oral tradition, transferred some of the heroic traits of Old Testament figures Moses and Daniel to modern labor leaders, especially John L. Lewis. These songs supply the listeners with both "aesthetic and ideological documents of the emergence of southern black workers' new political consciousness and resurgence of unionism as a powerful social movement." And the lyrics, she suggests, offer "potential solutions to both economic and social inequities."[75]

This is an important point. This transference continues the "narrative" of the spirituals from before the Civil War. The struggle for dignity of labor, a living wage, and freedom from abuse—the hallmarks of American unionism—continued the antebellum quest of African-American slaves. It establishes the justice of the singer's cause, and it establishes the foundation of unions against avaricious mine owners or steel manufacturers as a noble undertaking, one of good versus evil. The mythic status accorded Lewis, Joe Hill, Mother Jones, John Henry and others achieved in these songs is part of that "story."

From his years in the South and from working on social justice issues, Gellert instinctively understood this concept. In still another installment of his "Negro Songs of Protest" series in *New Masses* (May 1933), his comments in the introduction indicate that he believes that additional songs of protest were "cropping up the length and breadth of the Southland" as part of a simmering rebellion against the brutal reign of Jim Crow in the South. He name-checks a litany of "racial heroes," including John Henry, Steel Driving Sam, Long Gone John Stagolee, and Casey Jones, whom he calls "strong men—half legend, half real, who dare to stand toe to toe with the Oppressors of the Race—and win—or die trying."[76]

It is no coincidence that the stories of the heroic "steel-driving man" John Henry first emerge during these years. Nelson's meticulous research suggests that Henry was a real man who died, probably from overwork, abuse, and disease, as a prisoner in Virginia's infamous convict lease labor system, laying steel in the western part of the state, perhaps around 1873. The earliest version of the song is noted by a collector of African-American songs in 1917, and it was apparently well established by then. Sandburg helped popularize it with his songbook in the early 1920s, and "John Henry" soon became associated with the textile mills in Georgia and Carolinas, due in part to an early recording by Fiddlin' John Carson. Hugo Gellert used the dramatic drawing of a powerfully muscled John Henry to illustrate the cover of his brother Larry's book *Negro Songs of Protest* in 1936; by this point, the song was entrenched in labor and radical circles, appearing wherever the CIO unionized workers. In time, folklorists at the Library of Congress would "call it the most researched folk song in the United States."[77]

Most of the many variants of the song draw a strong connection between John Henry and the Old Testament hero Samson—John Henry in bondage to the state is a dramatic link to the blind and bound Samson, surrounded by Philistines. It is a formidable image, one that resonates at an unconscious level and has propelled the story of John Henry into iconic status in America's national narrative. Like Joe Hill and Mother Jones, Green writes that the myth of John Henry transcends the actual events of his life: "John Henry in ballad, rhythmic chant, children's story, and pictorial form comes closer than any other folk hero to personifying our work experience."[78] John Henry's story is all the more remarkable in that it emerged at a time when the status of African-Americans in the United States had rarely been lower and their lot more despised.

Still, it is the "common" laborer—who defied possible job termination, violence, and even death threats to support his or her right to unionize—that is labor's true hero, particularly when that laborer must also overcome the barrier of the era's institutional southern racism. In the May 11, 1939, issue of *Daily Worker*, Lee Collier's article featured the optimistic headline "Portrait of a New Southerner: The Land of Cotton Is Ringing to Songs of Negro and White Unity and People's Dixie." In it, Collier credits "the workers of Birmingham" with a protest-oriented rewrite of the spiritual "Joshua Fought the Battle of Jericho" (usually written as "Joshua Fit the Battle of Jericho"):

> *Black and white together, we'll win the vote, win the vote, win the vote*
> *Going to build our promised land.*
> *When we stand together, we'll be free, we'll be free, we'll be free*
> *Going to build our promised land.*
> *The Communist Party will lead the fight, lead the fight, lead the fight*
> *Going to build our promised land.*
> *The 10th Convention's coming, get ready now, get ready now, get ready now*
> *Fighting for our promised land.*
> *Get new members and pay our dues, pay our dues, pay our dues*
> *Fighting for our promised land.*[79]

While this song in itself is fascinating, in part because of the unique verse by verse transition from the inspirational to the prosaic, the article includes a second adapted song. In a state where the song "Dixie" has sacred connotations, it took a brave African-American worker to sing these lyrics to that familiar music: "Side by side we'll wage our fight / Equality for black and white / On the way, every day, making way for Socialism."[80]

However, the depth of Birmingham's gospel–union marriage is an outlier throughout most of the South. The CIO's tenacious, long-standing involvement in Memphis, especially among local, rather than national, companies and industries, meant that the city's African-Americans enjoyed a small degree of employment security in those settings.[81] As elsewhere, when African-Americans and labor unions joined forces, the transformation of spirituals into labor songs continued.

At a Memphis meeting of the CIO-affiliated United Cannery, Agricultural, Packaging, and Allied Workers Union (UCAPAWA) in 1940, black cotton worker Hattie Walls transformed the spiritual "The Old Ship of Zion" into "Union Train." Because of its popularity there, both Woody Guthrie and Pete Seeger took "Union Train" to CIO unions elsewhere as an organizing song.[82]

The writings of the indomitable Lucy Randolph Mason, the longtime southern ambassador for the CIO, provide insight into the events and personalities involved in the labor movement's struggles in the South, especially as they relate to the end of legalized discrimination against blacks. This particular note is from a section of her book that chronicles the almost religious fervor that African-Americans in Memphis felt and expressed for the CIO. She describes the "deeply religious" meetings where songs and the Lord's Prayer were still "lined out." "I think I never heard people pray more sincerely," she adds, "than did those humble union folk."[83]

Still, state government opposition (often aided by the Ku Klux Klan and various paramilitary groups) meant that there were few unions elsewhere in the South. But there were some pockets of musical resistance, usually in conjunction with labor union involvement. For example, in 1933, the *Labor Defender* magazine printed a first-person report from writer Rose Bradley, recently returned from the eastern shore of Maryland, where she witnessed a number of violent acts against African-Americans, including the torture and lynching of a black man on October 18. Bradley returned to Baltimore for a public presentation on her findings in November. According to her account, more than 1,500 people ("at least a third of them white") attended. Bradley writes that "773 were delegates, elected from lodges, churches, fraternal orders, trade unions and mass organization." On the same page are the lyrics to a song "Sung by the Share Croppers Delegation at the Farmers 2nd National Conference," based on the spiritual "We Shall Not Be Moved:"

> *Oh—we're from Alabama—we shall not be moved*
> *Just like a tree that's planted by the water—*
> *We shall not be moved.*
> *We fight against evictions, etc.,*
> *We fight against the terror, etc.*[84]

Seven years later, Korson recorded miner Charles Langford singing another version of "We Shall Not Be Moved" in Columbus, Ohio, showing the remarkable appeal and adaptability of the old spiritual: "John L. Lewis is our leader / We shall not be moved / Jus' like a tree dat's planted by de water / We shall not be moved."[85]

Richmond, Virginia

Considering the widespread bias against African-Americans during this period, the presence of *any* articles sympathetic to blacks—even in communist or socialist publications—is rare indeed. So Richard Frank's essay in *New Masses* on May 15, 1934, is unique in both its positive presentation of African-Americans and its detailed overview of spirituals used in labor actions across the United States. He treats this development as something of utmost significance. Frank notes that African-American music has an "irresistible attraction even for ruling-class whites" and that it is uncommonly influential on white American culture: "Many of the songs sung by white workers are Negro. When the American revolutionary movement finds expression in Negro music, therefore, it is expressing itself in a medium capable of arousing not only the twelve or fifteen million Negroes of America, but also all the toiling masses of America who for generations in one form or another have made Negro music their own."[86]

Frank cites the example of "one of the women comrades" in Charlotte, who adapted the old spiritual "In That Great Gettin'-Up Mornin'" into "In That Great Revolutionary Morning." Like Bradley, he also celebrates the transformation of "We Shall Not Be Moved" by "Negro share-croppers in Alabama." When he told members of the Unemployed Council of Richmond about the introduction of the song "In That Great Revolutionary Morning," Frank says they "spontaneously" created additional verses of their own. He also writes of attending a "party," apparently while still in Richmond, in the home of a "Negro comrade, where the workers sang spirituals for amusement." He called the singing "magnificent" and added that the tunes were usually sung with the "old religious" lyrics: "But occasionally some comrade would inject lines of real class significance. A group of young men stood in a circle. One would tell the others to be silent, and would then sing to them a song containing words which had just come into his mind. The others would listen attentively, swaying rhythmically and joining him in singing the refrain, until they too had learned the words. Then they all sang together until another comrade would make them pause to learn his new words. Here was folk-music in the making."[87]

Frank's mere presence at an African-American party in Richmond in 1934 is startling enough, and his outspoken support of the Russian Revolution would have doubtless given the respectable citizens of that town more than a little cause for alarm. Frank continues, writing that he believes that the "great Red heart of the American Revolution" could be found in the "voices of those singing workers"—what he calls "the voice of the masses," the "army of the future," with everyone marching and singing "these same revolutionary Negro folk-songs."[88]

Accounts from a strike by African-American tobacco workers in Richmond, Virginia, from 1937 yield more instances of the use of spirituals in a labor action. Dangerous conditions, overt racism, and inadequate pay for workers in the sprawling Carrington and Michaux tobacco plant prompted first a "wildcat walk-out" and later a more organized strike. The *Richmond Planet*, the city's African-American weekly newspaper, noted that as the strikers picketed the plant, they did so "singing, with a gusto born of courage and determination at the top of their voices, 'We Want Better Wages.'"[89] The union held meetings at the nearby Leigh Street

Church, where they sang "hymns" and added "lyrics of their own." Among the songs sung was the spiritual "We Shall Not Be Moved." The unrest continued for years and a fourth strike in August 1939, called by the Tobacco Stemmers and Laborers Union, saw the black strikers joined by two hundred white members of the CIO-affiliated Amalgamated Clothing Workers of America Richmond local, followed by members of several other white unions. Accounts from the strike indicate that black workers sang often during the round-the-clock picketing and, as we have seen from earlier examples, presumably at least some of the songs were spirituals or at least based on spirituals.[90]

Another *New Masses* article, this one from May 1930, recounts a meeting of the National Textile Union in Charlotte. While waiting for the meeting to begin, writer Grace Lumpkin writes that the workers—strikers from Gastonia and Bessemer City—first sang "Solidarity," then "Ella May's 'ballets.'"[91]

Gastonia, South Carolina

Lumpkin's mention of both Gastonia and Ella May (sometimes known as Ella May Wiggins) and her "ballets" is significant in that it shows how, ten years after the event, both had achieved legendary status in union circles. The Gastonia Textile Strike (April–September 1929) created both unique union songs and another well-known labor "martyr" on the order of Joe Hill—Ella May. As with many of these strikes, union action was prompted by abominable conditions, demands for increased production, lower salaries, and the addition of more "stretch-outs" per worker—the number of machines an individual simultaneously operated. The massive workforce at the Loray Mill in Gastonia included a night shift composed primarily of the much cheaper (and more docile) women and children workers. Management-sponsored violence escalated into murder, including the shooting of May, who was one of the leaders of the strike and a talented songwriter.[92]

The surviving records are too spotty for us to know how many of the union songs from Gastonia were based on old spirituals. The songs of May and her fellow songsters "gave mill workers an effective voice for their discontent" and were "enthusiastically accepted" and used by striking mill workers, but they do not indicate the melodies on which those songs were based.[93] However, in an article in the *Sunday Worker*, Randall states that May "borrowed her tunes from the starving little churches she had attended in North Carolina."[94] The bulk of the strikers, both black and white, were intensely religious and began conducting religious services the first Sunday of the strike. While they sang "Solidarity Forever," one observer said that they also "continued to use spirituals and hymns at strike meetings."[95] Another participant reported that the strikers would request new labor songs from May, "the minstrel of our strike," on a daily basis. Once she had completed those songs, "the singers would drift into spirituals or hymns and many a 'praise-the-Lord' would resound through the quiet night."[96]

Alan Lomax and Woody Guthrie cite May's "Toiling on Life's Pilgrim Pathway" in their book *Hard Hitting Songs for Hard-Hit People*. Although he does not indicate which hymn or spiritual the song is based on, Guthrie adds this note: "When Religion turns into hunger, Church songs are changed quick and easy into Fightin' Songs." The "I.L.D." is the legal arm of the Communist Party of the United States of America. The melding of religious and labor sentiments is clear throughout the song: "Now the South is hedged in darkness / Although they begin to see / Come and join the textile union / Also join the I.L.D."[97]

Among those present at the Gastonia strike was organizer Fred E. Beal, who wrote about his experiences in *Proletarian Journey* eight years after the event. As the workers began assembling in a ramshackle union headquarters to vote on a motion to strike, Beal noted that they arrived "singing whatever songs came to their minds": "From experience I knew the tremendous value of singing the right songs on a picket line. These workers knew none of the union's strike songs. To overcome this, I typed a number of copies of 'Solidarity' and told them to sing it to the tune of 'Glory, Glory Hallelujah.' It comes to me only now that it is also the tune of 'John Brown's Body' and was perhaps somewhat inappropriate for Southerners."[98]

After the unanimous vote to strike, a large crowd of workers began picketing at the mill. But as the mill's owner began taking names of the strikers and threatening to blacklist them, many in the crowd began drifting away. Beal and his fellow organizers desperately sought to rally the workers. At last, Beal cried, "Sing 'Solidarity.'" At that, the disorganized group began to march:

> The timid ones had been swayed by the militants; the revival spirit again gripped the crowd. From a window of one of the mills a worker shouted that the bosses had locked them in until quitting time but that they were coming out to join us. We answered with a cheer and sang louder, more sincerely than ever, "For the Union makes us strong."
> The strike was on.[99]

Also present in Gastonia was writer Mary Heaton Vorse, who was standing near Ella May when she was gunned down. Vorse wrote a novel based on Gastonia, titled *Strike!*, published in 1930. It was the first of several novels written in Gastonia's aftermath, the best known being Sherwood Anderson's *Beyond Desire*, published in 1932. Vorse writes movingly of the desperate circumstances facing the strikers and, in one section, depicts a sympathetic preacher and several strikers sitting in the store, "their shoulders relaxed, their heads bent together, singing a spiritual: 'My Lord, what a mornin' / When the sky come tumblin' down.'"[100]

In addition to providing Beal's and Vorse's firsthand accounts of the power of singing, the significance of the Loray strike, for our purposes, is twofold. First, it marks one of the earliest instances where commercial recordings were made of union songs and distributed to a wider audience.[101] Second, as mentioned earlier, the brutal slaying of songwriter Ella May made the national news in both union and nonunion circles. Less than a month after her death, the popular magazine *The Nation* published a tribute, titled "Ella May's Songs," and reprinted some of her haunting lyrics.[102] The author of the article, Margaret Larkin (a popular singer herself), then wrote a second, similar account of Ella May's death and its aftermath in the November 29, 1929, issue of *New Masses*.[103] Both articles also brought a greater awareness to the concept of using existing melodies for protest-related purposes.

Labor Colleges

Concurrently, the leadership of the American labor movement had seen as early as the beginnings of the twentieth century the need for training for future labor leaders. Several "labor colleges" were founded, most notably the Work People's College in Duluth, Minnesota (1907), Brookwood College in Katonah, New York (1907), Commonwealth College in Mena, Arkansas (1922), and the most famous, Highlander College in Monteagle, Tennessee, established in 1932.[104] A host of well-known labor activists passed through the doors of these schools and some left with more than leadership skills—they took with them an understanding of the importance and power of music to the union movement. One such attendee was songwriter/activist Lee Hays. Hays is mentioned in an article from August 1, 1939, when *New Masses* returned to the topic of African-American sacred music and unionization. In it, Hays uses the word "hymn" to describe some of the songs listed in the articles.[105] However, when the lyrics are printed, it seems more likely that they are actually based on spirituals. While at Commonwealth, Hays and John Handcox, of the Southern Tenant Farmers' Union (STFU), came under the influence of African-American preacher and song-leader Claude Williams, who preached the gospel of using "traditional folk songs, primarily spirituals, to communicate themes of social protest."[106]

In the article, Hays tells of attending a black church in Mena, where the congregation began singing "Let the Will of the Lord Be Done." Before Hays could suggest changing the lines to "Let the will of the people be done" or "Let the will of the union be done," the African-American song-leader interrupted, urging him not to change the lyrics of the song. But Hays persisted and recommended various "parodies," the common term at the time for alternate lyric versions, for any union meeting or action: "Organize! Today! / Let the will of the Lord be done." Other couplets urged workers to organize "on the farm" and "in the fields." This is a standard spiritual format. Hays also lists additional examples of spirituals used this way by sharecroppers. "Some of them we introduced," he notes, "some of them we overheard":

> *Somebody's knockin' at your door.*
> *Knocks like a union, etc.*

When the struggle's over
We shall all be free
In the new society.

It's a wonderful union,
And it's good enough for me.

Hays ends by adding that the version of "Jesus Is My Captain" had traveled from a North Carolina textile mill strike throughout the South and recently arrived in New York City, where it was featured in the recent May Day parade: "The union is a-marchin' / We shall not be moved!"[107]

At Commonwealth, Hays helped organize the Commonwealth Players, a performing company that took to small towns through the Deep South theatrical productions that emphasized education and organizing, then made the plays themselves available to local unions. The plays always featured plenty of catchy songs, sometimes led by Hays's distinctive rolling bass voice, and sometimes by Williams himself. It was also during the plays that songs such as "No More Mourning," "Roll the Union On," "What Is That I See Yonder Coming," "Let the Will of the Lord Be Done," and "When the Struggle's Over We Shall All Be Free, in the New Society" were first sung. Sometimes at meetings in isolated rural areas, Williams would sing "We Shall Not Be Moved," but kept the original words to the hymn handy just in case "gun thugs" should appear unexpectedly.[108]

While at Commonwealth, and sometimes traveling as far as Chicago to support other union actions, Hays also rewrote "Come to Jesus" as "Join the Union" and wrote a set of union-oriented lyrics for the old spiritual "When the Saints Go Marching In." According to several accounts, Hays's bass could revive spirits during tedious tasks and stiffen flagging resolve during dangerous encounters. A few years later, he wrote about those times, the cold nights traveling, singing hymns and spirituals for comfort, and their "perfect blends of tones and feelings and fears." Hays, who later spent time with the STFU, transformed numerous other hymns and spirituals into protest songs before and after joining the protest-oriented folk group the Almanac Singers. Hays's vision helped shape the focus of the loosely knit assembly of singer/songwriters that would, at different times, include Woody Guthrie, Bess Lomax Hawes, Earl Robinson, and Pete Seeger.[109]

As for Williams, he was asked by the CIO to move to Memphis to establish a series of institutes to support the UCAPAWA's efforts to unionize the city's food-processing plants. In the face of opposition from the infamous Boss Crump political machine, Williams met with both black and white workers in any available church, home, or union hall, where the gatherings were invariably filled with prayer, hymns, and "traditional spirituals converted into union songs."[110] Death threats eventually forced Williams to leave Memphis, but he would eventually become an influential voice in both the integration of the United Auto Workers and voter registration drives in the Deep South during the civil rights movement.[111]

Tom Tippett served a similar function as Hays at Brookwood. Tippett was a former coal miner who became an official with the United Mine Workers. He was present at some of the bloodiest strikes of the era, including Elizabeth, Marion, Gastonia, and Greenville, and wrote a book, *When Southern Labor Stirs*, detailing what he saw. At Marion, Tippett writes that religious songs from neighboring churches were sung at the strike meetings and were "later transcribed into songs of the strike." He writes movingly about the early days of the Marion strike, "the picket lines at night with their camp-fires burning; the women and men stationed there chanting rewritten Negro spirituals across the darkness to inspire faith and courage." At a similar strike in Danville, which also ended badly for the workers, he says that religious songs "were re-written into labor songs about the struggle" even as the strikers struggled to continue their daily lives: "In Danville, as elsewhere, the strike with its singing workers, released from the long and dreary hours in the mill, was in many ways beautiful." Still later at Danville, Tippett observes that the frenzied activity in the union headquarters included "mimeographing songs composed by strikers themselves to tell the history of their struggle." Finally, Tippett records the scene at a large hall designed to hold "600 or 700 people" but jammed with 1,500 strikers, who "sang a strike song to the music of 'Jesus Saves'" as they waited for the meeting to begin, singing "lustily." Even as the hall "resounded with familiar hymn tunes," led by the former choir director in the cotton mill's church, Tippett said workers found a "new religion."[112]

Other schools related to American labor also published songbooks. The University of Wisconsin School for Workers published a series of such books, beginning in 1924, as the *School for Workers Songbook*. Songs were divided by topic into chapters, including "Good Fellowship Songs" and "Spirituals and Folk Songs."[113] Denisoff notes that the significance of the labor colleges was in their role providing both songs and singers to the CIO and other labor and civil rights–related groups. The other labor school, Highlander, of course, would endure and become an influential factor in the American civil rights movement of the 1950s and '60s.[114]

Still another organization that aided in the widespread dispersal of protest songs of African-American origin was the Southern Tenant Farmers' Union, founded by a branch of the Socialist Party in 1934. One of the few racially integrated groups of its kind, STFU's activities featured singing, according to cofounder H. L. Mitchell, and their meetings were filled with religious fervor and music:

> There was quite a lot of singing, especially among the Negro members who were quite good singers. They would sing the old Negro spirituals. Many of them are songs of protest that grew out of conditions that existed before slavery was abolished. Some of the spirituals seemed to fit in with the union program. One of them, for instance, was selected as the official union song. It was "We Shall Not Be Moved." It went something like this: "Just like a tree planted by the water, we shall not be moved," and the words were added, "The union is a'marching, we shall not be moved."[115]

In February 1935, the union invited Jennie Lee, a former member of the British House of Commons, to address STFU members at a mass meeting in Marked Tree, Arkansas. Despite official oppression and threats of violence from planters, an estimated two thousand people marched in "orderly" fashion, two by two to the union hall, lifting their voices in "triumphant tones," and they sang what he identified as a union song, "We Shall Not Be Moved."[116]

As mentioned earlier, among the workers who were active with STFU was John Handcox, an African-American sharecropper who had also studied with Claude Williams at Commonwealth. Handcox wrote a number of protest songs based on spirituals and other religious music sources. One of his best-known numbers was adapted from "Roll the Chariot On," composed during a strike in Arkansas in 1936: "If the governor is in the way / We're going to roll it over him / We're goin' to roll the union on."[117] The revised spiritual was, for many years, associated with CIO's chief organizer Allan Haywood. Haywood was a familiar sight at union conventions, meetings, and rallies, and members fondly recalled how he would "boom out" the lyrics to "Roll the Union On."[118]

A natural preacher, Handcox traveled widely, singing the songs he had grown up listening to in church for both unions and communist groups. He later told Silverman that he didn't begin to write songs until he had joined the union, in order to "point out to people when they were working and not getting anything out of it."[119] Handcox's success was one of the reasons the American Communist Party so heavily used and promoted African-American sacred music as a suitable—and effective—means of protest.[120] Lomax and Guthrie cite his composition "No More Mournin'," calling it an "old, old Negro spiritual." Handcox sang it at STFU "meetings all over the south, and by now it's spread through the whole country": "Oh, freedom, oh, freedom / And before I'll be a slave / I'll be buried in my grave / Take my place with those who loved and fought before." Also attributed to Handcox is "Raggedy Raggedy Are We," based on the melody from "How Beautiful Heaven Would Be," and featuring the lines, "We don't get nothing for our labor / So hungry, hungry are we."[121]

According to Guthrie, a new set of lyrics to the pre–Civil War spiritual "We Shall Not Be Moved" was first sung by strikers at the Rockwood, Tennessee, hosiery plant in 1938, and the song was quickly adopted by labor movements across the United States. However, a quote from A. B. Brookins at the Third Annual Convention of the STFU in 1937 suggests that variations on the spiritual were known to strikers long before the hosiery action: "As I climb up to the highest hill of elevations, I will always be singing my union song, that we shall not be moved." As with so many other spirituals, the song's format makes it easy to adapt to individual situations—one of the reasons it would become one of the standard songs of the civil rights movement thirty years later: "We're not afraid of gun thugs / We shall not be moved."[122]

With financial assistance from a church in New York and the STFU, Hays and a photojournalist coproduced the documentary *America's Disinherited* in 1936. Filmed in the Mississippi Delta and rural Arkansas, the film "introduced New York's left-wing audiences" to the desperate conditions facing southern sharecroppers. At one point, black and white strikers are shown marching together and singing "Black and white together / We shall not be moved."[123]

There are, of course, other examples in the 1930s of the use of revised spirituals or at least camp-meeting hymns popular with black and white audiences. In Detroit, the *Daily Worker* reported that African-American workers in June 1934 protested the arrest of a fellow worker (who had allegedly attacked a white woman) by singing an adaptation of another old spiritual. The song, reworked from the original by songwriter Maurice Sugar, is interesting in that each succeeding verse shows the increasing militancy of the singers:

> *Bosses and judges, list'n t' me*
> *You ain't goin' t' jail James Victory*
> *I'm tellin' you*
> *He's goin' free,*
> *Black workers, white workers, joinin' with me*
> *They ain't goin' t' jail James Victory*
> *I'm tellin' you*
> *He's goin' free,*
> *Black workers, white workers, fightin' with me*
> *They ain't goin' t' jail James Victory*
> *He's goin' free.*[124]

Sugar, who was also a union lawyer, rewrote a number of well-known popular songs, including "The Soup Song" and "Sit-Down," both of which were common among labor unions.[125] The singing of rewritten spirituals and religious songs continued during the United Automobile Workers (UAW) strike in Flint, Michigan (December 1936–February 1937). Buoyed by the widespread use of song during the General Motors strike in Flint earlier in 1936, the UAW exhibited a renewed interest in the singing of labor songs "as both a valuable tool for rousing workers during a strike and vital 'for the enrichment of a real working class culture.'"[126]

Vorse's beautifully written articles on this strike and others make frequent mention of the singing, including versions of "We Shall Not Be Moved." Another religious song, "Hold the Fort," is mentioned during a tour she made through the Flint plant during a heavy snowfall.[127] Later in the strike, Vorse records the singing of the same two religious protest songs during a diversionary tactic that enabled strikers to occupy Chevrolet No. 4 and hasten the successful end of the labor action.[128]

From the *Sunday Worker* article mentioned above from September 1939, Randall reprints "a moving song" sung by relief clients in a Chicago picket line. The song, set to "the rich tune of an old spiritual," is directed at Senator Scott W. Lucas, who had voted to cut funding for a work program:

> *O-O-O what Lucas done to us.*
> *He took the milk from the babies,*

He never shall be reelected
For what he done to us.

In citing the song creators, Randall quotes Sainter L. Avery, chairman of Alliance Local 45 on Chicago's South Side, already known as a "Negro ghetto" in 1939: "We make up songs about everything we feel and are fighting for." According to Randall, Avery's ancestors, "slaving in the cottonfields of the South, may have added verses to the spirituals or the numerous work songs of America's black millions." A number of the Alliance locals organized choruses "to fill the cultural as well as the purely economic needs" of the union membership in Chicago: "At any Chicago unemployed demonstration, there is always a group of Negro singers from Local 45 to entertain and help mobilize the crowd with their latest songs. One song, praising the International Labor Defense for its fight to keep a crippled Negro who had been framed from being executed, and rendered by a quartet from Local 45 brought down the house at a benefit party in Chicago one night last year. The refrain of the song runs, 'O, the ILD / Took a man from a tree.'"[129] The "tree," Randall notes, is a direct reference to lynching and would be immediately apparent to African-American listeners.

According to Guthrie, "The Union Fights the Battle of Freedom," based on the spiritual "Joshua Fit the Battle of Jericho," was first composed by the South Side Negro Chorus of Local 76 of the ILGWU (International Ladies' Garment Workers' Union) during the Chicago Newspaper Guild strike in 1938: "The union fights the battle of freedom, freedom, freedom / And the bosses come tumbling down."[130]

A little-known but fascinating footnote in American protest history occurred in 1939 in Missouri's "Bootheel" region, where thousands of sharecroppers, under the direction of the Reverend Owen and Zella Whitfield, staged a spontaneous sit-down demonstration that stretched for miles along Highways 60 and 61 to protest conditions that even the federal government admitted were as bad as slavery—perhaps worse. And throughout the meetings and the long, dismal demonstrations, first on the highway and later in nearby swampy bottomlands, protest spirituals were sung.[131]

The Communist Party's influence in labor eventually waned, but not before African-American party members gave a number of old gospel songs and spirituals a decidedly Marxist spin, including this version of "Give Me That Old-Time Religion" secularized as "Give Me That Old Communist Spirit," where each stanza ends, "It was good enough for Lenin, and it's good enough for me." In reaction to the spurious trial of nine young African-American men in Scottsboro charged with raping two white women in 1931, party members transformed the song as follows:

The Scottsboro verdict,
Is not good enuf for me.
It's good for big fat bosses,
For workers double-crossers,
For low slaves and hosses,
But it ain't good enuf for me.[132]

And in the *Daily Worker* in the early 1930s, Mike Gold wrote a series of columns titled "The Negro Reds of Chicago." While chronicling protests resulting from the "killing of Negro workers" and "mass evictions on the South Side," Gold noted that African-Americans in 1932 were singing another variation, "Gimme that new communist spirit," which he said had "dozens" of verses: "Many such new songs and singers. [*sic*] At mass meetings their religious past becomes transmuted into a Communist present."[133] While the party was overtly antireligious, even the most jaded white communists were eventually forced to admit the power and the effectiveness of the black sacred music of African-Americans, where a "throbbing note of protest" could be found in the spirituals and where they "were living prophesies of deliverance." The pages of *The Liberator* in 1931 feature another adaptation of what the unnamed writer calls "an old nineteenth-century slave song" to create "No Mo', No Mo'."[134]

The use of spirituals by American labor as the basis for protest songs gradually spread as more African-American workers joined unions. Many undoubtedly were effective—and are still sung today. Joe Glazer, dubbed "labor's troubadour," writes in the book of the same name that when he was organizing southern textile mills in the late 1940s, he continually heard new versions of old spirituals and gospel hymns, including a remake of "Since I Been Introduced to the House of the Lord, I Ain't No Stranger Now": "Since I been introduced to the CIO / I ain't (no, I ain't) no stranger now." A second transformed hymn Glazer collected (and later recorded) was a version of "Let the Light of the Lighthouse Shine on Me," designed to tout the CIO: "No starvation wages, no more misery / Since the light of the union has shined on me." Still another rewritten gospel hymn first heard by Glazer while working various southern textile training institutes soon became one of his favorites, "Farther Along": "Cheer up my brothers, live in the sunshine / We'll understand it all by and by." Glazer writes that he first heard the union version of "I'll Overcome Some Day" ("We Shall Overcome") in 1947 from Agnes Martocci Douty, who learned it at Highlander College, which eventually came to be called the Highlander Folk School. Glazer records that he "sang it all through the South as a union song for years before it became a civil rights song." He also suggests that his recording of his arrangement in 1950 is the "first" modern recording of the song.[135]

However, for all their seriousness of intent, not every adaptation trips easily off the tongue, as evidenced by this final reworked labor song collected by Richard and JoAnne Reuss and featuring new words to "John the Revelator," still another old spiritual:

> *Tell me, who's that a-writing?*
> *Karl Marx is a-writing.*
> *And what's he writing?*
> *He's writing a manifesto,*
> *And signed it with the Communist seal.*[136]

THE BEGINNINGS OF THE MODERN CIVIL RIGHTS MOVEMENT, THE INFLUENCE OF RADIO, AND THE RISE OF GOSPEL MUSIC

People need work music. People need music to march by and to fight with, and if you composers don't dish it out right on the split second, you'll find folks passing you up and making up their own and playing and singing it.

—WOODY GUTHRIE

The songs of the working people have always been their sharpest statement and the one statement which cannot be destroyed. You can burn books, buy newspapers, you can guard against handbills and pamphlets, but you cannot prevent singing.

—JOHN STEINBECK

A people who can sing will make revolution; a people without spontaneous song will never defy the gods.

—F. BROWN

Much more occurred in the African-American struggle for equality in the late 1920s to the prewar 1940s than just the adoption of spirituals and the grudging acceptance of blacks into the labor movement, of course. By the 1920s, the African-American diaspora had helped awaken black political activism and gave savvy politicians the numbers they needed to influence policy in Cleveland, Pittsburgh, and, most notably, Chicago and New York.

In Chicago, Oscar De Priest became a kingmaker on the city's South Side and wielded power for decades. Meanwhile, in Harlem, a "machine" was created that aligned with labor and built the foundation for a series of strong African-American leaders for many years to come.[1] It was on Chicago's vibrant South Side in the late 1920s and early '30s that the next evolution in the history of the protest spiritual occurred. It was a new permutation of the basic musical form—the spiritual with the blues beat. As we shall see, this innovation—called gospel (sometimes black gospel)—reached further still into the consciousness of white America and would play an important role in the history of black sacred music and the ongoing civil rights movement. The spirituals, especially those that could be adapted for use as a vehicle of defiance and protest, survived gospel but were forever musically changed.[2]

With Franklin Roosevelt's election in 1932, black America had, if not a champion, then at least a sympathetic, progressive administration in the White House. Guided by his wife, Eleanor, the president regularly broke precedent, inviting numerous African-Americans, including musicians, college glee clubs, and jubilee groups, to the White House. Among the more notable examples, on a visit to Nashville the Tuskegee College choir sang at Roosevelt's mother's birthday party in January 1933, and the president requested that they sing at the White House shortly thereafter, despite intense opposition from southern politicians.[3] On other occasions, the Roosevelts stopped at Fisk University while in Nashville and heard the Fisk Jubilee Singers perform spirituals as tens of thousands of African-Americans lined the streets to glimpse the couple.[4] The June 10, 1933, edition of the *Chicago Defender* printed a photograph of the Morehouse College Quartet under the caption "Sings for the President," reflecting an event from "a few weeks ago" when the group "was presented at the White House."[5] *The Crisis*, the journal of the National Association for the Advancement of Colored People (NAACP), reported in the July 1933 edition (fig. 6) that the Glee Club of the Hampton Institute had entertained guests at the White House, including the former prime minister of France. The Morehouse College Glee Club performed again for the president that summer with "a program of songs and spirituals." *The Crisis*, which trumpeted the event, included a photograph of the Morehouse College Quartet.[6]

Later, during World War II, the Roosevelts invited the jubilee-turned-gospel group the Soul Stirrers to perform during a visit to the White House by Winston Churchill. The Soul Stirrers had been performing songs such as "Precious Lord" and "I'm a Soldier" at various USO shows at a time when black performers were still a rarity. Anthony Heilbut adds this wry parenthetical to a paragraph on the Soul Stirrers' performance at the White House: "It's gratifying to know that before he died, Winston Churchill heard a little Dr. Watts."[7]

In addition to the Roosevelts' personal and often very public support of blacks, Roosevelt's New Deal policies aimed at ending the crushing Great Depression were among the first to include African-Americans and served as a significant catalyst in blacks' shifting their allegiance to the Democratic Party.[8] African-American

July, 1933

THE
CRISIS

FIFTEEN CENTS

A RECORD OF THE DARKER RACES

FLINT-GOODRIDGE HOSPITAL · MAX YERGAN

OUR CLASS STRUGGLE · HISTORY OF THE NEGRO

FIGURE 6

In July 1933, *The Crisis* reported that the Hampton Institute's Glee Club had entertained guests at the White House.

newspapers wrote endless columns praising the Roosevelts' support as an unprecedented "example of interracial behavior."[9] In Arthur Raper's powerful indictment of African-American poverty in the South, *Tenants of the Almighty*, is a poem from "folk poet" Louisiana Dunn Thomas, wife of a black tenant farmer, who equated Roosevelt with a well-loved biblical liberator, a familiar—but still potent—image from the Old Testament and spirituals: "God has sent a Moses / To lead his people free."[10]

As suggested earlier, from a black sacred music standpoint, the most significant event of this era was the rise of gospel music. Gospel music combined religious lyrics, the biblically based storytelling of the spirituals, the close harmonies of jubilee, the rough-edged testifying voices of African-American preachers, and the beat and improvisational musical and lyrical characteristics of the blues. Fueled by the compositional skills of former bluesman Thomas A. Dorsey, the organizational abilities of his partner Sallie Martin, and the transcendent voice of Mahalia Jackson, gospel swept out of Chicago's black churches in the early 1930s and quickly became the dominant form of African-American sacred musical expression.[11]

While Dorsey styled himself the "father of gospel music," other composers at the time had been writing in a similarly "loose" compositional style, including William Henry Sherwood, Lucy Campbell, and Charles A. Tindley. Tindley's most famous compositions include "Stand by Me," "Beams of Heaven," "We'll Understand It Better By and By," and a number that would play a significant role in the evolution of the signature song of the civil rights movement, "I'll Overcome Some Day."[12] Popular jubilee groups, such as the Golden Gate Quartet (which dropped the "Jubilee" from their name during this period), the Soul Stirrers, the Dixie Hummingbirds, and many others, gradually moved to gospel by singing the songs of Dorsey, Tindley, Campbell, W. Herbert Brewster, and others. "The appeal of Dorsey's compositions," writes Jerma Jackson, "combined with innovative strategies of organization, would soon give gospel a following great enough to rival that of secular music."[13] This was due, in part, to Dorsey's "sketchy" published scores, which provided the new style with its "first wide-scale avenue of dissemination."[14]

As early as 1942, Arna Bontemps wrote that gospel music was "church music that can hold its own against anything on the hit parade."[15] The many attractions of gospel music would prove to be an important element in the widespread use of sacred music during the civil rights movement, a little more than a decade later. The best-known religious artist at the time was Sister Rosetta Tharpe, a guitar-playing evangelist who added a pronounced swing beat to both the old spirituals and the new gospel songs. During the World War II years, her hits "Strange Things Happening Every Day," Dorsey's "Rock Me," "This Train," "God Don't Like It," and "Up Above My Head I Hear Music in the Air" were the first gospel songs to top the Harlem Hit Parade's national "race" sales and airplay charts. Tharpe was so popular that the U.S. government even asked her to join country star Roy Acuff in recording a series of public service announcements on the deadly effects of venereal disease both for public consumption and for broadcast on Armed Forces

Radio. This was one of the first times that black and white performers had received equal billing, certainly on a national stage.[16] Tharpe's songs, too, would endure into the civil rights era.

However, as Tharpe's star slowly waned, no artist would come to dominate a musical genre like Mahalia Jackson eventually came to dominate gospel music. Jackson is easily the most political of all major gospel artists as well. As early as the summer of 1942, Jackson was singing at rallies and fund-raising events for African-American Alderman William L. Dawson in Chicago's District 1.[17] Dawson won and became only the third black U.S. representative in the twentieth century and the first to chair a standing committee. Dawson would eventually serve for thirty years in the House.[18] In August, following the Democratic Party convention in Chicago, Jackson publicly supported Franklin Roosevelt. Jackson said she "worked hard for Roosevelt. I went around all the different districts for him, because he said he'd put meat on the table."[19] Thus began a long and mutually beneficial relationship between gospel artists and the Democratic Party.

In the world of popular music, white Americans of the day rarely had the opportunity to hear or see black artists, whether they performed religious *or* mainstream music. Save when the popular *Rudy Vallée Show* (which regularly featured black artists) went on a three-month hiatus and Louis Armstrong hosted a replacement series titled *Harlem* in 1937, blacks were rarely, if ever, heard on radio.[20] In the 1930s, the few remaining independent radio stations soon fell to the dominant NBC and CBS networks, both of which rarely aired performances or recordings by African-American musicians for fear of alienating southern advertisers, listeners, and station owners. As a result, white swing bands and singers dominated Depression-era radio, even though the roots of jazz—and many of the best bands—came from African-American communities and neighborhoods. Only occasionally would a program with "liberal credentials," such as the *Rudy Vallée Show* or *Shell Chateau*, air music by blacks. To hear radio broadcasts of African-American musicians ranging from Duke Ellington to the Golden Gate Quartet, listeners had to turn to the networks' "sustaining-time" (public service) programming, which usually broadcast at odd hours.[21] Only four radio stations in 1943 featured programming tailored for black audiences.[22]

Major recording labels like Decca did sign and release music by black jazz artists, such as Armstrong, Chick Webb, Ella Fitzgerald, and others, on their "race" labels, but little of it reached white audiences.[23] Still, some white listeners did manage to find their way to the hot jazz of the 1940s, and their attitudes would lay the foundation for the more widespread acceptance of black popular music, particularly among teenagers and young adults in large urban areas in the 1950s. According to David Riesman, "Hot jazz lovers are protestors. They are individualists who reject contemporary majority conformities."[24]

While gospel was in its ascendancy in the African-American community, when white audiences actually *did* hear black sacred music, it was usually in the form of the arranged spirituals which, as we have seen, continued to be performed and sometimes preserved. The preservation and presentation of the spirituals was a part of a wider process of acculturation, exposing white America to African-Americans and African-American achievement in a positive light. Decades of minstrelsy, the demeaning "coon songs," and racist depictions of blacks in the media first had to be overcome. This process was slowed by the limited public media options open to African-Americans throughout much of the United States, not just the South. A number of extraordinarily talented artists and groundbreaking events did move the process along, although at what must have felt like an excruciatingly slow pace to most African-Americans. But the process did begin to happen in the late 1930s.

New York City's two "Spirituals to Swing" concerts placed black sacred music in the public spotlight during this era. In his long career, John Hammond was a talent scout and music promoter who is credited with "discovering" (i.e., bringing to the attention of white record labels and listeners) artists like Count Basie, Benny Goodman, Billie Holiday, and others (including, years later, Aretha Franklin, Bob Dylan, and Bruce Springsteen). It was Hammond who first proposed a concert featuring the best in black music, but he could find no sponsors until the Marxist weekly *New Masses*, one of the few journals of any kind to cover African-American musicians, stepped up. Hammond assembled a virtually all-black lineup in Carnegie Hall that exposed gospel, blues, and jazz to an integrated audience, most of whom were hearing it for the first time.[25] The sold-out first concert on December 23, 1938, included Tharpe and Mitchell's Christian Singers, as well as Count Basie, Sidney Bechet, Big Bill Broonzy, and others. (Broonzy's set on the Spirituals to Swing stage included his ever-evolving "Just a Dream," which featured this particularly "audacious" verse, *especially* for 1938: "I dreamed I was in the White House, sitting in the President's chair / I dreamed he shaked my hand, said 'Bill, I'm glad you're here.'")[26] A second concert, on December 24, 1939, featured the Golden Gate Quartet, along with the integrated Benny Goodman Sextet, Sonny Terry (who performed "The New John Henry"), Broonzy, Basie, and others.[27]

The influence of the Spirituals to Swing concerts on mainstream popular music is "difficult to deny," but just as important were the "social and political implications" of the concerts: "The racial impact cannot be overlooked as African-American artists were being presented to an integrated audience at Carnegie Hall at a time when such an occurrence was, if not unheard of, extremely rare." Hammond's reasons for the sponsoring the concerts were influenced by his own political activism: "The strongest motivation for my dissent was jazz. I heard no color line in the music. To bring recognition to the Negro's supremacy in jazz was the most effective and constructive form of social protest I could think of."[28] Hammond later told Studs Terkel that the two Spirituals to Swing concerts were the most "exhilarating moment" in his life: "I would say less than 10 percent of the audience for the 1938 concert was black, alas. It was a jazz audience. Some were obviously politically aware folk. To have any black people downstairs in Carnegie Hall was a political gesture in itself. My very own conservative Republican family was up in a box loving it."[29]

Hammond was friends with Barney Josephson, the force behind the Café Society nightclub in New York City, one of the first major venues anywhere in the United States to promote African-American artists to mixed audiences. Café Society, which opened five days after the first Spirituals to Swing concert, "broke" a host of major black artists to white audiences, including Lester Young, John Coltrane, Lena Horne, Sarah Vaughan, and Charlie Parker. Among the religious artists featured at various times were the Golden Gate Quartet, Mitchell's Christian Singers, Tharpe, and the Dixie Hummingbirds (then billed as the Sewanee Quintet). During World War II, the Gates (as they were popularly called) wrote and recorded "a topical spiritual" titled "Stalin Wasn't Stallin'," which was featured on a *March of Time* newsreel and became one of the first hits on the pop charts by an African-American group. Their Café Society engagements also led to a contract with CBS Radio. Josephson's commitment to racial equality was such that he bought advertisements in African-American newspapers, including the *Amsterdam News*, the *Pittsburgh Courier*, and the *Chicago Defender*, inviting blacks to his club in the very-white One Sheraton Square in Greenwich Village.[30]

The Gates would remain one of the most visible African-American sacred artists through the war, recording hits like "The Preacher and the Bear," "Coming in on a Wing and a Prayer," "Shadrack," and "Joshua Fit the Battle of Jericho," and were exceeded only by the Mills Brothers and the Ink Spots in popularity. Through their nearly fifty-year career, the Golden Gate Quartet also recorded a number of "protest" spirituals, including "If I Had My Way," "Way Down in Egypt's Land," "Wade in the Water," and "Swing Low, Sweet Chariot." They also performed repeatedly in the White House at the request of Eleanor Roosevelt and at FDR's inauguration, exposing white audiences to black sacred music every step of the way.[31]

Two early patrons of Café Society were Abel and Anne Meeropol, who had adopted the children of Ethel and Julius Rosenberg. (The Rosenbergs had been arrested for allegedly providing the Soviet Union with state secrets and would be unjustly executed a few years later.) One evening at the club, Abel (writing as "Lewis Allen") gave Josephson a song he had written about the epidemic of southern lynchings, titled "Strange Fruit." Josephson offered the lyrics to Billie Holiday, who sang it as her final encore that evening:

> Southern trees bear strange fruit
> Blood on the leaves and blood at the root
> Black bodies swinging in the southern breeze
> Strange fruit hanging from the poplar trees.

At the end of the song, Stephenson recorded, "Absolute silence. And then— boom! Big explosion. The audience really exploded, to the point where they rose to applaud." Word of mouth on the song—and Holiday's performance—quickly spread throughout the city and it was featured in *Time* magazine, eventually to become a mainstay of the protest movement.[32]

The 1930s also saw the long-overdue rise and gradual acceptance of a handful of talented, classically trained African-American singers, all of whom kept an arranged form of the spiritual, including protest spirituals, before the white public. Marian Anderson, one of America's greatest contraltos, initially gained prominence in the mid-1930s, performing concerts and recitals in Europe before finally overcoming deep-rooted prejudice among audiences in the United States to become one of the country's most significant classical artists.[33] In addition to her extensive classical repertoire, Anderson sang numerous spirituals in her recitals, in part due to her longtime friendship with Hall Johnson. The Hall Johnson Negro Choir was, along with Wings over Jordan, the best-known African-American choir in the United States, appearing on national radio programs and providing music for several motion pictures, including both the Broadway and film versions of *Green Pastures.* Working with Johnson's arrangements, Anderson championed such spirituals as "Fix Me, Jesus," "Deep River," "Certn'y Lord," "Dere's No Hidin' Place Down Dere," and "Roll, Jerd'n Roll."[34]

However, as the title of Raymond Arsenault's book—*The Sound of Freedom: Marian Anderson, the Lincoln Memorial, and the Concert That Awakened America*—suggests, Anderson's contribution to civil rights included a well-documented use of spirituals as a public protest against racism. Anderson had originally been scheduled to perform in Washington, D.C.'s Constitution Hall. However, the Daughters of the American Revolution (DAR), who operated the building as a public trust, had a policy forbidding African-American artists. Angered by the DAR's racism, Eleanor Roosevelt resigned her membership in protest. Two members of Franklin D. Roosevelt's cabinet, Walter White and Harold L. Ickes, arranged for Anderson to sing on the steps of the Lincoln Memorial to a national radio audience on Easter Sunday, April 9, 1939.[35] For African-Americans, it was a powerful and perhaps even pivotal moment in American race relations, in part because even the actual dedication of the Lincoln Memorial years earlier, on Memorial Day 1922, had been marred by racism. Arriving African-American dignitaries that day were shuttled to a segregated seating area in the rear. Many left in "disgust" and anger. "Nothing," one author noted, "symbolized the triumph of segregation more profoundly."[36]

The *Time* magazine account of Anderson's concert was more interested in which politicians from which party were *not* in attendance for fear of offending southern constituents ("For all who did not, New Dealer Ickes as Secretary of the Interior made things doubly uncomfortable by proffering the Emancipator for a backdrop") than the music itself. Still, according to *Time*, Anderson sang "America," "Ave Maria," and the spiritual "My Soul's Been Anchored in the Lord."[37] Anderson's autobiography notes that she also sang the spirituals "Gospel Train" and "Trampin'."[38] When Anderson was belatedly permitted to sing in Constitution Hall by a chastened DAR four years later, she was accompanied by German refugee Franz Rupp on the piano as she sang the spiritual "Let Us Break Bread Together" to yet another national radio audience. When told she had become a "symbol of democracy" to a nation embroiled in a second world war, Anderson later said that the Easter Sunday event was "more than a concert." Standing on the steps of the Lincoln Memorial before seventy-five thousand people felt like "singing for an entire nation." She "carried the inspiration" of that concert with her, she said, wherever she sang in the decades that followed.[39] Some writers saw the performance as a "testament to racial solidarity and a signal event of the fledgling civil rights movement."[40]

A week later, in an event that was equally significant in the eyes of the African-American press, the Roosevelts hosted the state visit of King George VI and Queen Elizabeth at the White House. Among the performers were the North Carolina Spiritual Singers, under the auspices of the Works Project Administration's Federal Music Project, along with Anderson, who again sang "My Soul's Been Anchored in the Lord." The evening's program featured African-Americans' contributions of to their country's music and drew effusive praise.[41] Anderson later would sing at the inaugurations of both Dwight Eisenhower and John F. Kennedy and would remain active through the course of the civil rights movement in the 1960s.[42] Though the event on the steps of the Lincoln Memorial was little remarked on at the time, some scholars, including Scott A. Sandage, claim that not only did the "modern civil rights movement come of age" on that Easter Sunday, but that its combination of sacred song and mass protest also "constituted a tactical learning experience that contributed to the civil rights movement's strategies of nonviolent action." Held tightly in the shared memories of African-Americans, it was not a coincidence, Sandage argues, that Dr. Martin Luther King, Jr.'s "I Have a Dream" speech—which ends with the words of a spiritual—was delivered from the same steps as Marian Anderson's concert.[43]

Paul Robeson's presence as a major African-American artist illuminates more than forty years of American life. One of the nation's greatest bass-baritones, he was a College Hall of Fame football star, a groundbreaking operatic performer, a recording artist, a Broadway star, a fearless activist, and a civil rights crusader.[44] Like Anderson, he was justly celebrated for the spirituals he sang, sometimes as the first African-American to perform on some of the world's preeminent stages. A *New York Times* reviewer wrote after one such concert that Robeson's spirituals had "the ring of the revivalist" and were a "cry from the depths, this universal humanism that touches the heart." The reviewer hailed Robeson's interpretation and conviction: "Sung by one man, they voiced the sorrow and hopes of a people."[45]

Robeson is now best known for his rendition of "Old Man River" in the stage and film versions of *Showboat*, though his *Othello*, both on Broadway and in London, is still celebrated in the histories of the stage. His heroic, very public lifelong struggle against racism and the dreaded House Un-American Activities Committee may not be widely remembered today, but as the best-known African-American not named Joe Louis in the 1930s and '40s, that aspect of his complicated life may have had a more lasting impact.[46] In 1939, Robeson was cast as the lead in the Broadway musical *John Henry*. While the production lasted only for five performances, two members of the chorus—folk/blues singer Josh White and a very young Bayard Rustin—became friends. When White formed Josh White and the Carolinians, he invited Rustin to become a member. The group had a regular gig at Café Society and released the well-received album *Chain Gang* on Columbia Records. Rustin, of course, would become one of the most significant strategists of the civil rights movement.[47] On the eve of World War II, when radio was the dominant form of home entertainment, Robeson, accompanied by the American People's Chorus, performed "Ballad for Americans," an eleven-minute choral work written by John La Touche, with music by Earl Robinson. Network radio rarely featured African-Americans in a positive light, since such performances were censored in the South, but on this occasion Robeson sang the words "Man in a white skin can never be free / while his black brother is in slavery" to an audience of millions.[48]

Although not as well known as Anderson and Robeson, African-American singers Jules Bledsoe and Roland Hayes also specialized in arranged spirituals and performed in both classical and popular venues throughout the United States and abroad. Bledsoe's career had been stagnating until he performed a recital in New York's Town Hall in 1939 that included both spirituals and a section titled "Songs of Freedom and Hope." In Bledsoe's introduction, he dedicated the songs "to those in the world who are in need of freedom and hope; in other words, true Democracy."[49]

Still, African-Americans on national radio networks remained something of a rarity. One exception was the Wings over Jordan Choir, which sang every Sunday morning on the CBS radio network from 1938 through 1949. Through the years, a number of notable black singers, authors, and politicians appeared on the show, including Langston Hughes and Adam Clayton Powell, Sr. Traveling in buses, the choir toured the United States, sometimes singing for integrated audiences. The group sang hymns, spirituals, and gospel songs, including "I've Been 'Buked and I've Been Scorned," "Amen," "Swing Low, Sweet Chariot," "Trampin'," "Over My Head (I Hear Music in the Air)," "I Cried and I Cried," and "Rock-a My Soul."[50] During one such tour in 1939, Wings over Jordan performed before eighteen thousand people in Baltimore and fifteen thousand people in Washington, D.C. By June 1940, 107 CBS affiliates carried their radio program and the National Association of Broadcasters presented them the Peabody Award for outstanding public service.[51] Listening to the Wings over Jordan's early Sunday morning performances was a ritual in many African-America households, and the group did much to expose black sacred music to white audiences.[52]

Few people worked as hard on behalf of African-Americans as Eleanor Roosevelt. Throughout her life, the wife of the president used every means possible to bring the races together, and she even became a member of both the NAACP and the Congress of Racial Equality (CORE) in 1945.[53] In addition to her personal influence, Eleanor (like her husband) made frequent use of radio, sometimes appearing with African-American artists, to further her aims. Through her support, often in her very popular syndicated "My Day" newspaper column, word of progressive radio programs—such as *Immigrants All, Americans All*; *The Negro*; and *Freedom's People*—reached wide network radio audiences.[54] Supported by the Office of Education, *Immigrants All* featured several episodes that timidly explored the black experience in American history. While the series, which aired from 1938 to 1939, disappointed many African-Americans, it did pave the way for the somewhat more forthright series *The Negro*.[55] *The Negro* was designed, in part, to counter to the racist, demeaning images of African-Americans, most notably as portrayed in the popular *Amos 'n' Andy* radio show. However, as the original team of consultants and scriptwriters included no African-Americans, *The Negro* had a rocky road before even reaching the airwaves in 1938. Unpaid "advisers" W. E. B. Du Bois and Alain Locke were belatedly invited to read the initial script. Both found it offensive and made numerous suggestions. Roy Wilkins of the New York offices of the NAACP wrote, "This script reads like a history of the progress of white people using the labor and talents of Negroes." Eventually, a somewhat altered script was grudgingly approved, and the show aired later that year. For all its flaws, *The Negro* did include a performance of James Weldon Johnson's "Lift Every Voice and Sing," often called "The Negro National Anthem," and a long section on the history of the Fisk Jubilee Singers.[56]

Much more successful was the national broadcast of the series *Freedom's People*, which aired on the NBC radio network beginning in 1942. While the first episode concentrated on the least controversial aspect of African-American history—music—it provided a positive and sometimes inspirational vehicle for performances by Josh White, Count Basie, Paul Robeson, the Southernaires, the Golden Gate Quartet, and black collegiate choral groups from Tuskegee Institute, Howard University, and Fisk University. Even the opening theme music, a choral medley drawn from "My Country 'Tis of the Thee," "Go Down, Moses," and "Lift Every Voice," presented a different picture of African-Americans to white listeners. In *Freedom's People*, Irve Tunick's script revealed the history of African-Americans through their music. One vignette identified "Steal Away to Jesus" as "a message not just about the escape to physical freedom but also about the quest for religious liberty." Josh White sang "John Henry." But according to Barbara Dianne Savage, *Freedom's People*'s most riveting sequence came when Robeson sang a "protest spiritual," "No More Auction Block for Me."[57] *Time* magazine called Robeson's performance "towering" and noted that he also sang "Swing Low, Sweet Chariot."[58] *New Masses* responded with a short history of African-Americans on broadcast radio in addition to reviewing *Freedom's People*, which it deemed "excellent." One reviewer particularly praised Robeson's "No More Auction Block for Me," quoting Robeson as saying that "the promise of the Emancipation Proclamation must be realized."[59]

However, it was not until an episode on African-American achievements in athletics that *Freedom's People* made a "direct reference to segregation and an outright appeal to black patriotism." The segment, which was broadcast in November

1941, featured a rendition of the spiritual "Climbing Jacob's Ladder" before Joe DiMaggio was interviewed as saying that Negro Leagues star Satchel Paige was one of the best pitchers he ever faced. Live interviews were conducted with Olympian Jesse Owens and heavyweight champion Joe Louis. Spirituals and black gospel songs were highlighted in other episodes as well. A narrator told the story of Phillis Wheatley's family, accompanied by excerpts from the spiritual "Sometimes I Feel Like a Motherless Child" in one episode, while groups ranging from the Leonard De Paur Chorus to the Golden Gate Quartet performed in others.[60] Again, this would have been a rare opportunity for many white Americans to hear authentic African-American sacred music, performed by some of its greatest practitioners.

Also on radio were two series on CBS produced by Alan Lomax and Nicholas Ray, *The American School of the Air* on Saturday mornings (1939) and *Back Where I Come From* (1940), which featured Leadbelly, Josh White, the Golden Gate Quartet, and Woody Guthrie and were broadcast during prime listening hours.[61] An article titled "Folk Songs in the White House" in the March 3, 1941, issue of *Time* details a White House concert from the week before titled "An Evening of Songs for American Soldiers." Hosted by Alan Lomax, the lineup included "Joshua" White (who performed "John Henry" and "Man Goin' Round' Takin' Names") and the "foot-tapping" Golden Gate Quartet (which performed "Noah" and "Things Are Gonna Come My Way"). All the performers, including Burl Ives, were drawn from the CBS series *Back Where I Come From*.[62]

The first half of a groundbreaking episode of the popular CBS series *The Spirit of '43*, titled "Heroines in Bronze," was built around the lives of three African-American pioneers, Phillis Wheatley, Sojourner Truth, and Harriet Tubman, with the second half devoted to contemporary black women, including Mary McLeod Bethune. "Heroines in Bronze" was the first national radio broadcast devoted to African-American women and, with the support of the Urban League, drew the support of New York Governor Thomas Dewey and President Roosevelt. The program featured a number of spirituals, including "Nobody Knows the Trouble I've Seen," "I Know the Lord Has Laid His Hands on Me," "No More Auction Block for Me," "Go Down, Moses," "Walk Together Children," and "I Thank God I'm Free at Last."[63] In late 1942, the title of the series *Freedom's People* was changed to the less confrontational *Jubilee* and became more of a variety show featuring African-American artists. In addition to the great jazz groups of the day, *Jubilee* at different times featured the Hall Johnson Choir and Ethel Waters.[64]

How significant were these and other radio programs in preparing both blacks and whites for the sustained civil rights movement of the 1950s and '60s? In "Radio Fights Jim Crow," Savage states that many of the creators of the radio programs would remain involved in the movement in the years to come: "I think that very specific and strong lessons were learned during the production of these radio shows. Both about the importance of mass media, but also I think about the centrality of mass media to the struggle for racial equality in this country. And a recognition that radio, and then television, of course, which was the medium of the civil rights movement, would and could play a really central role. That media, race and politics are intertwined." As another historian wrote, radio helped create the first few "cracks in the wall of racial segregation."[65]

As for the artists who had begun singing with the labor movement and the various socialist (and sometimes communist) organizations of the 1930s, a handful coalesced in an informal group called the Almanac Singers. The *Daily Worker* reported that the Almanac Singers came together at the Youth Congress in Washington, D.C., in early 1941.[66] Just a few months later, another article in the *Daily Worker* stated that singer/songwriters Lee Hays, Millard Lampell, and a young Pete Seeger actually formed the Almanacs in Greenwich Village in December 1940. But then, that discrepancy was the sort of laissez-faire attitude and narrative that was to be expected of a group whose members at various times included Woody Guthrie, Allan Sloane, Bess Lomax, Baldwin Hawes, Gordon Friesen, Sis Cunningham, Josh White, Arthur Stern, Cisco Houston, Brownie McGhee, Sonny Terry, and Earl Robinson. In fact, the Almanacs split into several incarnations when participants had competing engagements.[67]

As a biracial group, the Almanac Singers were a rarity, and the African-American artists, McGhee, Terry, and White, maintained solo careers as well. Despite crisscrossing the country on behalf of the CIO and recording a number of union songs (including one based on a spiritual, "Roll the Union On"), the group was "better known in bohemian and communist circles" than in the general labor movement.[68] Still, as a *Daily Worker* article from 1941 notes, the Almanacs sang spirituals and the blues and believed that the "songs of the Negro people are the most fertile field for folk songs in the world." The same reporter also reviewed one of their concerts and hailed their rendition of "John Henry" as one of the "best songs of this nature."[69] One of the Almanac Singers' most enduring songs, "Talking Union," was based on a spiritual that began, "If you want to get to heaven, let me tell you what to do." With lyrics written by Seeger and Lampell, and an assist from Hays, "Talking Union" became a prototype for the "talking" folk songs of the 1950s and early '60s and included the often-quoted line, "Take it easy . . . but take it!"[70] The Almanac Singers disbanded during World War II, in part because of a violent reaction to several songs they had recorded earlier in opposition to America's potential involvement in the conflict. Still, they were instrumental in helping launch the career of Seeger, who would remain a potent musical force through the civil rights movement and beyond.

One of the Almanac Singers' favorite cities was Detroit, where some members later relocated, perhaps because of the presence of a supportive, labor-based audience. African-Americans had slowly warmed to labor, and some important black church leaders in Chicago had supported A. Philip Randolph's push for a porters' union.[71] An event in Michigan that, while significant at the time, would have even broader implications in the years to come was the 1941 United Automobile Workers strike at the massive Ford Motor Company complex in Dearborn, Michigan. The plant employed sixty thousand African-Americans—few of them in the union. But when the strike was called, black workers sided with the UAW. Their actions, Lichtenstein writes, and their rejection of "Ford paternalism" by a "strategic minority," ensured both a victory by the union and the "subsequent labor alignment" with African-Americans in Detroit. It also provided one of the catalysts for the NAACP, the Urban League and, eventually, the southern civil rights movement.[72]

The Reverend C. L. Franklin, who arrived at New Bethel Baptist Church in Detroit in 1946, quickly became one of the most influential black preachers in the United States. Franklin, the father of singer Aretha Franklin, soon mobilized the church into sustained political activity. Some New Bethel deacons were active in the UAW, and he formed a political action committee to spur voter education and registration. One of Franklin's actions was to invite Adam Clayton Powell (and later Dr. Martin Luther King, Jr.) to speak from the pulpit, and he also urged that his parishioners support Democratic candidates.[73]

With the possibility of a two-front war looming, African-American leaders considered Roosevelt's Selective Service and Training Act, passed on September 16, 1940, to be a "milestone for black soldiers" because of two antidiscrimination clauses. The first clause enabled all American males aged between eighteen and thirty-six to enlist. The second clause, for the first time, expressly prohibited discrimination by race. A third clause, however, gave the Department of War the final authority on selection. It quickly became obvious that both the army and several individual states found numerous reasons to reject African-American applicants. This was possible at a time when most draft boards in both the North and South had no black members and more than 75 percent of the African-American inductees who failed the Army Classification Test came from the southern and border states, though illiterate whites were routinely admitted.[74]

At the onset of World War II, the number of African-Americans in the army was strictly limited and most were assigned to noncombat units. The navy allowed blacks to work only in the mess halls or as personal valets, while the coast guard and marines excluded them entirely. Military bases were more segregated than were the surrounding towns in the North, while in the American South, black soldiers were barred from the USO, theaters, and base exchanges. Even the chapel services were off-limits. African-American soldiers who did manage to enlist received virtually no protection on or off the military bases, especially in the South, where harassment and assault were common.[75]

While the United States Army and Navy were, eventually, slowly integrated, discrimination in the military did not disappear. Despite an unbroken history of gallant service by African-Americans, numerous books have detailed the horrendous, sometimes deadly treatment black soldiers and sailors received, some of it condoned and encouraged by the very officers charged with enforcing equal treatment in the ranks.[76]

At the same time, mobilization for what appeared to be another world war gave blacks additional leverage in the ongoing struggle for equal rights. Randolph, now president of the Brotherhood of Sleeping Car Porters, supported by Bayard Rustin (who later became one of Martin Luther King, Jr.'s closest advisers) and others, threatened to lead a large and potentially embarrassing march on the Washington Monument in July 1941 if the administration did not mandate an end to discriminatory practices in the area of military-related hiring. President Roosevelt and other political leaders convinced Randolph to cancel the event; in return, in June 1941 Executive Order 8802 was issued, establishing the "Fair Employment Practices Committee," which required equal participation by all races in employment the war effort. No company could afford to miss participation in the massive defense buildup because of discrimination. Consequently, the number of African-Americans working in manufacturing jumped from a half million in December 1941 to 1.2 million in August 1942.[77] It is interesting to contemplate, had the march actually taken place, *which* protest spirituals and labor songs the marchers would have sung. Randolph's Brotherhood provided one more component for the future of civil rights in the United States—a key member of the Brotherhood of Sleeping Car Porters was E. D. Nixon, who would later lead the Montgomery NAACP and recruit the young Rev. Martin Luther King, Jr., to lead the city's fledgling bus boycott.[78]

Reagon has identified forty songs "created by the black community during World War II" that she considered "historical documents" of a time when mainstream media paid little attention to African-Americans. Among the most influential of those songs was the "gospel ballad" known alternately as "World War II Ballad," "Oh, What a Time," or "Pearl Harbor." The song, performed in a call-and-response format in the style of a black preacher, featured a melody that had been used in songs chronicling several previous events that had affected the black community, from natural disasters to the sinking of the *Titanic*. "World War II Ballad" was sung by the Percy Wilburn Quartet, "Oh What a Time" was performed by the Georgia Sea Island Singers, and "Pearl Harbor I and II" were recorded by the Soul Stirrers.[79]

While the lyrics in all three versions primarily recounted the events of the war, one section directly addressed the navy's overt racism in trying to at first deny, then marginalize, the heroic efforts of African-American sailor Doris (sometimes written as Dorie) Miller, a cook who grabbed a machine gun, an action expressly forbidden to blacks, and shot down an unknown number of Japanese airplanes. The lyrics tout the efforts of the "colored press," specifically the *Pittsburgh Courier*, to publicize Miller's actions.[80]

Somewhat less overt is "God's Mighty Hand," released on the Matchbox label. Like the previous song, it features a talking historical narrative set to a familiar tune. The song's lyrics subtly indicted U.S. racism as one of the causes of the era's misfortunes—from the Great Depression to the war. Also from that era, Reagon cites the song "I Am American," which was heard and collected during a performance in a sanctified church congregation, sung in a call-and-response format. Amid the straightforward patriotic lyrics, one couplet subtly urges listeners to regard all people as equal: "When you walk down the street / Smile at everyone you meet."[81]

Perhaps the best known of the African-American religious songs recorded during World War II was the Soul Stirrers' "Why I Like Roosevelt," written by Otis Jackson. Similar to the "Pearl Harbor" songs, "Roosevelt" is a rambling, historically based narrative. It "clearly links" the president with poor blacks and includes a litany of advances for blacks initiated during Roosevelt's administration, including the promotion of the first African-American general in the army, Benjamin O. Davis. Eleanor Roosevelt also receives praise for her efforts on behalf of racial justice. The final section laments Roosevelt's death in office, equating him with Abraham Lincoln:

> *God Almighty knew just what was best*
> *Knew that the president needed a rest*
> *His battle done fought, victory done won*
> *Our problems had just begun*
> *When your burden get so heavy, you don't know what to do*
> *Call on Jesus, He's a president, too.*[82]

The African-American soldiers, sailors, and pilots who returned to the United States after the war were changed by what they had seen and heard. To many, fighting oppression and fascism abroad while they were denied the right to vote at home created a disconnect that demanded action. While stationed in India, some black members of the military even studied India's nonviolent struggle for independence.[83] The Reverend Harold Toliver vividly remembered what it was like to be a returning African-American veteran, facing "prejudice, racism, intolerance," the same problems as before. While some blacks became discouraged, Toliver believes that the "majority" instead "rededicated themselves to the struggle." Ultimately, "if the war did nothing else to me as a minister—or just as an ordinary person— it made me more determined to give what little energy I had to bringing people of the world together."[84]

In the eyes of some historians, for all its horrors, the "Great War" proved to be a catalyst in the African-American struggle for equality, providing the "forge" in which long-suppressed anger was "shaped into new expressions of protest." Fighting against fascism and racism abroad and returning to find racism at home "galvanized anger and transformed it into political and social activism."[85] Or, as a slogan among black draftees put it, "Here lies a black man killed fighting a yellow man for the glory of a white man."

Not surprisingly, membership in the NAACP grew by 900 percent following the war.[86] The NAACP, from its earliest days, saw the value of singing black sacred protest music. Rebecca de Schweinitz notes that "singing Freedom Songs seems to have been a standard part of NAACP youth council activities at least as early as the mid-1940s."[87] A registration drive in Atlanta in 1946 saw eighteen hundred African-Americans register to vote. In 1947, three thousand blacks in Winston-Salem registered and helped elect the city's first African-American alderman. But in the Deep South, where an estimated 95 percent of the black workers were employed by whites, many whites used the specter of job loss—or worse—to dissuade black workers from registering.[88]

There were other noteworthy changes looming in American life during the tumultuous postwar period. For one, the GI Bill made education accessible to all veterans. As one African-American serviceman observed, the new access to education "made us a far more democratic people."[89]

At war's end, more than a half million African-Americans had joined the CIO-affiliated unions, including those in the South, where they learned invaluable organizing *and* singing skills. Seymour Martin Lipset writes that for many Americans, black or white, organizational and leadership skills can only be acquired in religious organizations, unions, and political parties—and politics (save for a brief time when the communist and socialist organizations in the South were active) were off-limits to southern blacks.[90] Not coincidentally, the labor movement was weakest in the South as well.

However, directed singing with an eye toward social and political transformation was a long-standing, almost ubiquitous by-product of African-American religious institutions in the South. In segregation, as T. V. Reed writes, their churches became the de facto political arena for blacks, creating "tightly knit black communities, and in those communities the churches became the heart of social and political as well as religious life." African-American ministers, pastors, and elders provided political leadership to their congregations, large and small. And churches provided the necessary infrastructure—organizational and fund-raising—when black discontent coalesced into black protest.[91] By the mid-1950s, black churches would be a recognizable force in American politics.

The social justice–oriented liberalism of the New Deal and the Roosevelt era eventually ran its course in post–World War II America. One of its last gasps was in Henry Wallace's quixotic presidential campaign and in the founding of People's Songs Inc. in early 1946 from the ashes of the Composers' Collective. People's Songs attracted the Almanac Singers (especially Pete Seeger and Lee Hays), Alan Lomax, and other musicians interested in using folk songs to effect change.[92] The organization, which published *People's Songs* (sometimes called *People's Songs Newsletter*), was most visible during the presidential campaign of Wallace and the Progressive Party in 1948.

Resources were scarce, production was amateurish, and issues were sometimes late, but *People's Songs* earned a loyal audience. It was also a vehicle for exposing spirituals, usually with rewritten lyrics, to new audiences. The second issue (March 1946) included a revised version of "The Gospel Train (Get on Board Little Children)," now titled "Keep That Line A-Moving." Co-lyricist Charlotte Anthony told the magazine that she had heard the original phrase from a picket captain while singing on the sound truck "at the Western Union picketline" and turned it into a song. On this "union train," the lyrics say, there is "no color line."[93]

Seeger's involvement in the Wallace campaign (along with the publication's inevitable cash-flow issues) meant there was no time to prepare the October 1947 issue. The organization did release a "campaign folio" in August 1948 that sold "four or five thousand copies," titled *Songs for Wallace, 2nd Edition*. Once again, a number of spirituals were revived and revised to promote Wallace and the Progressives, including "Great Day." In the same issue, Paul Robeson rewrote the lyrics to "Get on Board" and "Old Time Religion" as "We'll All Join Gideon's Army" and suggested that they be sung in succession. Like "Great Day," the lyrics promised, "No Jim Crow class aboard this train / There's room for many-a-more!" Also in the issue, an unnamed author (perhaps Seeger or Hays) introduced a revised version of "Hallelujah, I'm a-Travelin'" (based on "Revive Us Again") and noted that the author was "a southern Negro farmer" who had been involved in a bloody race-related riot in Columbia, Tennessee, in February 1946 that resulted in the deaths of two blacks in police custody and the arrest and imprisonment of many more. The lyrics explain why the author must remain anonymous:

> *I'm paying my fare*
> *On the Greyhound bus line*
> *I'm riding the front seat*
> *To Nashville this time*
> *Stand up and rejoice!*
> *A great day is here!*
>
> *We are fighting Jim Crow, and the Victory is near!*
> *Hallelujah, I'm a-travelin', Hallelujah, ain't it time?*
> *Hallelujah, I'm a-travelin', Down Freedom's main line!*

The allusions to later civil rights–era freedom songs are unmistakable. Even that hoary chestnut "Battle Hymn of the Republic/John Brown's Body" was again dusted off and included as "Battle Hymn of '48." The Almanac Singers also contributed their rewritten version of the spiritual "The Old Ship of Zion" ("Union Train").[94]

The most intriguing song, perhaps because it is set to the haunting, defiant spiritual "We Shall Not Be Moved," is "Let's Get Out the Vote." The new lyrics, by the "Gloversville—'Wallace for President Committee,'" compare Wallace to Roosevelt and celebrate the African-American/labor union connection, claim that both "the elephant and the donkey" will be voted out of office, and denounce the "Taft–Hartley slave bill"—even as it urged listeners to vote in the upcoming election.[95]

From the standpoint of the civil rights movement of the 1950s and '60s, the inclusion of "We Will Overcome" in the September 1948 issue of *People's Songs* is particularly interesting because it speaks to the long, uninterrupted use of the song in times of political and social turmoil. The article's unnamed author notes that the "simple and moving hymn" is "especially thrilling" when its origins are considered: "It was learned by Zilphia Horton of the Highlander Folk School in Tennessee, from members of the CIO Food and Tobacco Workers Union. Many a visitor to the south has never forgotten hearing the rich harmonies of some little band, and the determination in these words, even though surrounded on all sides by hate, Jim Crow and all the forces of power and money."[96]

As we have seen above, the revision is based on a hymn by gospel composer Charles Tindley.[97] Over the next few years, the "Will" in the title is eventually replaced by "Shall," but the song is otherwise little different from what would become the anthem of the civil rights movement:

> *We will overcome, We will overcome, We will overcome some day.*
> *Oh, down in my heart, I do believe, We'll overcome some day.*
> *The Lord will see us through*
> *The Lord will see us through, some day.*
> *We're on to victory*
> *We're on to victory, some day.*

The article also includes a message from Horton, who writes that this version was first sung in Charleston, and that the "strong emotional appeal and simple dignity" of the song on listeners "sort of stops them cold silent."[98]

The November 1948 issue reported how Seeger and Wallace once used spirituals to silence an "organized, egg-throwing block of hecklers" in an otherwise friendly Winston-Salem audience:

> Seeger stood up and announced that he was going to sing a familiar old hymn. "We're going to change only one word in the hymn, and where you hear it, you'll understand why," he said. Then he sang, and all the Negro and white people there promptly began to sing.
>
>> *Farther along they'll know all about it,*
>> *Farther along, they'll understand why,*
>> *Cheer up, my brothers, live in the sunshine,*
>> *They'll understand it all by and by.*
>
> The entire audience turned and faced the hecklers and sang directly to them. They had always sung "Farther along *we'll* know all about it" but never before had they sung the old hymn with more conviction.[99]

The publication's most public moment came at the Progressive Party's nomination convention in Philadelphia in July 1948. A host of well-known singers, including Robeson and Seeger, were joined by a large chorus singing numerous spirited songs in support of Wallace, including the revised spiritual "Great Day, the People Marching" and "The Battle Hymn of '48."[100]

Wallace's decisive defeat, the rise of the anticommunist hysteria, and the group's mounting debt ultimately ended People's Songs Inc. as an effective organization by the end of 1948.[101] From its ashes, however, arose People's Artists, which in May 1950 transformed *People's Songs* into a monthly folk-oriented publication of songs and news, *Sing Out!*, which focused on "world peace, political repression, and civil rights."[102] Seeger joined yet another socially aware group, the Weavers, which sold two million copies of Leadbelly's "Goodnight, Irene," perhaps the first "folk" song to sell more than a million copies.[103]

The use of spirituals in the labor movement did not end at that point, of course. For instance, in the late 1940s, the CIO's United Packinghouse Workers of America employed a number of unique approaches, including the creation of traveling musical and theatrical troupes designed to organize farmers in Nebraska and Iowa—usually at county fairs. One such group, the Union Caravan, "borrowed the idea and performers" from the Progressive Party's "Wallace Caravans" and performed throughout Iowa in the fall of 1949. The interracial group included well-known singer Marianne "Jolly" Smolens, actor Herschel "Hesh" Bernardi (who would later appear widely on American television), and African-American Juanita Griffin, who served as the group's "lead" singer. Songs included "Down Freedom's Main Line," "Hallelujah, I'm a Bum," and "Oh Freedom."[104]

Other changes were afoot, however—changes that shook the very core of African-American life. For one, the postwar years saw the advent of the first powerful radio stations to broadcast black music and programming. The arrival of three African-American veterans carrying boxes full of records at the doors of the 50,000-watt AM station WLAC (1510 kHz) in Nashville was a significant milestone in 1946. The station reached a good portion of the continental United States. "There was a lot of stations as strong as that," singer James Brown once said, "but I never seen one cover as much of it as LAC did. And LAC was all we had."[105] WLAC quickly switched to broadcasting black music and made an immediate impact.

In 1947, there were three thousand disc jockeys in the country, but only sixteen were black.[106] Still, *Ebony* magazine breathlessly identified the sixteen "sepia spielers" as part of a "boom that has skyrocketed the chatter chaps to a new peak." The longest-tenured DJs were Jack L. Cooper, with twenty-five years of radio experience (WSBC in Chicago), and Boss Harris (KING in Seattle), but the majority had two years or less. Cooper was reported to be the highest-paid African-American DJ, grossing $180,000 per year on his program, with a staff of ten writers and announcers. According to *Ebony*, Cooper "sells 50 white and Negro sponsors 41 hours of time weekly on four stations . . . most colored radio jivesters seek and get an interracial audience."[107]

WLAC's broadcasts, which included heavy programming of gospel music, covered most of the South and Southeast and bulged northward strongly into Indiana, Ohio, Illinois, and Michigan. While there were other stations playing black music in the 1950s and early 1960s, most were in the larger cities, with limited coverage. John L. Landes writes that WLAC's reach extended to the "hinterlands" and for the first time brought the music of legendary blues, rhythm and blues, and later soul artists "to a generation of blacks not well served by the local media." Nearly as important, according to the longtime WLAC disc jockey Bill "Hoss" Allen, the audience for their African-American programming was 50 percent white. At one point, WLAC DJ Gene Nobles was even elected as "favorite deejay" of the all-white University of Mississippi.[108]

Other stations followed, adding not only African-American music, both sacred and popular, but black DJs as well. What would become the nation's other most significant black-oriented AM radio station, WDIA (1070 kHz) in Memphis, installed the city's first black disc jockey on October 25, 1948, and soon switched to solely African-American music programming. Singer Lou Rawls says that the station's impact was "enormous," as "hundreds of other radio stations across the U.S. were influenced by WDIA, and black radio spread coast to coast."[109] Louis Cantor estimates that WDIA reached "an incredible 10 percent of the total black population of the United States" as the first "all-black station in the nation to go 50,000 watts."[110] By the mid-1950s, approximately six hundred stations broadcast black programming and, according to Rawls, "WDIA influenced them all."[111]

This figure is noteworthy, since as early as 1949, magazines were trumpeting the "forgotten 15,000,000" African-Americans as a demographic with increasing postwar buying power—and influence.[112] An article in the *Pittsburgh Courier* claimed that "many civic leaders below the Mason Dixon line are of the opinion that [black radio] will do more for lowering jim-crow barriers than flowery oratory."[113] Even though television grew rapidly in popularity in the 1950s, African-Americans rarely saw black faces or heard black issues discussed, leaving local radio stations as their information and entertainment medium of choice.[114] With that in mind, Newman identifies four ways that black radio in the 1950s contributed in a meaningful way to both African-American consumer and political power: "It integrated black working-class and lower-income consumers, especially, into the mainstream of American consumer culture; it provided a cross-class space (similar to black churches and black lodges) for the expression of racial pride and identification; it provoked some black listeners, especially those in the middle classes, to consider the consumer realm as a realm for protest; and it sparked national interest in the phenomenon of the 'Negro market,' which made boycotting for civil rights an increasingly effective tactic."[115] Or, as legendary Memphis DJ (and later Detroit radio station owner) Martha Jean "The Queen" Steinberg once said, "Black radio was God-directed for the salvation of this nation and the world."[116] Cantor does not to use Steinberg's emphatic language but thoughtfully notes that while African-Americans did not "begin to tear down the legal walls of segregation" until the advent of the civil rights movement in the 1950s and '60s, "WDIA certainly helped set the stage for the changes to come. At the very least, they promoted the self-esteem of black people, and helped raise expectations to a level where the long struggle against racism could finally begin."[117]

Another significant change during this period was the arrival of the portable transistor radio in 1947. Within a decade, radio's listenership, especially among the young, had shifted from homes to automobiles—and wherever automobiles went. Susan J. Douglas says transistor and car radios helped young people "stake out their social space" by "blanketing" a given area with their music.[118]

Almost simultaneously, the arrival of the transistor was accompanied by a new kind of disc jockey, who "compelled listeners to identify with particular stations, and often eased and even celebrated a new merger between black and white culture." When the radio was a piece of furniture, situated prominently in the living room, young people had little choice but to listen to their parents' choice of programming, be it the latest hit by Bing Crosby or the latest episode of *The Shadow*. When television arrived in U.S. homes, it took the place of radio and continued that domination. With the transistor radio, however, black and white teenagers could listen to what they wanted, where they wanted to listen to it. These new DJs were among the first to exploit those differences, replacing smooth-voiced disc jockeys playing the latest Dean Martin–Perry Como record with a fast-talking DJ steeped in black music and slang. Radio, ultimately, became an "agent of desegregation." It was in radio that "cultural and industrial battles over how much influence black culture was going to have on white culture were staged and fought." Douglas concludes, "It was that whites themselves—the DJs, the performers, and their fans—embraced a hybridity that confounded and defied the existing racial order. And it was precisely because of radio's invisibility that such hybridizations could flourish."[119]

As early as May 31, 1952, *Billboard* magazine headlined an article "White Fans Hyping R&B Platter Sales," which reported that—at least in Southern California—"a major portion of the r.&b. sides now being sold are bought by Spanish and mixed-nationality buyers." The distributors attributed the increased sales to the "new audience to the work of a group of leading d.j.'s, mostly on indie outlets." At Dolphin's Hollywood Records Shop, then open twenty-four hours a day, seven days a week, John Dolphin himself "reports that about 40 percent of his retail business now comes from white buyers, where previously his trade was almost entirely Negro buyers." The article concludes by quoting promoter Ralph Bass and others saying that the new audience has also spurred an increasing number of concerts with rhythm and blues and jazz artists.[120]

Two years later (and just weeks before the *Brown v. Board of Education* decision), *Billboard* featured a front-page story with the title "Teen-Agers Demand Music with a Beat, Spur Rhythm-Blues," with a subtitle of "Field Reaps $15,000,000; Radio, Juke Boxes Answer Big Demands." The article claimed that R & B records, "once limited in sales appeal to the relatively small Negro market," had "blossomed into one of the fastest growing areas of the entire record business." By now, there were seven hundred DJs exclusively airing rhythm and blues. In addition to the independent labels that had specialized in R & B and gospel (including Peacock, Specialty, Aladdin, and Imperial), the "major" labels were now actively signing, recording, and promoting African-American artists for white audiences.[121]

As African-Americans and whites interacted more often, both during and after World War II, in part because of the mass migrations, radio created what Douglas calls "trading zones" between the cultures. The rise of network television marked the end of the monolithic radio networks, enabling the appearance and viability of the numerous independent radio stations that provided the music that many of their listeners had rarely been able to hear in the past—gospel, rhythm and blues, country and western.[122]

The late 1940s and early '50s saw a second widespread change in the delivery of popular music, one that would extend the "trading zones" and further pave the way for the impact of black sacred music in the civil rights movement—the humble 45-rpm record. In June 1948, RCA Victor Records introduced the micro-groove long-playing 33 1/3–rpm vinyl 12-inch record, quickly dubbed the "LP." Just before the end of the year, CBS (Columbia Records) introduced the vinyl 45 (often called "the single") with its distinctive 1 5/8–inch hole in the middle. RCA also unveiled both a series of expensive radio–phonograph players designed to play the LP, costing anywhere from $200 to $600, and a small, mostly plastic $12.95 record player, designed to play only the much cheaper 45s. Of the 45 player, Philip Ennis writes, "It was this machine that was probably the single most important piece of technology facilitating rocknroll's [*sic*] appearance."[123]

Audiences and artists soon diverged—with adult-oriented musicians and singers and their fans gravitating toward the LPs, and rock and roll and rhythm and blues artists gravitating toward the cheaper and more portable 45s and their players. Whereas vinyl record players were once large consoles designed to fill a room for family listening, 45s and transistor radios (and later cassettes, CDs, and MP3s) could be taken elsewhere, where like-minded teens could listen to "their" music. It is in peer groups, Simon Frith argues, that music helps teenagers "learn the rules of the social game." "Youth culture," he writes, becomes "classless" and young people "have more problems in common with each other than with the adults of their own class or sex."[124] Rhythm and blues (and later rock and roll) was *not* your parents' music. And for young people seeking a form of self-expression, that was a *good* thing.

There were also economic reasons for the change in musical tastes and the slow but steady rise of African-American music. The recession of the immediate post–World War II years heavily affected blacks, who suffered the "last hired, first fired" policies of big business between 1946 and 1949. The Korean War, however, encouraged still another migration of African-Americans into the large urban areas, creating an even greater audience for black music programming, which was broadcast into white and black homes in the early 1950s.[125]

Concurrently, the arrival and gradual dominance of television leeched most of the national advertising dollars away from the big radio networks. Local independent radio stations were left with the cheaper alternative to the big network comedies and dramas, local DJs playing recorded music. Subsequently, independent radio stations could be and were more responsive to local tastes with their programming. In 1953, 270 radio stations (out of 2,700 total stations) programmed African-American music (blues, rhythm and blues, and/or gospel) exclusively.

By 1956, there were 400 such stations. According to Jonathan Kamin, this meant that rhythm and blues "became the first black music adapted to white tastes to be readily available to those who would seek it out."[126]

Most concerts and dances in the South had long been segregated, but when whites began attending the R & B shows, accommodations were gradually made. If there was a dance floor, sometimes only a rope separated the races. It was when the ropes came down that authority figures in the South became concerned—and come down they did.[127] A number of musicians from the era remember the phenomenon with pleasure, including Ralph Bass, who recalls that the integrated dance floors were instituted, in part, by promoters eager to squeeze in more paying customers, regardless of race: "The blacks on one side, whites on the other, digging how the blacks were dancing and copying them. Then, hell, the rope would come down and they'd all be dancing together. And it was a revolution. Music did it. We did it as much with our music as the civil rights acts and all of the marches, for breaking the race thing down."[128] J. Fred MacDonald (among others) also believes that the first volleys of the civil rights movement—the Supreme Court's *Brown v. Board of Education* decision, the use of federal troops to integrate Central High School in Little Rock, and the Montgomery bus boycott—were accepted by American young people (including many in the South) "with more understanding than might have been expected" because of their introduction to R & B and rock and roll performed by African-American musicians: "Through the new black music . . . a generation of white youngsters, protected from black realities by a tradition of segregation and bigotry, learned to appreciate Afro-American attitudes and realities. Dancing, working, relaxing, and singing to rhythm and blues, white listeners of radio in the 1950s came to know better than their parents the illogical nature of racism. Within a few years it would be this generation that would join with youthful blacks to form the idealistic vanguard of the civil rights movement of the 1960s."[129]

Long before some white musicians became popular, they began emulating the style of their black counterparts. In Memphis, Elvis Presley and his band, as well as Jerry Lee Lewis, Carl Perkins, Roy Orbison, Charlie Rich, Johnny Cash, and others, bought their flashy clothes at Lansky Brothers on Beale Street—a clothing store that had previously catered exclusively to African-Americans, including B. B. King, Isaac Hayes, and a number of R & B bands and gospel groups. According to Rich, "We would dress like the blacks did. That was kinda the 'in thing' to do, and a little bit of the rebel."[130] And many teenagers then—as now—emulated the clothing styles of their musical heroes, black or white. Obviously, Bass (and to a lesser degree MacDonald) may overstate the case somewhat for the impact that rhythm and blues and rock and roll had on the civil rights movement. Still, the gradual acculturation of African-Americans into the public consciousness of white America is no small issue.

The biographies of proponents of the new music, such as Alan Freed and Dick Clark, suggest that the simple of act of playing black music on (formerly) white radio and having black and white artists tour together was revolutionary for the time. Freed, for instance, thought nothing of kissing black female performers onstage or embracing black male singers, though he "had no desire to become embroiled in social conflict and he bristled at any suggestion that he was a racial do-gooder."[131] While Clark "sweated out" the first time his popular television series *American Bandstand* featured even one African-American couple dancing amid the whites, he was instrumental in introducing a number of black artists to white America, including Chuck Berry and James Brown. Clark called rock and roll "the most subtle form of integration that ever existed."[132] John A. Jackson paints a less flattering picture of Clark's efforts in integrating *American Bandstand*'s audience, dancers, and featured musicians. Though the rock and roll tours that bore his name were integrated, Jackson writes, "when it came to integrating *American Bandstand . . .* Clark was a lot less ballsy." Still, according to Clarence Collins of the Imperials, Clark's integrated live music "Caravan" tours, performing to integrated audiences, "got [blacks and whites] in there together and eventually in the South they forgot all about what color you were."[133]

As early as 1951, Alan Freed's "Moon Dog House Rock and Roll Party" was attracting tens of thousands of radio listeners in Cleveland, and his integrated concerts (featuring the Dominoes, the Orioles, the Moonglows, and others) were sensational successes throughout the country, but especially in New York, where he later relocated.[134] By July 1955, tastes were changing so quickly that *Variety* would feature a headline proclaiming, "R&B Cracking Racial Barriers in Southwest Where It's Bigger'n Ever." The article notes the considerable gains that R & B sales and artists had made in Texas, Oklahoma, New Mexico, Kansas, and Missouri, "where hillbillies have been thrown for a loss." As one promoter noted, "It's a new thing for the whites while the Negroes have had it all along."[135]

Consequently, after World War II and into the early 1950s, white audiences across the United States slowly at first, then more rapidly, became aware of black singers and musicians and, with time, became fans of those artists. The pioneering success of gospel artists such as the Golden Gate Quartet, Sister Rosetta Tharpe, Wings over Jordan, and a handful of others paved the way for the postwar gospel "boom." As Jackson points out, though African-Americans may have remained on the "margins of industrial development,"

> The gospel music industry opens a window into a corner of the industrial economy where African Americans played a significant role, as well as into the ways that the expansion of material values and the development of technologies of mass production and communication influenced African American life. Considering gospel music musicians, the communities of which they were a part, and the audiences who embraced them makes it possible to examine some of the ways in which African Americans contended with a society marked not simply by racial discrimination, but by the growing influence commerce wielded over daily affairs.[136]

For instance, DoVeanna S. Fulton Minor maintains that for religiously oriented African-American women unwilling to embrace the blues or the blues lifestyle and constrained from preaching or testifying in the patriarchy of black Baptist churches in particular, gospel music provided a "a degree of power in the church through an oral discourse that is the descendant of the liberation narratives of slave Spirituals." Minor's thesis suggests that African-American women gospel singers could use, for example, the traditional spirituals about the biblical flood "as a metaphor" for the horrendous 1927 Mississippi River flood—which, by extension, creates a compelling vehicle to "take a radical position and 'preach' against injustices and discrimination."[137]

The female gospel artist who most forcefully "preached" in the pre–civil rights era was Mahalia Jackson. Jackson, as mentioned earlier, had been politically active in Democratic Party politics as early as the 1930s. In late 1946, Jackson wrote President Harry Truman directly, asking him to intervene in the case of a family member she felt had been treated badly in a pension/retirement issue. The matter was reconsidered and settled in the family's favor. As Jackson's biographer Laurraine Goreau wrote, "It was a family debt Mahalia would soon pay—and gladly."[138] (Years later, while on a national television program, she commented to Joey Bishop on what Heilbut calls "her fervent attachment to the Democrats": "Roosevelt fed me when I was *hongry. A*-men.")[139]

After several unsuccessful singles for the Apollo label, Jackson's version of "Move on Up a Little Higher" broke nationally, selling an unprecedented two million copies in early 1947. Under the astute booking of former William Morris Agency agent Harry Lenetska and ceaseless promotion on Studs Terkel's Chicago radio program, "Move on Up" was the first step in establishing Jackson as a household name with white as well as black audiences. Sallie Martin, Thomas Dorsey's sharp-tongued business manager, had her own opinion as to the reason for Jackson's success with the song: "It's all those political meetings she goes to."[140]

The song itself is transcendent, a surging, triumphant tour-de-force, an irresistible gospel song that would eventually sell more than eight million copies.[141] Terkel has said that it is, perhaps, something more than just a marketing phenomenon: "Consider this. In scores of thousands of homes, among the devout and God-fearing, oh yeah, and in taverns and pool parlors, too, lowly spirits are lifted by a soaring, winged voice. Again and again and again, this record is played on phonographs and jukeboxes. The grooves are worn deep and needles are dulled, but they keep on listening, through scratch and static, to this voice."[142]

But "Move on Up" has an added dimension, something that resonated at an even deeper level in the black community. The song was composed by the Reverend W. Herbert Brewster, a legendary preacher/composer in African-American circles, but little known in the white community outside his native Memphis. Brewster's large and prosperous East Trigg Baptist Church had mounted large-scale theatrical productions performed to gospel music about challenging topics (including one about the Nat Turner slave revolt) since the 1940s. He had also bravely written pamphlets and books that urged "a greater freedom for the black man."[143] Among the regular visitors to East Trigg were Elvis Presley, producer Jack Clement, and southern gospel star James Blackwood. All were attracted to the stirring gospel music (led by Queen C. Anderson and the Brewsteraires) and Brewster's eloquent sermons, which frequently featured "the theme that a better day was coming, one in which all men could walk together as brothers."[144]

In the years before *Brown v. Board of Education* or the Montgomery bus boycott, Brewster was creating gospel songs that spoke directly to the yearning of African-Americans to be free in their own country. While detailed interviews with the man are rare, he was interviewed by Reagon as part of a Smithsonian-sponsored symposium on gospel music concerning the use of civil rights–related lyrics (though the term was not in common currency at the time of the song's release) in "Move on Up":

> The fight for rights here in Memphis was pretty rough on the Black church. The lily white, the black and the tan were locking horns; and the idea struck me and I wrote that song "Move on Up a Little Higher." We'll have to move in the field of education. Move into the professions and move into politics. Move in anything that any other race has to have to survive. That was a protest idea and inspiration. I was trying to inspire Black people to move up higher. Don't be satisfied with the mediocre. Don't be satisfied. That was my doctrine. Before the freedom fights started, before the Martin Luther King days, I had to lead a lot of protest meetings. In order to get my message over, there were things that were almost dangerous to say, but you could sing it.[145]

African-American audiences knew Brewster's widely popular gospel songs, such as "Move on Up ("all God's sons and daughters will be drinking that healing water"), "I'm Climbing Higher and Higher" ("and I won't come down"), "These Are They" ("they're coming on up, coming on up through great tribulation"), and "Surely God Is Able" ("to carry you through"). As Heilbut writes, these were "meant to function as both gospel songs and codified political statements."[146] In *The Gospel Sound: Good News and Bad Times*, Heilbut is even more explicit: "Reverend Brewster is a beautiful example of the progressive impulses nurtured by gospel and developed in the freedom movement."[147] In a compilation of "golden age" gospel songs, Heilbut calls "Move on Up" a "barely disguised freedom song."[148] In *The Fan Who Knew Too Much*, he also identified "How I Got Over" as one of Brewster's compositions that "included coded references to social mobility and political empowerment."[149] Brewster would long remain a potent force in Tennessee politics as a confidant of both Senator Albert Gore, Sr., and Martin Luther King, Jr. He continued pastoring East Trigg and writing complex, compelling gospel songs until his death in October 1987.[150] "Brewster's political boldness and courage," writes Heilbut, "combined with his brilliant development of black folk art, is a thrilling realization of the best impulses in gospel. On the strength of his achievement he should be a culture hero of the first rank."[151]

Brewster was not the only one writing gospel songs with strong civil rights overtones, of course. Within the African-American community, Tindley's earlier gospel songs "Beams of Heaven" and "We'll Understand It Better By and By" were considered to have social as well as religious themes, such as this line from latter: "We'll tell the story how we've overcome."[152] Some of the lines in "Beams of Heaven" seem even more direct: "There is a God that rules above / With hand of power and heart of love / If I am right, He'll fight my battle / I shall have peace someday."[153]

Late in the summer of 1948, while still enjoying the runaway success of "Move on Up," Jackson received a call from U.S. representative William L. Dawson, who had represented Chicago's South Side since 1939. According to Goreau, Dawson is reported to have said, "Everybody says Harry S. Truman doesn't have a chance at being elected, Mahalia, but I'm going to turn my district out. He's been speaking his mind on equal rights to my certain knowledge since 1940, and I want you to sing for our meetings here in Chicago." Shortly thereafter, Goreau writes that "300,000 people heard Jackson in Chicago." Truman was one of them and the president asked Jackson to accompany him on the campaign tour, which included stops in Ohio, Missouri, Indiana, and Illinois. On election night, Jackson and her friends listened to election returns in Chicago and heard reports of not just Truman's upset victory, but also the victories of Adlai Stevenson for governor of Illinois and Paul Douglas for senator—both of whom she had campaigned for. The Trumans, in return, invited Jackson to the White House to sing, where she received a personal tour from the president himself.[154]

Jackson's newfound fame with all audiences was not lost on the popular entertainers of the day. Ed Sullivan's variety series *Toast of the Town* (later *The Ed Sullivan Show*) was one of the most popular in the early days of television. Sullivan was also among the first TV promoters to book African-American singers and musicians, despite the objections of southern stations, and featured the Ink Spots as early as his second show in June 1948. He spotlighted Mahalia Jackson for the first time in January 1949, further cementing her status among viewers, white and black. In short order, she was featured for the first time in *Ebony* magazine, signed to national powerhouse Columbia Records, and was spotlighted a second time on Sullivan's show.[155] Each event furthered her name recognition in white America.

The combination of composer Thomas Dorsey and Jackson was crucial in still another way. Eyerman and Jamison write that "the most important single element of the black music tradition that would be mobilized in the civil rights movement was the gospel blues"—as written by Dorsey and sung by Jackson. This "updated" "swing-like" gospel would inspire both "the emergent soul music of Ray Charles" and the pervasive, influential freedom songs of movement: "From a base in the segregated black church—a kind of submerged social network where forms of social solidarity could be preserved and reproduced—both gospel music and the civil rights movement would lead to profound processes of cultural transformation."[156]

But if it was a good time for Mahalia Jackson, it was not a good time for many other black Americans. The late 1940s and early 1950s were the age of loyalty oaths, the House Un-American Activities Committee, the postwar "white flight," attacks on America's unions, blacklisting, and the continued repression of African-Americans.[157] Despite the fact that 252 bills against discrimination were introduced in Congress between 1937 and 1950—with seventy-two of them introduced in the 1949–50 session alone—Martha Biondi notes that "these bills failed to produce a single new law." Progressive lawmakers were thwarted at every turn by a cabal of longtime Southern congressmen. One such man was Senator Theodore Bilbo of Mississippi, who actively advocated violence against African-Americans trying to vote. Bilbo, a self-professed Ku Klux Klan leader, was noted for his violent, racist rhetoric, including this chilling statement from a speech in 1946: "I call on every red-blooded American who believes in the superiority and integrity of the white race to get out and see that no nigger votes . . . AND THE BEST TIME TO DO IT IS THE NIGHT BEFORE."

Despite many comments like this one and serious allegations of accepting bribes, the Senate did little in response to Bilbo's words and deeds.[158] In much of the country, particularly in the South, African-Americans found little or no protection under the law, making overt protest dangerous, even deadly. Still, the spirit that inspired the spirituals to challenge the de facto slavery that endured under Jim Crow and "the absence of mass protest did not signify passive acceptance of the status quo. If whites controlled the outer reality, they could not control the inner spirit. Through the years of Jim Crow, when America's laws said that blacks could not vote, share restaurant facilities, or go to school with whites, the black struggle to overcome oppression gathered strength."[159]

And black musicians still managed to offer sly—and sometimes overt—observations on the state of U.S. race relations during those days. In 1943, the Fairfield Four recorded "Don't Let Nobody Turn You Around" for the Library of Congress, which almost certainly contains an early civil rights message. Anthony Heilbut writes that the Fairfield Four's classic "No Room in the Inn" (recorded in 1951), "with its vision of workers, oppressed by management," is a "proto–civil rights complaint."[160] Composer Otis Jackson, who wrote a number of civil rights–related gospel songs, composed "I'm So Grateful to the NAACP" for the Gospel Pilgrims in December 1950, a musical "thank-you" for the organization's help in overturning a death verdict for three African-Americans the previous year. Guido Van Rijn notes that the 45 was released on the Atlantic label, which would continue to release socially conscious songs in the decades to come. In 1952, the Echoes of Zion released "Keep Still (God Will Fight Your Battles)," an unrestrained condemnation of "America's failure to live up to the preamble to the Declaration of Independence."[161]

Two gospel songs from 1951 depict Jesus as liberator, and Louis-Charles Harvey relates both of them to the African-American fight for freedom and civil rights, "This Same Jesus" and "Oh Yes He Set Me Free." "This Same Jesus" references both

Paul and Silas in prison and Moses leading his people to safety from Egypt. In both cases, these familiar tropes from Civil War–era spirituals would be resurrected during the civil rights movement.[162] Later, two important deaths would generate additional gospel and blues paeans. The brutal murder of Emmett Till in 1955 by two white men who alleged that he had been disrespectful to a white girl prompted the song "The Death of Emmett Till" by Madame A. C. Bilbrew and the Ramparts. (The song was rerecorded and rereleased by Brother Will Hairston in 1969.) The passing of revered African-American educator and activist Mary McLeod Bethune was the topic of Otis Jackson's "The Life Story of Madame Bethune," recorded and released that year by the Dixie Hummingbirds on the black-owned Peacock label.[163]

On the secular music side of the aisle, Big Bill Broonzy's popular, at least in some circles, "Black, Brown and White," also released in 1951, is startlingly direct. Broonzy, a close friend of Mahalia Jackson, recorded the song following a successful tour of the Continent traveling with a white band and performing before white audiences:

> They say, "If you was white, should be all right
> If you was brown, stick around
> But as you'se black, umm, brother,
> Get back, get back, get back."[164]

There were some advances for African-Americans during these years, including the arrival of Jackie Robinson onto baseball's formerly all-white diamonds in 1947, the slow rise of the first African-American movie stars Harry Belafonte and Sidney Poitier, and the emergence of the Congress of Racial Equality and its nonviolent efforts at desegregating northern swimming pools, restaurants, shopping malls, movie theaters, and playgrounds.[165] CORE's leadership included James Farmer, Bayard Rustin, and A. J. Muste; long before the justly famed freedom rides of the 1960s, CORE activists were making similarly courageous public treks against segregation.[166]

Meanwhile, as mentioned above, popular music, particularly jazz and R & B and Mahalia Jackson's gospel music, integrated for the first time into white culture. The broad acceptance of jazz, which in the postwar era was dominated by African-Americans, was another step in the gradual transformation of American views toward race, in part because it was the one musical genre where "the assaults, responses, exchanges, challenges, inversions, and rejections between blackness and whiteness were launched, issued, and played out during the postwar era." It was also during that time that jazz, according to historian Jon Panish, "had its most profound impact on U.S. popular culture."[167]

For many African-Americans, the first steps toward public activism finally began to emerge in the 1950s. On October 4, 1950, Mahalia Jackson became the first black artist since Duke Ellington and His Orchestra (and the first gospel artist) to sing in New York's Carnegie Hall, before a sold-out crowd and numerous national and international reporters and critics. Jackson chose Representative Adam Clayton Powell, still one of only two blacks in Congress and an outspoken advocate of civil rights, to provide "entr'acte remarks."[168] Within a few years, Jackson would achieve a popularity among black and white artists rivaled only by jazz artists like Ellington, Louis Armstrong, and Ella Fitzgerald.[169]

The year 1950 saw a number of firsts for African-Americans, some because of litigation, some because of the threat of litigation, and some because progressive white Americans took the initiative—the first blacks admitted to a handful of southern law schools, the first blacks (including Marian Anderson) selected to serve as alternate delegates to the United Nations, the first black doctors admitted to the American Medical Association. Also that year, Ralph Bunche became the first African-American to receive the Nobel Peace Prize (five years later he became the first black to serve as undersecretary of the United Nations), Gwendolyn Brooks received the Pulitzer Prize for Poetry, and Althea Gibson became the first black accepted to play tennis at the U.S. National Championships. Within two years, the platforms of both major political parties contained explicit (if toothless) rejections of bigotry and segregation.[170]

The early 1950s were marked by both the "Red Scares" fueled by the incendiary rhetoric and activities of Senator Joseph McCarthy and the escalation of the cold war against the Soviet Union and its allies. While in the United States, the quest for "the free world" was severely hampered as "southern apartheid became an international embarrassment to the U.S. government." Events abroad, particularly the sometimes painful but ultimately successful independence struggles of the former African colonies of western Europe, further motivated African-Americans in their own centuries-long struggles for civil rights.[171]

The next link in the chain that would lead to the civil rights movement was the Supreme Court's decision on five school segregation cases knitted together by the NAACP. This action, following more than fifty years of often quiet court cases and organizational efforts by the NAACP, culminated on May 17, 1954, in what would become known as *Brown v. Board of Education*.[172] The Court ruled that previous decisions supporting "separate but equal" educational opportunities for African-Americans were invalid and therefore violated the Fourteenth Amendment's Equal Protection Clause.[173]

Violence and massive resistance by southern whites against the decision was immediate and widespread—and continued for more than a decade. Alas, the Court delayed requiring immediate compliance and President Dwight Eisenhower repeatedly declined to support the ruling in public, save for a few vague comments about "respect for the law."[174] In retrospect, Michael J. Klarman insists that the case for *Brown v. Board of Education* as the catalyst of the civil rights movement is overstated, in part because it was "almost completely nullified for a decade south of the border states" and that the first major civil rights action—the Montgomery bus boycott—was still several years away. Nevertheless, he writes, *Brown* is important for a number of other reasons: "The Court's ruling plainly raised the salience of school segregation, encouraged blacks to litigate against it, changed the order in which racial practices would otherwise have been contested, mobilized extraordinary resistance to racial change among southern whites, and created concrete occasions for street confrontations and violence."[175]

For many African-Americans, however, the effect of *Brown v. Board of Education* was electrifying. Former marine Robert F. Williams, who would later gain notoriety for his public support of armed resistance by blacks against the federal government, wrote at the time, "My inner emotions must have been approximate to the Negro slaves' when they first heard about the Emancipation Proclamation. Elation took hold of me so strongly that I found it very difficult to refrain from yielding to an urge of jubilation. . . . On this momentous night of May 17, 1954, I felt at last the government was willing to assert itself on behalf of first-class citizenship, even for Negroes. I experienced a sense of loyalty that I had never felt before. I was sure that this was the beginning of a new era of American democracy."[176]

And even more eloquent words on *Brown* were written by the acclaimed African-American writer Arna Bontemps in the April 1965 edition of *Harper's Magazine*:

> While this was a landmark, it provoked no wild optimism. I had no doubt that the tide would now turn, but it was not until the freedom movement began to express itself that I felt reassured. We were in the middle of it in Nashville. Our little world commenced to sway and rock with the fury of a resurrection. I tried to discover just how the energy was generated. I think I found it. The singing that broke out in the ranks of protest marchers, in the jails where sit-in demonstrators were held, in the mass meetings and boycott rallies, was gloriously appropriate. The only American songs suitable for a resurrection—or a revolution, for that matter—are Negro spirituals. The surge these awakened was so mighty it threatened to change the name of our era from the "space age" to the "age of freedom."[177]

5

MONTGOMERY

Black Sacred Song in the Modern Civil Rights Movement

Yet, even here amid dangers, and here amid temptations, let the "Alleluia" be sung by others and by us, too. . . . Therefore, my brethren, let us sing now, not for the delights of peace, but for the solace of our labor. Just as travelers are accustomed to sing, sing but advance; solace your labor by singing; do not love inactivity; keep singing and keep progressing. . . . If you are progressing, you are advancing; but progress in well-doing, progress in good faith, progress in good deeds. Keep singing and keep advancing.

—SAINT AUGUSTINE

It was all part and parcel of the big left turn middle class college students were making. . . . So we owe it all to Rosa Parks.

—DAVE VAN RONK

Black sacred music is the primary reservoir of the Black people's historical context and an important factor in the process of social change.

—WYATT TEE WALKER

Even as *Brown v. Board of Education* was met with often violent opposition in the South, Representative Adam Clayton Powell had been working with State Department officials to arrange a series of international tours and "cultural" programs abroad featuring African-American artists. On November 18, 1955, he announced tours featuring Louis Armstrong, Dizzy Gillespie, and Count Basie to Communist-controlled Eastern Europe, as well as Asia and Africa. A week later, the Interstate Commerce Commission issued rulings that banned racial segregation in passenger bus and train waiting rooms.

Several southern states immediately announced that they would resist the measures.[1] In Chicago, Mahalia Jackson continued her political activities as well. In the summer and fall of 1954, she joined Representative Dawson in supporting young Cook County clerk Richard Daley's candidacy for mayor, singing at rallies and precinct meetings, sometimes accompanied by Thomas Dorsey: "But Mahalia's hidden strength lay in her living room. There was no day when preachers were not visiting Mahalia Jackson. And in Chicago, the reverends controlled a lot of votes."[2] Later, after Daley's new "machine" had swept the polls, she joined the newly elected Mayor Daley, Joe Louis, Senator Everett Dirksen, Walter Reuther, Jesse Owens, and others at Chicago's huge Bud Billiken Parade. At one point, Daley pulled her over and said, according to Goreau, "Anything I can do for you, Mahalia, you just let me know."[3]

But most blacks knew that white politicians would do very little for them, particularly in the South. As mentioned earlier, the August 1955 murder of fourteen-year-old Chicago native Emmett Till in Money, Mississippi, just months after the *Brown v. Board of Education* announcement, was, in the eyes of many scholars, another milestone in the civil rights movement. The intense national media coverage of Till's brutal slaying and the subsequent release of his killers created both an outcry and a national debate on Jim Crow. And the next generation of young African-American leaders soon to be coming of age in Nashville, Montgomery, Albany, and elsewhere were horrified at the lynching and its all-too-predictable outcome. Consequently, the murder had the effect of "radicalizing" these new student leaders, a number of whom began "embracing ideas of activism." This may have been because they, too, felt "vulnerable." It was a harsh reality that few in either the black or white communities would work toward justice—at least until, as one commentator noted, "the Till lynching pushed them toward political activism."[4]

One of the places where these student leaders were nurtured and equipped for the battles ahead was at the Highlander Folk School. From 1932 to 1962, first as Highlander College, then as Highlander Folk School, it trained southern labor organizers and, later, civil rights activists in Monteagle, Tennessee.[5] Cofounder Myles Horton's wife, Zilphia, active in Highlander's drama and music programs, was frequently invited to lead the singing at both the local and state meetings of the new CIO unions as early as 1938. In 1939, Zilphia led the singing of labor songs at the new Textile Workers Union of America's Constitutional Convention in Philadelphia; the songbook *Labor Songs*, featuring songs she had collected for use at Highlander, was published by the union.[6] As noted above, Myles Horton credits Zilphia with adapting "We Will Overcome" into "We Shall Overcome." The song came to Highlander with strikers from the American Tobacco Company action in Charleston in 1945. It was another early Highlander, Pete Seeger, who is credited with changing the "Will" to "Shall."[7]

Other influential singers who came to Highlander included Guy and Candie Carawan, Woody Guthrie, Lee Hays, Waldemar Hille, and Seeger. Even after

Zilphia's accidental death in 1956, civil rights–related singers such as Fannie Lou Hamer and Bernice Johnson Reagon also came to Monteagle to study at Highlander. Horton called Zilphia "the moving spirit in shaping the singing and music program at Highlander."[8] Also attending one of the many organizing sessions at Highlander in the summer of 1955 was Rosa Parks from Montgomery, Alabama.[9] At Highlander, Parks learned what would be called "freedom songs" and the principles of civil disobedience.[10]

But the leaders of Highlander, along with numerous African-Americans who had been working toward civil rights in the United States, were feeling the pressure from Senator Joseph McCarthy and the infamous House Un-American Activities Committee. Among those under assault was frequent Highlander visitor Seeger who, in 1956, was sentenced to a year in jail for ten counts of contempt. He actually only spent a few hours in jail while his attorney raised bail: "But it wasn't a waste of time. There were two young black men in the cell with me, eating baloney sandwiches and singing. They taught me this fine old spiritual, 'If that judge believe what I say / I'll be leaving for home today.'"[11]

The primary participants in the Montgomery bus boycott are well-known to even casual readers of American history: E. D. Nixon, former president of the Montgomery NAACP and head of the local chapter of the Brotherhood of Sleeping Car Porters; Parks, a soft-spoken seamstress, active church member, and secretary of the NAACP; Jo Ann Robinson, English professor and leader of the Women's Political Council (WPC); and, of course, Dr. Martin Luther King, Jr., the newly arrived pastor of Dexter Avenue Baptist Church in Montgomery (fig. 7).[12] King's father, Martin Luther King, Sr. (often called "Daddy King"), was an influential pastor himself in Atlanta and had been active in civil rights and segregation issues since the 1930s. Of his son, King wrote in his autobiography that Martin had a "fine, clear voice" and that he "loved" church, with a pronounced "feeling for ceremonies and ritual" and displayed a "passionate love" for "Baptist music."[13] King's wife, Coretta, whom he met while she was attending the New England Conservatory of Music, was an accomplished musician (both keyboards and trumpet), singer, and even choir director.[14] Like her husband, she was steeped in the traditions and performance of black sacred music.

The Montgomery bus boycott itself has been admirably chronicled by a number of first-rate scholars, each choosing a different aspect of the events.[15] But in brief, Nixon and others in Montgomery had been waiting for an opportunity to challenge the city's rules regarding bus ridership—blacks deferred to whites, even in the "black" sections of the buses, and were subject to frequent verbal and sometimes physical abuse. When Parks refused to give up her seat to a white man and was arrested on December 1, 1955, she called her friend and longtime political activist Nixon. Nixon first contacted attorney Fred Gray, who had previously worked on other civil rights causes, but who was out of town that day. Nixon's next call was to Clifford Durr, a white former official in FDR's New Deal administration. His wife,

FIGURE 7

Dr. Martin Luther King, Jr., is well known to
even casual readers of American history. Martin
Luther King, Sr., said his son had a "fine, clear
voice" and a passionate love for Baptist music.

Virginia Durr, had occasionally hired Parks to tailor clothes for the family, and the Durrs were responsible, at least in part, for Parks's presence at Highlander.[16]

Nixon then called Robinson and others in the WPC, which had also contemplated calling for a bus boycott. The group met, Robinson returned to Alabama State College to print thousands of leaflets, and the ad hoc group rallied many of the city's pastors to the cause, calling for a bus boycott on Monday, December 5, and a mass meeting that evening at Holt Street Baptist Church.[17] The committee then considered several names before deciding on the Montgomery Improvement Association (MIA), with relative newcomer King, the pastor of Dexter Avenue Baptist, as its president. Fearful of spies, someone suggested, "Maybe we ought to just sing and pray," and refrain from using names. Nixon angrily spoke against the idea. From that first evening, mass meetings would continue for a year in different churches on Monday and Thursday nights.[18] It was Parks who initially urged King to become active in the Montgomery NAACP following his call to Dexter Avenue.[19]

Dexter Avenue itself had a history of activism, beginning with King's predecessor, Vernon Johns, who had assumed the pastorate in 1948. Johns had been trained in the social gospel and preached tirelessly against discrimination with sermon titles such as "Will There Be Segregation in Heaven?" Harassed by the Montgomery police for his militancy, Johns once sought to ride in the "whites only" section of a bus and ate in a white restaurant. Dexter Avenue was also one of the sponsors of the WPC, which challenged segregation and urged blacks to register to vote.[20]

After the successful one-day boycott, Coretta King writes in her autobiography that her husband was "almost panicked" at the prospect of appearing before reporters and television cameras to articulate the MIA's vision at the 7 P.M. mass meeting at Holt Street Baptist Church. However, as King and his friend and second in command, the Reverend Ralph Abernathy, approached the church, they were met by thousands of people standing outside, "listening to loudspeakers, and singing hymns." The crowd, as well as the singing, "inspired Martin." However, the crush was so great, neither King nor Abernathy was able to push into Holt Street. The crowd, Coretta King writes, lifted the two men and passed them "hand to hand over their heads to the platform."[21]

So, on Monday evening, before "5,000 hymn-singing blacks," along with several television camera crews and reporter–editor Joe Azbell of the *Montgomery Advertiser*, the movement was officially launched. The popular hymn "Onward, Christian Soldiers," a nineteenth-century children's "marching hymn" by Sabine Baring-Gold, is noted by several participants as the first song to be sung.[22] In his autobiography, Abernathy alone of the participants remembers "Leaning on the Everlasting Arms (What a Fellowship, What a Joy Divine)" as the first hymn sung. To him, it thus "became the first hymn to be used" in the movement and the crowd "rocked the rafters" when they sang it.[23]

Both hymns were popular and well known by those in attendance. With its heavily cadenced marching imagery, "Onward, Christian Soldiers" was an astute choice for a population that had chosen to walk rather than continue to ride segregated buses.[24] According to one observer, during the singing of the hymn, "the voices thundered through the church."[25] In his account of the boycott, *Stride Toward Freedom*, King remembered it this way: "The opening hymn was the old familiar 'Onward Christian Soldiers,' and when that mammoth audience stood to sing, the voices outside swelling the chorus in the church, there was a mighty ring like the glad echo of heaven itself."[26] Reagon writes that the martial allusions in the lyrics were another reason that the hymn "became the contemporary freedom anthem" of the Montgomery bus boycott.[27]

Following sermons by King and Abernathy, the meeting closed with the patriotic song "My Country 'Tis of Thee."[28] In Abernathy's account, however, the meeting closed with an unnamed "rousing hymn": "The huge church trembled from the vibrations. Later, I wondered what the white sheriff's deputies must have thought, parked a block away, hunched down in their cars, ordered to report everything they saw and heard. The sight of five thousand blacks in attendance must have impressed them, but the sound of our cheers and singing must have unnerved them even more."[29]

Azbell wrote a firsthand account of the meeting for the Montgomery newspaper and indicated that several other hymns were sung in addition to those listed above, both by participants inside the church building and by the large crowd standing outside, though he does not identify the songs. Considering that the coverage of civil rights events by southern newspapers generally ranged from condescending to vitriolic, Azbell's carefully observed account is intriguing. He likened the meeting to "an old-fashioned revival with loud applause added." For Azbell, the event "proved beyond any doubt" that African-Americans were capable of a "military discipline," but one "combined with emotion."[30] At least according to one observer, that night harked back yet again to the spirit of Moses the Deliverer: "God sent Moses to the children of Israel to get them out of Egypt. He sent Martin Luther King in this particular instance to lead our people.[31] As for Azbell, memories of that night still moved him, years after the event: "I've never heard singing like that. . . . They were on fire for freedom."[32]

And the Montgomery bus boycott was begun as thousands of African-Americans faithfully avoided taking the buses on which they had been scorned and abused for so long. City and bus officials were impervious to reason and in the months ahead responded with threats, bribery, bullying, violence, and ultimately the wholesale arrest of participants. The first meetings set the model for subsequent mass meetings. King recalled that people from all walks of life arrived hours early to the appointed churches, with latecomers standing outside. To pass the time, some read or talked. But many of the others joined in the group-singing of "hymns . . . unaccompanied lined tunes of low pitch and long meter." King admitted that he was "moved by these traditional songs, which brought to mind the long history of the Negro's suffering."[33]

King's sermons in those meetings "always contained the hope for freedom, and he always related it to his current struggles to attain freedom in this world."

To do that, King drew on a "hope that stretched back to the beginnings of the black Christian community": "All he had to do was restate that hope for freedom in the songs and language of the people and they would respond to the content of the message. That was why King used the language of the so-called 'Negro Spirituals' in his sermons in black churches."[34] Or, as another writer put it, "King quoted from biographers, historians and poets, but more often than not, the spirituals fired his vision."[35]

Coretta King's memories of the meetings were that each one began informally with various hymns and spirituals, including "Lord, I Want to Be a Christian in My Heart," "Oh, Freedom over Me," "Before I Be a Slave, I'll Be Buried in My Grave (and Go Home to My Lord and Be Free)," and "Go Down, Moses." Following her husband's message, there would be another song, a prayer, a benediction, then another prayer. Following the final prayer, the participants would return home "feeling good and inspired and ready to go back the next morning to a long day of hard work." But because of the lift they had received at the meetings, Coretta believed that participants "could take it a little better" and the daily grind of work "that had been difficult became easier."[36]

In addition to the aforementioned "Onward, Christian Soldiers," two more traditional hymns were sung frequently throughout the boycott, "Lift Him Up" (not inappropriate considering King and Abernathy's "rock star"–styled entrance into Holt Street on December 5) and "Leaning on the Everlasting Arms."[37] Reagon writes that those who sang "Lift Him Up" in Montgomery believed the words suggested that with Jesus as the leader and defender of their cause, even the racists of Montgomery could be transformed—and encouraged to operate in good faith in the negotiating sessions: "How to reach the masses, men of every birth / For an answer Jesus gave the key / And I, if I be lifted up from the earth / Will draw all men to me." For "Leaning on the Everlasting Arms," in the dangerous city of Montgomery in 1955 and '56, the lyrics created a "safety zone" for singers at mass meetings, and it was understood at the time to be a "freedom hymn": "Leaning on the everlasting arms / Leaning on Jesus, Leaning on Jesus / Safe and secure from all alarm."[38]

In a letter Seeger received during the bus boycott, Montgomery resident Hannah Johnston wrote that there was "a great deal of singing" during the mass meetings, both hymns and spirituals. The spirituals sung most often during the meetings included "Steal Away," "Old Time Religion," "Shine on Me," "Ain't Gonna Study War No More," "Swing Low, Sweet Chariot," "I Got a Home in That Rock," and "Poor Man Dives." The words of "Poor Man Dives" had a particular resonance: "Rich Man Dives lived so well / When he died he went to Hell / Poor Man Lazarus, poor as I / When he died he had a home on High."[39]

The longer the boycott continued, the greater the violence that flared against the participants. On the evening of January 30, 1956, while King was speaking at another meeting, his home—with Coretta and their infant daughter Yolanda in the house—was bombed. When King reached his house, a large crowd had already gathered, along with several Montgomery city officials. Though no one was injured, the crowd was "angry and aroused." At one point, Coretta writes, a spontaneous version of "My Country 'Tis of Thee" was sung and the milling crowd only dispersed at King's repeated requests.[40]

By February 22, city officials had indicted more than one hundred people who had been identified as "leaders" of the protest. Word quickly spread and as each leader, led by Nixon, arrived at the police station to surrender, they passed through a phalanx of cheering supporters. After each $300 bail had been posted, the protestors gathered again at Dexter Avenue Baptist Church for a prayer meeting.

Bayard Rustin—who was a member of a pacifist organization, the Fellowship of Reconciliation, at the time—came to Montgomery at the suggestion of FOR board member Lillian E. Smith and the recommendation of his mentor A. Philip Randolph. Once there, he performed a variety of tasks for King and the MIA. Rustin wrote draft appeal letters, made telephone calls, and would "help compose songs." As he told Raines, "I was a singer and I wrote songs and they were topical about what was happening and Abernathy would usually introduce them."[41] In an article published just a few months after the event, Rustin wrote that earlier that day a "song had been adopted" as the "theme song for the movement." It was a rewritten version of the spiritual "Give Me That Old-Time Religion," and, according to Rustin, the new lyrics proclaimed the "essential elements of a passive resistance struggle—protest, unity, non-violence and equality." The song was sung that evening at Dexter Avenue:

> *We shall all stand together*
> *'Til every one is free.*
> *We know love is the watchword*
> *For peace and liberty*
> *Black and white all are brothers*
> *To live in harmony.*
> *We are moving on to vict'ry*
> *With hope and dignity.*[42]

The use of spirituals and gospel songs in all later movement events is relatively well documented, but this is one of the first references to a protest spiritual being used in Montgomery. The significance of such songs may not have been immediately recognized, and other such protest spirituals may have been sung—but not recorded. Alas, Rustin, who was a gifted singer and musician, does not identify the writer of the new lyrics nor indicate whether other such spirituals were sung in Montgomery. However, Alfred Maund covered the mass arraignment for *The Nation* and also notes the singing of "Give Me That Old-Time Religion," only this time with the proper arrangement of verses (the first verse is sung three times): "We are moving on to victory / With hope and dignity / We will all stand together / Until we all are free / Black and white both are brothers / To live in harmony."

Maund attributed the new lyrics to King himself and writes that the meeting closed with "Nobody Knows the Trouble I've Seen."[43] While King was certainly capable of recasting lyrics to old hymns, he makes no mention of the fact in his autobiography, nor is there an indication in his later writings that he rewrote any other spirituals.

Pete Seeger had heard the new spiritual and he quickly wrote the MIA: "I understand you have some songs you made up. Could you possibly send me the words?" This may indicate that "Give Me That Old-Time Religion" was not the only such rewritten spiritual. Nixon responded with a copy of the revised lyrics. Upon receiving Nixon's letter, Seeger, who had long sung revised spirituals as protest songs and was always looking for more, was delighted: "I'd heard songs like that on and off. The poetry of it! 'My feet is sore but my heart is light.'"[44]

Jo Ann Robinson recalled that the first mass meeting after the arrests was scheduled at the First Baptist Church and that the crowds thronged to the building, filling it for hours before the official 7:00 P.M. start time. While they waited, "thousands of people . . . sang and prayed to Almighty God for four hours, until the ministers came." According to Robinson's memoirs, after King and the others left the courtroom, they walked to the Dexter Avenue Baptist Church, where a forty-five-minute "spiritual meeting" was held, again accompanied by prayer and unidentified religious songs. At the close of the meeting, Robinson confirmed Rustin's story that the group left the church singing the rewritten version of "Give Me That Old-Time Religion."[45]

King's trumped-up arrest and subsequent trial had a galvanizing effect on boycott supporters, especially when the national news media reported their vivid accounts of the assaults and humiliations they had suffered at the hands of white bus drivers. When word of King's conviction—he was given a choice of a $500 fine or 386 days at hard labor—was announced, African-Americans who had gathered outside the courthouse spontaneously sang, "We ain't gonna ride the buses no more." And for the most part, John A. Salmond writes, they didn't.[46]

While the histories of the civil rights movement do not generally begin mentioning freedom songs or revised spirituals until at least the first wave of protests in 1960, African-American sacred songs, some clearly referring to the protest spirituals from the Civil War era, were sung at the MIA meetings. Most of the records of Montgomery mention sacred music in passing, and only then generically as "hymns." For example, a *New York Times* article from February 24, 1956, reporting on a mass meeting held the previous night at the First Baptist Church, stated that the boycott was by then "eighty days" old. The meeting opened, once again, with "Onward, Christian Soldiers" and later included "Lift Me Up." It closed with a greeting from the Reverend A. W. Wilson, vice president of the Negro Alabama Baptist Convention: "No other race but the Negro race could smile as we have smiled tonight, and sing as we sang tonight and get happy and shout as we have shouted tonight."[47]

However, Reagon writes that boycott participants and supporters in Montgomery were among the first to utilize black sacred protest songs and song-leaders to "mobilize" the emerging movement. One song-leader was Mary Ethel Dozier Jones. Along with Minnie Hendricks and Gladys Burnette Carter, Jones was a member of the Montgomery Gospel Trio and verified both the presence of such songs in Montgomery and that the trio existed before the boycott:

> I was in elementary school; in 1954 I was ten years old. Pretty soon after the first mass meeting in 1955 we started singing for the Montgomery Improvement Association. We were doing songs of the movement, "This Little Light of Mine, I'm Gonna Let It Shine." "We Shall Overcome" came later. We would make up songs. All the songs I remember gave us strength to go on. . . . It was kind of spontaneous; if someone started beating us over the head with a billy club we would start singing about the billy club, or either that person's name would come out in a song.[48]

In 1963, Guy Carawan recorded Dozier, Hendricks, and Carter singing three protest spirituals from the Montgomery boycott, "We Are Soldiers in the Army," "Keep Your Hand on the Plow," and "This Little Light." Carawan accompanied the three on guitar, and the bass voice of Sam Collier, who would become a well-known civil rights activist, can be heard in the mix as well. According to Carawan's liner notes, through the boycott and beyond, members of the MIA had to contend with constant threats and violence, but "singing became a strong force in unifying people in their struggle." Of the three, all teenagers or preteens at the time, Carawan writes, "These young women who sing spiritual and gospel songs that express the spirit of freedom have sung often for this organization and for many other groups in Montgomery. They are used to the fact that these meetings may be harassed by police or white hoodlums and that they have to be careful about where they go, what they do and what they say. Songs like 'We Are Soldiers,' 'Hold On' and 'This Little Light' are some of their best and have helped to lift the spirits of many people in Montgomery."[49]

Likewise, in Stewart Burns's collection of documents from the Montgomery bus protest, at least some of those hymns or spirituals are mentioned by name. For instance, Donald T. Ferron's recollections of the MIA's standing-room-only mass meeting of February 27 indicated, once again, that the crowd outside Holt Street Baptist Church was much larger than the one inside. Ferron arrived just before 5:00 P.M. and, until the announced 7:00 P.M. meeting time, reported "an informal, unplanned, undirected, yet cooperative, concerted singing and humming of hymns and spirituals." The arrivals of King, Abernathy, Hubbard, and others were accompanied by the singing of the hymn "Guide Me o'er My Great Jehovah." Later, led by Abernathy, the congregation sang the spiritual "Lay Down My Burden." Sung near the closing was the hymn "Sweet Hour of Prayer" and, following an "introduction" by Abernathy, the spiritual "Steal Away" was sung. One more unidentified spiritual was also sung that evening.[50] At a subsequent meeting on March 1 at Hutchinson Street Church, congregants sang the spiritual "When the Saints Go Marching In" (popularized by both Mahalia Jackson and Louis Armstrong), the hymns "Leaning on the Everlasting Arms," "Jesus Keep Me Near the Cross," and "What a Friend We Have in Jesus," and closed with the spirituals "Nobody Knows the Trouble I've Seen" and "Steal Away," both having been employed by African-Americans during slavery.[51]

The MIA meeting on March 22, again, took place at Holt Street. According to Anna Holden, several "outside" media organizations, including newspapers from New York and Boston, NBC-TV, *France Soir*, and others, were in attendance. At this meeting, the spirituals "I'll Not Be Moved" and "Climbing Jacob's Ladder," and the gospel song "I'll Go, Send Me" were sung. Holden notes that attendees said they had arrived at 2:00 P.M. to have seats for the 7:00 P.M. meeting. The singing continued with "I Need You" and "I Want to Be Near the Cross Where They Crucified My Lord" (perhaps "Were You There When They Crucified My Lord?"). Following a "talk" by King, the congregation sang "I'll Not Be Moved" (perhaps "We Shall Not Be Moved") and "Nobody Knows." At one point, Dr. Moses Jones "substituted" "Walk Together Children" for the scheduled hymn. Also sung near the close of the meeting were the hymn "Pass Me Not, O Gentle Savior" and what Holden titled "God Be with Us."[52] Coretta King confirmed that the crowd that gathered outside the courtroom on March 22, when her husband was sentenced to 386 days of hard labor, erupted into "We Ain't Going to Ride the Buses No More" when she and Martin appeared on the courthouse steps.[53] Even from this small sample, it appears that black sacred song used for the purpose of protest was an integral part of the mass meetings.

Later in the spring of 1956, with financial resources rapidly being depleted, King called the most famous African-American male singer in the country, Harry Belafonte. The two met at the famed Abyssinian Baptist Church in Harlem and cemented Belafonte's intimate relationship with the civil rights movement. Belafonte writes that he immediately donated "significant" money for gasoline and food to the Montgomery Improvement Association. He organized house parties with various organizations to raise money and produced a fund-raising concert at Madison Square Garden with Frank Sinatra. "I gave a lot," Belafonte writes, "but I got a lot back."[54] Coretta King, along with Stanley Levinson, Ella Baker, and Rustin, also organized a benefit concert, at the Manhattan Center in New York on December 5, 1956, that featured Belafonte, Duke Ellington, and others. King sang a series of spirituals that had resonated during the boycott, including "Walk Together, Chillun," "Lord, I Can't Turn Back, Just Because I've Been Born Again," "Keep Your Hand on the Plow," and one she called one of "Martin's favourites," "Honor, Honor."[55]

In writing on the one-year anniversary of the boycott, Studs Terkel recalled that Mahalia Jackson woke him one night with a series of questions. By now, Terkel and Jackson had become fast—if unlikely—friends. Terkel had championed Jackson's music on his Chicago radio program and she had been a frequent guest on the show. According to Terkel's account, the two had bantered back and forth about a call from Abernathy on King's behalf, asking her to sing at one of their fund-raising rallies. Jackson had pretended to be uncertain:

> She lets out a long sigh. "What do you think I should do?"
> "When are you goin'?"
> "Day after tomorrow. Reverend Abernathy asks how much I'll charge." She laughs.
> "What'd you tell him?" As though I didn't know.
> "I said, 'Reverend Abernathy, I don't charge the walkin' people.'"

> Mahalia has found what she was looking for.

> Time passes, cataclysmically. The walking people of Montgomery set hearts on fire. So does song as well as the word. Martin Luther King knows what he's about in calling on Mahalia Jackson. He has found a way; so has she.[56]

Just Mahalia, Baby records minute details of the trip from Chicago. Jackson and her accompanist, Mildred Falls, were guests in the Abernathy home, which would be bombed shortly after she left. On December 6, 1956, St. John AME Church was "packed out" by midday to hear "the first big star to join them" in Montgomery. It did not take long, according to Goreau's account, for Jackson's singing—and the audience's ecstatic response—to have an impact on King: "Intellectual Martin Luther King had come to realize the role of the testifying, the shouting, the service of feeling, of seeking not so much with your mind as with your heart for the path to the soul. Hearing Mahalia this night, he would tell her he now knew fully what gospel music meant."[57] Jackson opened with "(I've Heard of a) City Called Heaven," which would become King's "favorite" during the civil rights movement's darkest days, according to Birmingham singer Cleopatra Kennedy.[58] It was followed by, among others, "All to Jesus, I Surrender," "I'm Made Over," "God Is So Good to Me," and "Move on Up a Little Higher." The concert closed with "Silent Night, Holy Night."[59]

It is "difficult to imagine" the pressures facing not only Jackson at that concert, but anyone in attendance, so real was the constant threat of violence to participants, their relatives, and their friends. As Craig Werner writes, "Again and again, movement veterans testify to the central role gospel music played in helping them find the strength to overcome their fears. So it was crucial that Mahalia was physically present while the police and the Ku Klux Klan—not always two distinct groups in the Deep South—circled the church." According to Werner, rapt listeners found "A City Called Heaven" particularly meaningful:

> When Mahalia sang "I've Heard of a City Called Heaven," she was reaching out for a home, trying to find a way to hold on to the belief that, someday,

things would change. That night in Montgomery, as the community gathered in the church prepared to take the movement to a new level, it was crucial that Mahalia acknowledged both the reality of the moan and the determination to "move on up a little higher."

The people heard Mahalia at the same time they heard King. And they found the strength to march out and meet "the man."[60]

After the concert, Jackson urged King to continue the struggle in Montgomery and find a way to involve more African-Americans across the United States. Back in Chicago, Jackson would declare of King, "I believe he is a black Moses, come to lead his people, and I believe God's going to part the waters."[61] The *New York Amsterdam News* reported that Jackson had received a "tumultuous reception" at the concert.[62]

"It is no accident," Reed notes, "that several of the freedom songs that emerged in Montgomery as symbols of their efforts had a whole lot of walking in them." In addition to "Onward, Christian Soldiers," he cites the spiritual "Walk Together Children" as being especially popular during the bus boycott: "Walk together children, don't you get weary / There's a great camp meeting in the Promised Land." Spirituals like "Walk Together Children" would be "deeply familiar to the respectable churchgoing folks at the heart of the Montgomery movement. They needed no changing come movement time, but were given new life and urgency by the movement."[63]

While black citizens of Montgomery continued their boycott, lawyers supported by the NAACP continued to push the Rosa Parks case through the courts. There was much else happening on the civil rights front, of course, in addition to Montgomery. The NAACP had filed desegregation lawsuits in more than 117 cities in 1955 alone and—still following the precepts of *Brown v. Board of Education*—thousands of African-American parents submitted applications for their children to enroll in previously all-white public schools.[64] Elsewhere, both during and in the months immediately following Montgomery, bus boycotts spread to Tallahassee, Miami, and Birmingham (where the Reverend Fred Shuttlesworth's home was bombed on Christmas Day, 1956).[65]

Parks remained active during this period as well. On Sunday, August 19, 1956, she joined the Reverend Robert S. Graetz and his family for a weeklong retreat at Highlander Folk School, a workshop on public school integration, but one with opportunities for group-singing. On the following Saturday, Graetz was notified that his home had been bombed and his family made plans to return early to Montgomery. At breakfast that morning, the other participants surrounded the Graetz family and sang, "We shall not, we shall not be moved; just like a tree that's planted by the water, we shall not be moved."[66]

The Supreme Court's ruling striking down Alabama's bus segregation laws was finally handed down on November 13, 1956, though following the rejection of the Montgomery City Commission's appeal, the ruling did not actually take effect until December 20, 1956. That night, a massive crowd gathered both inside and outside Holt Street Baptist Church for a climactic celebration. In addition to rousing speeches/sermons by King and others, Georgia Gilmore remembered that the crowd sang "freedom songs and spirituals," including "Swing Low, Sweet Chariot," "This Little Light of Mine," and "a whole lot of others." The following morning at 5:55 A.M., surrounded by reporters, King, Abernathy, Nixon, Glenn Smiley, and others boarded a bus near his house, where they were treated courteously.[67]

So how did the Montgomery bus boycott succeed for more than thirteen months despite economic pressure, physical attacks, mass jailings, bombings, and the sheer logistics of transporting tens of thousands of workers every day? Certainly the organizational brilliance of the WPC and the MIA played a role. And the importance of the African-American churches and their supportive pastors and congregations to the success of the boycott cannot be overstated. The churches "provided the emerging movement with its vast communication network, its organized congregations, and its cultural and financial resources." King, though new to the leadership, also instinctively knew the sustaining power of the emotional mass meeting/church services, which featured the ecstatic singing of sacred African music and fiery preaching—as well as strategy.[68] The Monday and Thursday night meetings may have been the tipping point, just as they would be a few years later in Birmingham. In his account of the boycotts, King pointedly wrote, "The mass meetings accomplished on Monday and Thursday nights what the Christian Church had failed to accomplish on Sunday mornings."[69] On those nights, Edward P. Morgan noted, "one of the local churches was filled to the rafters with gatherers singing hymns, spirituals, and freedom songs and responding enthusiastically to the oratory of Martin Luther King Jr., Ralph Abernathy, and other local preachers. The church meetings drew together blacks of all social classes and forged a sense of collective power."[70] With the successful completion of the actions in Montgomery, Shuttlesworth, who would become a national figure during the Birmingham campaign, again cited the hymn that he believed initiated the bus boycott: "That's what many people don't understand about what happened back in the Deep South, that here I am. That this is my duty. I've got to do something, and God is with me. And if God is with me, how can you lose, 'leaning on the Everlasting Arm'?"[71]

With Montgomery as a catalyst, more sacred protest music was generated throughout the country during this period, including "Eyes on the Prize," an adaptation of a Holiness hymn known by various names (including "Gospel Plow," "Keep Your Eyes on the Prize," "Keep Your Hand on the Plow," and "Hold On"), and rewritten by civil rights activist Alice Wine in 1956. It was later performed (as "Keep Your Hand on the Plow") by Mahalia Jackson with the Duke Ellington Orchestra at the Newport Jazz Festival in 1958, by Bob Dylan on his debut album (1962), and by Pete Seeger with the Student Nonviolent Coordinating Committee Freedom Singers at Carnegie Hall (1963). It would remain a prominent freedom song throughout the history of the movement, and was "specially meaningful for the freedom riders and the sit-in students, who faced long spells of being 'bound in jail' up to and including Mississippi's notoriously brutal Parchman Prison Farm."[72] The lyrics, which vary widely among the various versions, are best known for their references to Paul and Silas during their imprisonment in Philippi in the Book of Acts in the New Testament (16:11–40). Silverman writes that Wine was from Johns Island, South Carolina, and that she was "one of the first proud products" of the new voter education schools: "Freedom's name is mighty sweet / And soon we're gonna meet / Keep your eyes on the prize / Hold on, hold on, hold on, hold on."[73]

A popular gospel song that may have been inspired by the bus boycott is the Reverend James Cleveland's "Soldiers in the Army," copyrighted in 1956. Cleveland was Jackson's longtime friend (and accompanist) and was doubtless aware of her activities in Montgomery. One hint is the reference to the "gospel plow" again from "Eyes on the Prize": "I'm glad, I'm a soldier / I've got my hands on the gospel plow / I know one day I'll get old, and I can't fight any more / But I'll just stand here and fight anyhow."[74] However, the song (and the two are nearly identical) predates Cleveland who, like many gospel artists, sometimes rewrote and rearranged old spirituals. Silverman deemed it a spiritual and wrote that it was introduced to participants—which included veterans of the Montgomery bus boycott and unnamed gospel groups from Montgomery and Birmingham—at a civil rights–related workshop. According to Silverman, "Everybody present immediately realized the song's relevance to the struggle for equal rights that was underway."[75]

It was during this period that what may have been the first gospel song—indeed, *any* song—to mention King was released. In 1956, Brother Will Hairston of Detroit recorded a talking gospel blues number titled "The Alabama Bus—Parts 1 and 2" on black-owned JVB Records. Side 1 equates King with Moses, while side 2 draws parallels between King and Abraham Lincoln: "I wanna tell you 'bout the Reverend Martin Luther King / You know, they tell me that the people began to sing / You know, the man God sent out in the world."[76]

How significant was Montgomery? As James H. Cone has pointed out, at the time of the bus boycott, no sub-Saharan African nation had achieved independence from the western European powers. By the time of King's assassination, twelve short years later, the majority of those same countries were independent nations.[77] For James N. Gregory, the decision on February 23, 1956, to wholeheartedly support the nearly hundred black Montgomery citizens who had been indicted, and the immediate media coverage that followed, was "a pivotal point in the Montgomery struggle and perhaps in the American struggle against racial apartheid." Because of that date, the center of the movement for equal rights would move from New York to the South, a southerner would take the lead in the struggle, and it would be a "much broader and daring and powerful movement, a movement that ultimately drew thousands into acts of protest."[78]

The success of the bus boycott was one of the most significant catalysts for the civil rights movement, writes Ennis, because it began "a steady acceleration in organization and resolution challenging every facet of racial discrimination in the nation. Young people of both races were drawn into those struggles, sometimes as allies, sometimes as enemies. Their efforts to find justice were always accompanied by the sounds of popular music and its dances."[79]

Finally, the advent of the regular mass meeting in community churches was one last innovation from the Montgomery campaign that affected the African-American freedom struggle. Nearly one hundred mass meetings occurred between December 5, 1955, and the day blacks returned to the buses on December 21, 1956. The meetings were originally held every Monday and Thursday evening until the fall of 1956, when organizers reduced them to one night a week.[80] Virtually all participants and scholars have repeatedly cited the importance of the meetings. King observed later that it was the mass meetings that "generated the power and depth which finally galvanized the entire Negro community."[81]

However, most historians have overlooked the impact of the *singing* itself during those meetings. As we have seen, blacks have employed sacred music as, among other things, a vehicle of protest and resistance since their forced arrival on America's shores. Reagon writes that music "has always been integral to the Black American struggle for freedom."[82] And, she says, the singing, which made up a major part of each evening,

> really helped to create the culture of action, create the ambience that could sustain a movement of struggle. On some level, you have an intellectual thing you have to do to be involved in struggle and know where you want to be, but the other part is . . . how do you feel, do you feel like doing it? The idea that you're going to a mass meeting, and you're going to be talking about struggle, changes if you know that that mass meeting is going to be a powerful, powerful singing experience. You're being fed— you go to your meetings, you go to your marches, and you know that it is more than just getting your mind intellectually in line with what you believe in. You know there is going to be power because of the singing.[83]

Coretta King's memories of the renewing power of the combination of preaching, singing, and prayer in the mass meetings are in a similar vein. She recalled that there was "something" in the experience that gave participants "hope and inspiration." The more involved they became, "the more we had the feeling that something could be done about the situation, that we could change it."[84] It was during the Montgomery bus boycott that the tradition of singing black sacred music in mass meetings took hold and became one of the significant tools of African-Americans in their search for civil rights in this country.

The nascent civil rights movement finds the irresistible force it needs to face the country's immovable wall of racism in the sacred songs (and speeches and organization) embodied in the mass meetings. Those sacred songs, the spirituals (and later gospel), have been a powerful weapon in the history of African-Americans, bearing a message of defiance and hope, insurrection and peace, since the first slaves arrived in North America. The labor unions have used song as a tool for inspiration and organization for more than a century. When blacks first joined the unions, the spirituals were quickly assimilated into labor songs—the marriage increasing the potency and power of both. The Great Migration took southern song—sacred and profane—northward and created voting blocs too big for politicians to ignore. The African-American veterans from two world wars—where they fought and died for the freedom of others—returned with a renewed determination to fight for their own freedom. The social upheavals that followed created a new music and a generation not bound by the prejudices and tastes of their elders. Atrocities against blacks were, for the first time, covered by the national media, creating a climate ripe for change in the South. Various African-American protests followed—some successful, some not. When the Supreme Court announced the *Brown v. Board of Education* decision, those protests, given the weight of law, intensified until, in Montgomery, the work of a handful of freedom fighters, trained in the labor wars and at Highlander, led by a charismatic young preacher and a fearless seamstress, rocked a venerable old church with the thundering chords of "Onward, Christian Soldiers."

The years that would follow would take the first seeds of sacred protest song, the tenets of nonviolence, and the electrifying revival-styled format of the mass meeting across the United States. And they would be backed by the shared experiences of dozens of generations of slaves and former slaves, mill workers and coal miners, sharecroppers and barrelhouse pianists, students and soldiers, preachers and DJs and politicians all singing "Go Down, Moses," "We Shall Not Be Moved," "We Shall Overcome," and a thousand more like them in a grand concert that, in a remarkably short time, would rock both the nation and the world.

Music is our witness, and our ally. The
beat is the confession which recognizes,
changes, and conquers time.

—JAMES BALDWIN

Notes

Preface

The epigraphs to this preface are drawn from Leon F. Litwack, *Trouble in Mind: Black Southerners in the Age of Jim Crow* (New York: Knopf, 1999), xvi–xvii; and from CIO militant Harvey O'Connor, cited in Stuart Hall and Tony Jefferson, eds., *Resistance Through Rituals: Youth Subcultures in Post-War Britain* (New York: Holmes and Meier, 1975), 165.

1. Zora Neale Hurston, *The Sanctified Church* (New York: Marlowe, 1981), 69.
2. Ibid.
3. John Lovell, Jr., "The Social Implications of the Negro Spiritual," *Journal of Negro Education* 8, no. 4 (1939): 642–43.
4. Gavin Weightman, *The Industrial Revolutionaries: The Making of the Modern World, 1776–1914* (New York: Grove Press, 2007), 268.

Introduction

The epigraphs to this introduction are drawn from Lerone Bennett, Jr.'s introduction to Vincent Harding, *Hope and History: Why We Must Share the Story of the Movement* (Maryknoll, NY: Orbis, 1999), x; Malcolm O. Sillars, "Defining Movements Rhetorically: Casting the Widest Net," in *Readings on the Rhetoric of Social Protest*, ed. Charles E. Morris III and Stephen H. Browne (State College, PA: Strata, 2001), 115–16. The quotation that closes this introduction is drawn from Leonard E. Barrett, *Soul-Force: African Heritage in Afro-American Religion* (Garden City, NY: Anchor/Doubleday, 1974), 2.

1. Numerous books detail the widespread nature, multiple forms and sheer ferocity of slave resistance: John Hope Franklin and Alfred A. Moss, Jr., *From Slavery to Freedom: A History of Negro Americans* (1947; repr., New York: Knopf, 1988); John W. Blassingame, ed., *Slave Testimony: Two Centuries of Letters, Speeches, Interviews, and Autobiographies* (Baton Rouge: Louisiana State University Press, 1977); John Hope Franklin and Loren Schweninger, *Runaway Slaves: Rebels on the Plantation* (New York: Oxford University Press, 1999); Eugene D. Genovese, *From Rebellion to Revolution: Afro-American Slave Revolts in the Making of the Modern World* (Baton Rouge: Louisiana State University Press, 1979); and Junius P. Rodriguez, ed., *Encyclopedia of Slave Resistance and Rebellion* (Westport, CT: Greenwood, 2007), among others.
2. The literature is equally vast on the importance, content, and widespread commonalities among the songs and music of the primarily western and central African nations that provided the bulk of the slaves: Alan P. Merriam, *African Music in Perspective* (New York: Garland, 1982); A. M. Jones, *Studies in African Music*, vol. 1 (London: Oxford University Press, 1959); J. H. Nketia,

The Music of Africa (New York: Norton, 1974); and John Storm Roberts, *Black Music of Two Worlds* (New York: Praeger, 1972), among others.

3. J. H. Nketia, "The Musical Languages of Subsaharan Africa," in *African Music Meeting in Yaoundé (Cameroon), 23–27 February 1970*, organized by UNESCO (Paris: La Revue Musicale, 1972), 37.

4. Chief Fela Sowande, "The Role of Music in Traditional African Society," in ibid., 64.

5. Samuel A. Floyd, Jr., *The Power of Black Music: Interpreting Its History from Africa to the United States* (New York: Oxford University Press, 1995), 32.

6. See Henry Louis Gates, Jr., *The Signifying Monkey: A Theory of Afro-American Criticism* (New York: Oxford University Press, 1966) for a much more detailed, nuanced description of "signifyin'" and its importance in the history of African and African-American culture.

7. See Melville J. Herskovits, *The Myth of the Negro Past* (New York: Harper and Brothers, 1941); Roberts, *Black Music of Two Worlds*; and Dan Gorlin, *Songs of West Africa* (Forest Knolls, CA: Alokli West African Dance, 2000).

8. Again, the literature on this topic is extensive, including Eugene D. Genovese, *Roll, Jordan, Roll: The World the Slaves Made* (New York: Vintage, 1976), Kenneth M. Stampp, *The Peculiar Institution: Slavery in the Antebellum South* (New York: Vintage, 1989), and more.

9. Hall Johnson, "Notes on the Negro Spiritual," in *Readings in Black American Music*, 2nd ed., ed. Eileen Southern (New York: Norton, 1983), 274.

10. The Bible verses Colossians 3:22, Ephesians 6:5, and 1 Peter 2:18 all essentially repeat the same thing: "Slaves, obey your master." See *The New Interpreter's Study Bible, New Revised Standard Version with the Apocrypha* (Nashville: Abingdon Press, 2003). Unless otherwise noted, all biblical quotations in this volume are from the NISB.

11. The complex nature of the introduction of Christianity to the slaves and the religion they subsequently created has been the life's work of numerous excellent scholars. Good overviews can be found in Barrett, *Soul-Force*; Albert J. Raboteau, *Slave Religion: The "Invisible Institution" in the Antebellum South* (New York: Oxford University Press, 1978); C. Eric Lincoln, ed., *The Black Experience in Religion* (Garden City, NY: Anchor/Doubleday, 1974); and C. Eric Lincoln and Lawrence H. Mamiya, *The Black Church in the African American Experience* (Durham: Duke University Press, 1990), among others.

12. See the two monumental works of scholarship on the topic of spirituals, Dena J. Epstein, *Sinful Tunes and Spirituals: Black Folk Music to the Civil War* (Urbana: University of Illinois Press, 1977), and John Lovell, Jr., *Black Song: The Forge and the Flame; The Story of How the Afro-American Spiritual Was Hammered Out* (1972; repr., New York: Paragon House, 1986).

13. Various artists, *Folk Music of the United States: Afro-American Spirituals, Work Songs, and Ballads from the Archive of American Folk Song*, ed. Alan Lomax (Library of Congress Division of Music Recording Laboratory, Album 8, 1942); *The Ballad Hunter*, Parts 7 and 8, *Spirituals Through the Songs of Southern Negroes*, narrated by John Lomax (Library of Congress and the Archive of Folk Song, AFS L5, 1998).

14. William Francis Allen, Charles Pickard Ware, and Lucy McKim Garrison, *Slave Songs of the United States* (1867; repr., New York: Peter Smith, 1927), iv, 19.

15. In addition to Epstein, *Sinful Tunes* (particularly 217); Lovell, *Black Song*; and Allen, Ware, and Garrison, *Slave Songs*, among the earliest descriptions of the spirituals can be found in the writings of Col. Thomas Higginson, who directed an all-black regiment during the American Civil War. Higginson's

observations, and numerous others, can also be found in Southern's *Readings in Black American Music*. This brief summary of what the spirituals sounded like is also drawn, in part, from Robert Darden, *People Get Ready! A New History of Black Gospel Music* (New York: Continuum, 2004), 18–24, 72–77.

16. Robert Anderson, quoted in Raboteau, *Slave Religion*, 65.

Chapter 1

The epigraphs to this chapter are drawn from W. E. B. Du Bois, *The Souls of Black Folk* (1903; repr., McLean, VA: IndyPublish.com), 146, and Gloria Scott, cited by Margo V. Perkins in *My Soul Is a Witness: African-American Women's Spirituality*, ed. Gloria Wade-Gayles (Boston: Beacon, 1995), 128.

1. See George Pullen Jackson, *White and Negro Spirituals* (New York: Augustin, 1943); George Pullen Jackson, *White Spirituals in the Southern Uplands: The Story of the Fasola Folk, Their Songs, Singings, and "Buckwheat Notes"* (Chapel Hill: University of North Carolina Press, 1933); George Pullen Jackson, *Down-East Spirituals and Others* (New York: Augustin, 1942); and Newman I. White, *American Negro Folk-Songs* (Cambridge: Harvard University Press, 1928).

2. Miles Mark Fisher, *Negro Slave Songs in the United States* (1953; repr., New York: Russell and Russell, 1968).

3. See Alan Lomax, "Africanism in New World Negro Music," in *The Haitian Potential: Research and Resources of Haiti*, ed. Vera Rubin and Richard P. Schaedel (New York: Teachers College Press, Columbia University, 1975); Jones, *Studies in African Music*; and, most definitively, Lovell, *Black Song*.

4. Bernice Johnson Reagon, cited by Lisa Pertillar Brevard, "'Will the Circle Be Unbroken': African-American Women's Spirituality in Sacred Song Traditions,"

in Wade-Gayles, *My Soul Is a Witness*, 36.

5. Allen, Ware, and Garrison, *Slave Songs*, ii.

6. Epstein, *Sinful Tunes*, 192–201, 218–19.

7. The process of slave conversions was, not surprisingly, complicated and multifaceted. Where the Second Great Awakening camp meeting revivals included African-Americans, Christianity apparently spread quickly. In the Deep South, where religion was of little importance to the plantation owners, the process was more gradual. And, in the North, Richard Allen's Mother Bethel American Methodist Episcopal Church—the first church founded and governed by freed slaves—was established in Philadelphia in 1816. See Raboteau's *Slave Religion* as well as Lincoln and Mamiya's *Black Church* for a good overview of the spread of Christianity among slaves in the South and freed slaves in the North.

8. Raboteau, *Slave Religion*, 64.

9. "Religion So Sweet," in Allen, Ware, and Garrison, *Slave Songs*, 13.

10. Lovell, *Black Song*, 223.

11. Ibid., 223–24.

12. James H. Cone, *The Spirituals and the Blues* (New York: Seabury Press, 1972), 69–70.

13. Raboteau, *Slave Religion*, 90–92.

14. Wyatt Tee Walker, *Spirits That Dwell in Deep Woods: The Prayer and Praise Hymns of the Black Religious Experience* (Chicago: GIA, 1991), xiv, from the foreword to Volume III by Rev. Dr. Jeremiah A. Wright, Jr.

15. Lovell, *Black Song*, 224.

16. Ibid., 225.

17. Stephen Butterfield, *Black Autobiography in America* (Amherst: University of Massachusetts Press, 1974), 15–18.

18. Aaron, *The Light and Truth of Slavery* (Worcester, MA, 1843), quoted in V. P. Franklin, *Black Self-Determination: A Cultural History of the Faith of the Fathers* (Westport, CT: Lawrence Hill, 1984), 53.

19. Frederick Douglass, *My Bondage and My Freedom* (1855; repr., Urbana: University of Illinois Press, 1987), 281.

20. John W. Roberts, *From Trickster to Badman: The Black Folk Hero in Slavery and Freedom* (Philadelphia: University of Pennsylvania Press, 1989), 158.

21. Genovese, *Roll, Jordan, Roll*, 283.

22. The literature on the topic includes both insightful texts and faithful recreations of the music itself. See Kenneth Silverman, *Cultural History of the American Revolution: Painting, Music, Literature, and the Theatre* (New York: T. Y. Crowell, 1976), along with the recordings *Music of the American Revolution: The Birth of Liberty* (New World Records, CD 80276-2, 1996) and *American Songs of Revolutionary Times and the Civil War Era* (Folk American, CD 362, 2009). Silverman relates a letter from Nicholas Creswell, a London merchant, who in 1774 witnessed a "Negro Ball" where the slaves sang a number of songs, including those related to "the usage they have received from their Masters or Mistresses in a very satirical stile and manner" (*Cultural History*, 184). While this is not protest music per se, it does not appear that the slaves were exactly celebrating their treatment at the hands of their owners, either!

23. For more information on this fascinating, widely connected family, see Scott Gac, *Singing for Freedom: The Hutchinson Family Singers and the Nineteenth-Century Culture of Reform* (New Haven: Yale University Press, 2007), and Dale Cockrell, ed. and annot., *Excelsior: Journals of the Hutchinson Family Singers, 1846–1846* (Stuyvesant, NY: Pendragon Press, 1989).

24. Cockrell, *Excelsior*, 381. Andrew Ward's *Dark Midnight When I Rise: The Story of the Jubilee Singers Who Introduced the World to the Music of Black America* (New York: Farrar, Straus and Giroux, 2000) cites a letter from a John Davidson of New York, who writes that the Hutchinsons both sang and published "Room Enough" and "Turn Back Pharaoh's Army" (184).

25. Gac, *Singing for Freedom*, 21.

26. Jon Cruz, *Culture on the Margins: The Black Spiritual and the Rise of American Cultural Interpretation* (Princeton: Princeton University Press, 1999), 11–12.

27. Epstein, *Sinful Tunes*, 241–42.

28. W. E. B. Du Bois, *Black Reconstruction in America: An Essay Toward a History of the Part Which Black Folk Played in the Attempt to Reconstruct Democracy in America, 1860–1880* (1935; repr., New York: Atheneum, 1962), 125.

29. Willie Lee Rose, *Rehearsal for Reconstruction: The Port Royal Experiment* (Indianapolis: Bobbs-Merrill, 1964), 12–13, 90–91.

30. Booker T. Washington, *Up from Slavery* (1901; repr., New York: Penguin, 1986), 8–9.

31. Epstein, *Sinful Tunes*, 243–44.

32. Ibid., 245–46.

33. Ibid., 245.

34. Ibid., 275–76.

35. Ibid., 314–17, 260–70.

36. Ibid., 270–71.

37. Cruz, *Culture on the Margins*, 142–50.

38. Thomas Wentworth Higginson, "Negro Spirituals," *Atlantic Monthly*, June 7, 1867, 685.

39. Ibid., 686, 691.

40. Ibid., 692.

41. Ibid..

42. Ibid., 693–94.

43. Epstein, *Sinful Tunes*, 303–4.

44. Ibid., 304–9.

45. Allen, Ware, and Garrison, *Slave Songs*, 310–12, iii.

46. Reprinted, in part, in Southern, *Readings in Black American Music*, 175–202.

47. While Gustavus D. Pike's *The Jubilee Singers of Fisk University, and Their Campaign for Twenty Thousand Dollars* (Boston: Lee and Shepard, 1873) was the first of two accounts of the Fisk Jubilee Singers, a later book by J. B. T. Marsh combined both of Pike's books, updated

some of the biographies, and added songs that the Jubilee Singers had incorporated into their repertoire in the subsequent decade: see Marsh's *The Story of the Jubilee Singers: With Their Songs* (1881; repr., New York: Negro Universities Press, 1969). For more detailed recent scholarship on the influence of the Fisk Jubilee Singers, see Ward, *Dark Midnight*, and Toni P. Anderson, *"Tell Them We Are Singing for Jesus": The Original Fisk Jubilee Singers and Christian Reconstruction, 1871–1878* (Macon: Mercer University Press, 2010).

48. Allen, Ware, and Garrison, *Slave Songs*, preface by Harold Courlander to the 1995 ed. (Mineola, NY: Dover), n.p.

49. Several commentators, including Bernice Johnson Reagon, reiterate this important distinction between "arranged and notated spirituals" and the original improvised spirituals. See Marta J. Effinger, "An Interview with Bernice J. Reagon," *Footsteps: African American Heritage*, http://www.footstepsmagazine .com/ReagonInterview.asp; and Stephen Glazier, ed., *The Encyclopedia of African and African-American Religions* (New York: Routledge, 2001), 199–203.

50. Lovell, *Black Song*, 19.

51. Allen, Ware, and Garrison, *Slave Songs*, xxxviii–xlii.

52. Ronald Radano, "Denoting Difference: The Writing of the Slave Spirituals," *Critical Inquiry* 22, no. 3 (1996): 526.

Chapter 2

The epigraphs to this chapter are drawn from Perry Bradford, *Born with the Blues: Perry Bradford's Own Story* (New York: Oak, 1965), 21; Du Bois, *Black Reconstruction in America*, 124; and Charles Ball, a fugitive slave, whose words from 1859 are quoted in Franklin, *Black Determination*, 27.

1. Cruz, *Culture on the Margins*, 110.

2. Ibid.

3. Pike, *Jubilee Singers*, 182–83.

4. Kenneth A. Bernard, *Lincoln and the Music of the Civil War* (Caldwell, ID: Claxton, 1966), 95.

5. Ward, *Dark Midnight*, 176–77, 211–14.

6. Several biographies have been written about this singular American hero, including Catherine Clinton's *Harriet Tubman: The Road to Freedom* (New York: Little, Brown, 2004); Beverly Lowry's *Harriet Tubman: Imagining a Life* (New York: Doubleday, 2007); and Earl Conrad's *General Harriet Tubman* (1943; repr., Washington, DC: Associated, 1990). The earliest biography is Sarah Bradford's *Harriet Tubman: The Moses of Her People*, published in 1869, updated in 1886. Corinth Books reissued it in 1961.

7. *Freedmen's Record*, vol. 1, March 1865, cited in Blassingame, *Slave Testimony*, 457–65.

8. Lowry, *Harriet Tubman*, 198–99.

9. The familiar stories of Moses fill most of the Christian Old Testament books of Exodus, Leviticus, and Deuteronomy.

10. Darden, *People Get Ready*, 89–90.

11. Bradford, *Harriet Tubman*, 35–38.

12. Jerry Silverman, *Slave Songs* (New York: Chelsea House, 1994), 20.

13. Bruce Feiler, *America's Prophet: Moses and the American Story* (New York: William Morrow, 2009), 107.

14. Ibid., 125.

15. Lovell, *Black Song*, 326.

16. Christa K. Dixon, *Negro Spirituals from Bible to Folk Song* (Philadelphia: Fortress Press, 1976), 24.

17. Richard Newman, *Go Down, Moses: A Celebration of the African-American Spiritual* (New York: Clarkson Potter, 1998), 23.

18. Lovell, *Black Song*, 326–27.

19. Jon Michael Spencer, *Protest and Praise: Sacred Music of Black Religion* (Minneapolis: Fortress Press, 1990), 4–5.

20. Newman, *Go Down, Moses*, from the foreword by Cornel West, 9.

21. James Weldon Johnson, ed., with J. Rosamund Johnson, arr., *The Book of American Negro Spirituals* (New York: Viking, 1925), 13.

22. Lovell, *Black Song*, 386.

23. Conrad, *General Harriet Tubman*, 211–12, 230.

24. Moses's anger is kindled against his recalcitrant followers on several occasions, most notably upon his return to camp from communing with Yahweh, bearing the original Ten Commandments (Exod. 32). The Four Gospels provide different accounts of Jesus's anger with the money changers in the Temple (Matt. 21:12–13), the "cursing" of the barren fig tree (Matt. 21:18–20), and the hypocritical scribes and Pharisees (Matt. 23:1–36).

25. Bruce Feiler, *Abraham: A Journey to the Heart of Three Faiths* (New York: William Morrow, 2002), 157.

26. Ibid.

27. Roberts, *From Trickster to Badman*, 120–21.

28. Ibid., 149.

29. Albert Murray, *The Hero and the Blues* (1973; repr., New York: Vintage, 1995), 61.

30. Johnson, *Book of American Negro Spirituals*, 20–21.

31. Margaret Mitchell, *Gone with the Wind* (1936; repr., New York: Scribner, 1964), 308.

32. Roland Hayes, *My Songs: Aframerican Religious Folk Songs Arranged and Interpreted by Roland Hayes* (Boston: Little, Brown, 1948), 22.

33. Silverman, *Slave Songs*, 20.

34. Allen, Ware, and Garrison, *Slave Songs*, 94.

35. E. A. McIlhenny, *Befo' de War Spirituals: Words and Melodies* (Boston: Christopher, 1933), 248–49.

36. Pike, *Jubilee Singers*, 174–75.

37. Newman, *Go Down, Moses*, 78.

38. Henry H. Mitchell, *Black Church Beginnings: The Long-Hidden Realities of the First Years* (Grand Rapids, MI: Eerdmans, 2004), 43–44.

39. Lovell, *Black Song*, 234.

40. Walker, *Spirits That Dwell*, 20, 21.

41. Roberts, *From Trickster to Badman*, 152.

42. Lovell, *Black Song*, 329.

43. Several sources exist for the different stories behind "John Brown's Body" (or "The John Brown Song"), including Percy A. Scholes's article "John Brown's Body" in *The Oxford Companion of Music*, vol. 1 (London: Oxford University Press, 1983), 1001–2; George Kimball, "Origin of the John Brown Song," *New England Magazine*, n.s., 7, no. 4 (1890): 371–76; Charles Hamm, *Yesterdays: Popular Song in America* (New York: Norton, 1979); Sarah Vowell, "John Brown's Body," in *The Rose and the Briar: Death, Love, and Liberty in the American Ballad*, ed. Sean Wilentz and Greil Marcus (New York: Norton, 2005); and Epstein, *Sinful Tunes*.

44. Bernard, *Lincoln and the Music*, 100–101.

45. Frederick Douglass, *Life and Times of Frederick Douglass, Written by Himself: His Early Life as a Slave, His Escape from Bondage, and His Complete History* (1892; repr., New York: Collier, 1962), 321–24.

46. Bernard, *Lincoln and the Music*, 30–31, 50–51.

47. Epstein, *Sinful Tunes*, 259.

48. Cruz, *Culture on the Margins*, 155.

49. Allen, Ware, and Garrison, *Slave Songs*, xxxvii.

50. Marsh, *Story of the Jubilee Singers*, 228.

51. Bernard, *Lincoln and the Music*, 259–99.

52. Washington, *Up from Slavery*, 19–20.

53. Sojourner Truth, *The Narrative of Sojourner Truth* (1878; repr., New York: Arno Press and the *New York Times*, 1968), 126.

54. Bernice Johnson Reagon, *If You Don't Go Don't Hinder Me: The African American Sacred Song Tradition* (Lincoln: University of Nebraska Press, 2001), 118–19.

55. W. E. B. Du Bois, *The Autobiography of W. E. B. Du Bois: A Soliloquy on*

Viewing My Life from the Last Decade of Its First Century (New York: International, 1968), 251, 259.

56. Anderson, *"Tell Them We Are Singing for Jesus,"* 82, 125, 286.

57. Hamm, *Yesterdays*, 156.

58. Vowell, "John Brown's Body," 83–89, 363.

59. "Centennial Rites Hail Emancipator: Freeing of Slaves Is Marked by Capitol in Poetry, Song, and Kennedy Message," *New York Times*, September 23, 1962, 1, 50.

60. Brevard, "Will the Circle Be Unbroken," 45.

61. Ralph David Abernathy, *And the Walls Came Tumbling Down: An Autobiography* (New York: Harper Perennial, 1989), 433.

62. James Oliver Horton and Lois E. Horton, *In Hope of Liberty: Culture, Community, and Protest Among Northern Free Blacks, 1700–1860* (New York: Oxford University Press, 1997), 132–33.

63. *Jubilee and Plantation Songs: Characteristic Favorites, as Sung by the Hampton Students, Jubilee Singers, Fisk University Students, and Other Concert Companies; Also, a Number of New and Pleasing Selections* (Boston: Oliver Ditson, 1887), 34.

64. Hildred Roach, *Black American Music: Past and Present* (Malabar, FL: Krieger, 1992), 25, 35.

65. Fisher, *Negro Slave Songs*, 66–67.

66. Du Bois, *Souls of Black Folk*, 147.

67. *American Negro Songs and Spirituals: A Comprehensive Collection of 230 Folk Songs, Religious and Secular, with a Foreword by John W. Work* (1915; repr., New York: Negro Universities Press, 1969), 77–78.

68. Dorothy Scarborough, *On the Trail of Negro Folk-Songs* (Cambridge: Harvard University Press, 1925), 22–23.

69. Bradford, *Born with the Blues*, 22.

70. Lovell, *Black Song*, 226–28.

71. Ibid., 228.

72. Dixon, *Negro Spirituals*, 82–83.

73. Marsh, *Story of the Jubilee Singers*, 188.

74. Douglass, *My Bondage and My Freedom*, 170.

75. Marsh, *Story of the Jubilee Singers*, 188.

76. Hayes, *My Songs*, 98–99.

77. Mitchell, *Black Church Beginnings*, 43.

78. Hayes, *My Songs*, 121–22, 127–28.

79. Allen, Ware, and Garrison, *Slave Songs*, 55.

80. Ibid., 55.

81. Howard Thurman, *"Deep River" and "The Negro Spiritual Speaks of Life and Death"* (1945; repr., Richmond, IN: Friends United Press, 1975), 32.

82. Cornel West, "The Religious Foundations of the Thought of Martin Luther King, Jr.," in *We Shall Overcome: Martin Luther King, Jr., and the Black Freedom Struggle*, ed. Peter J. Albert and Ronald Hoffman (New York: United States Capitol Historical Society/Pantheon, 1990), 121–22.

83. Albert Sidney Beckham, "The Psychology of Negro Spirituals," *Southern Workman* 60 (1931): 391–94.

84. Blassingame, *Slave Testimony*, 593.

85. John Killens, cited in *Black Protest Thought in the Twentieth Century*, ed. August Meier, Elliott Rudwick, and Francis L. Broderick, 2nd ed. (New York: Macmillan, 1971), 423–24. Killens uses Foster's song as part of an argument to debunk the myth of the faithful slave. The slave owners with even an ounce of humanity, of course, had to convince themselves that their slaves were better off in their "care" and that they really loved their masters, even to the point of writing what he calls "improbable lyrics" like these and believing that their slaves really sang them: "*All de darkeys am a-weepin' / Massa's in the de cold, cold ground.* But my great-grandmother told me differently. 'We wept all right, honey! Great God Almighty! We cried for joy and shouted hallelujah,' when old master got the cold, cold ground that was coming to him."

86. Frederick Herzog, *Liberation Theology: Liberation in the Light of the Fourth*

Gospel (New York: Seabury Press, 1972), 211.

87. Spencer, *Protest and Praise*, 13.

88. Guy Carawan and Candie Carawan, *Ain't You Got a Right to the Tree of Life? The People of Johns Island, South Carolina—Their Faces, Their Words, and Their Songs* (New York: Simon and Schuster, 1966), 10.

89. Floyd, *Power of Black Music*, 40.

90. Marsh, *Story of the Jubilee Singers*, 53.

91. Cheryl Ann Kirk-Duggan, "Theodicy and the Redacted African-American Spirituals of the 1960s Civil Rights Movement" (Ph.D. diss., Baylor University, 1992), 103–4.

92. *American Negro Songs and Spirituals*, 49.

93. *The Big Book of Hymns* (Milwaukee: Hal Leonard, 1999), 24–25.

94. Lovell, *Black Song*, 230.

95. Lydia Parrish, *Slave Songs of the Georgia Sea Islands* (1942; repr., Hatboro, PA: Folklore Associates, 1965), 182–84.

96. William C. Banfield, *Black Notes: Essays of a Musician Writing in a Post-Album Age* (Lanham, MD: Scarecrow Press, 2004), 82.

97. Harold Courlander, *Negro Folk Music, USA* (New York: Columbia University Press, 1963), 67.

98. Bernice Johnson Reagon, quoted in Kirk-Duggan, "Theodicy," 142.

99. Lovell, *Black Song*, 287, 343.

100. Kerran L. Sanger, "Slave Resistance and Rhetorical Self-Definition: Spirituals as Strategy," *Western Journal of Communication* 59 (Summer 1995): 183.

101. Thurman, *"Deep River,"* 48.

Interlude

The epigraphs for this interlude are drawn from Cornel West, "Marcus Shelby and the Soul of the Movement," *Smiley & West*, NPR, January 7, 2011, https://www.smileyandwest.com/show-transcripts/smiley-west-featuring-marcus-shelby/; W. E. B. Du Bois, *The Souls of Black Folk: Essays and Sketches* (1953; repr., Greenwich, CT: Fawcett Premier, 1961), 148; and Reagon, *If You Don't Go Don't Hinder Me*, 10.

1. Du Bois, *Black Reconstruction in America*, 124.

2. In the decades that followed the Civil War, numerous writers lamented the passing of the spiritual, each apparently unaware of the previous predictions. Few, however, bothered to travel to the more rural areas of the South, where the spirituals were continuing to be sung. Some examples of the pronouncements lamenting the loss of this musical form include Scarborough, *On the Trail of Negro Folk-Songs*, 280–81; Henry Cleveland Wood, "Negro Camp-Meeting Melodies," *New England Magazine*, March 1892, 62; Marion Alexander, "Negro 'Spirituals,'" *Century Magazine*, August 1899, 577; Herbert Ravenel Sass, "I Can't Help from Crying," *Saturday Evening Post*, October 3, 1942, 16–17.

3. Both Leon F. Litwack's towering, Pulitzer Prize–winning *Been in the Storm So Long: The Aftermath of Slavery* (New York: Knopf, 1979), and his later, equally monumental *Trouble in Mind* use thousands of original sources to tell this brutal, shameful story of betrayal and abuse.

4. Litwack, *Trouble in Mind*, 379.

5. Mitchell, *Black Church Beginnings*, 167. Another excellent book on the black church after the Civil War is Albert J. Raboteau, *Canaan Land: A Religious History of African Americans* (1999; repr., New York: Oxford University Press, 2001).

6. Vincent Harding, *There Is a River: The Black Struggle for Freedom in America* (New York: Harcourt Brace Jovanovich, 1981), 265.

7. Mary R. Sawyer, "The Black Church and Black Politics: Models of Ministerial Activism," in *Down by the Riverside: Readings in African American Religion*,

ed. Larry G. Murphy (New York: New York University Press, 2000), 293.

8. Wyatt Tee Walker, *"Somebody's Calling My Name": Black Sacred Music and Social Change* (Valley Forge, PA: Judson Press, 1979), 24.

9. Ibid., 22.

10. Mitchell, *Black Church Beginnings*, 190–92.

11. There are several fine books on Allen and his hymnals, including Charles H. Wesley, *Richard Allen, Apostle of Freedom* (Washington, DC: Associated, 1935); Richard Allen, *Life, Experience, and Gospel Labors of the Rt. Rev. Richard Allen* (Philadelphia: Martin and Boden, 1833); and Eileen Southern, *The Music of Black Americans: A History*, 2nd ed. (New York: Norton, 1983), as well as additional research on the African-American churches in Philadelphia in Leon F. Litwack, *North of Slavery: The Negro in the Free States, 1790–1860* (Chicago: University of Chicago Press, 1961).

12. Jerma A. Jackson, *Singing in My Soul: Black Gospel Music in a Secular Age* (Chapel Hill: University of North Carolina Press, 2004), 12–13.

13. Work, *Folk Song of the American Negro*, 112.

14. Langston Hughes, "The Negro Artist and the Racial Mountain," *The Nation*, June 23, 1926, 693.

15. For a well-crafted overview of the evolution of popular music in the post–Civil War era, from minstrelsy to Tin Pan Alley, see Hamm, *Yesterdays.*

16. Several thoughtful books in recent years have examined the blackface minstrel phenomenon, most notably Eric Lott, *Love and Theft: Blackface Minstrelsy and the American Working Class* (New York: Oxford University Press, 1993); Dale Cockrell, *Demons of Disorder: Early Blackface Minstrels and Their World* (Cambridge: Cambridge University Press, 1997); Robert C. Toll, *Blacking Up: The Minstrel Show in Nineteenth-Century America* (New York: Oxford University Press, 1974); W. T. Lhamon, *Raising Cain: Blackface Performance from Jim Crow to Hip Hop* (Cambridge: Harvard University Press, 1998); and Lynn Abbott and Doug Seroff, *Ragged but Right: Black Traveling Shows, "Coon Songs," and the Dark Pathway to Blues and Jazz* (Jackson: University Press of Mississippi, 2007).

17. W. C. Handy, *Father of the Blues: An Autobiography* (1941; repr., New York: Da Capo, 1969), 62.

18. Toll, *Blacking Up*, 237–38.

19. James M. Trotter, *Music and Some Highly Musical People: Remarkable Musicians of the Colored Race, with Portraits* (1878; repr., New York: Johnson, 1968), 276–77.

20. Hamm, *Yesterdays*, 285–87.

21. Work, *Folk Song of the American Negro*, 90, 93.

22. Dale Cockrell, "Of Gospel Hymns, Minstrel Shows, and Jubilee Singers: Toward Some Black South African Musics," *American Music* 5, no. 4 (1987): 417–32.

23. Ward, *Dark Midnight*, 139.

24. *American Negro Songs and Spirituals*, 27.

25. Eileen Southern, *The Music of Black Americans: A History* (New York: Norton, 1971), 251.

26. Lovell, *Black Song*, 427–56.

27. Trotter, *Music and Some Highly Musical People*, 271.

28. Lynn Abbott, "'Play That Barber Shop Chord': A Case for the African-American Origin of Barbershop Harmony," *American Music* 10, no. 3 (1992): 290–93.

29. Work, *Folk Song of the American Negro*, 92.

30. Abbott, "Play That Barber Shop Chord," 306.

31. Johnson, *Book of American Negro Spirituals*, 35.

32. Alan Lomax, *Mister Jelly Roll: The Fortunes of Jelly Roll Morton, New Orleans Creole and "Inventor of Jazz"* (Berkeley:

University of California Press, 1950), 15–16.

33. Abbott, "Play That Barber Shop Chord," 303.

34. See Paul Oliver, *Songsters and Saints: Vocal Traditions on Race Records* (Cambridge: Cambridge University Press, 1984), for the most extensive research into this intriguing phenomenon and its equally fascinating counterpart, the so-called Jack-Leg Preachers, who were often found on competing street corners—preaching an unpolished gospel message for pennies—and would have a significant influence on the performance of gospel music.

35. Michael Hall, "The Soul of a Man," *Texas Monthly*, December 2010, 130–35, 206–7, 258, 260–61, 264.

36. Oliver, *Songsters and Saints*, 201–228.

37. William E. Barton, *Old Plantation Hymns: A Collection of Hitherto Unpublished Melodies of the Slave and the Freedman, with Historical and Descriptive Notes* (1899; repr., New York: AMS Press, 1972), 3, 33–35.

38. Eva A. Jessye, *My Spirituals* (New York: Robbins-Engel, 1927), 1–2.

39. Recent decades have seen numerous studies devoted to nearly every aspect of what is now commonly called the Great Migration, including Alferdteen Harrison, ed., *Black Exodus: The Great Migration from the American South* (Jackson: University Press of Mississippi, 1991); Joe William Trotter, Jr., ed., *The Great Migration in Historical Perspective: New Dimensions of Race, Class, and Gender* (Bloomington: Indiana University Press, 1991); Ira Berlin, *The Making of African America: The Four Great Migrations* (New York: Viking, 2010); Isabel Wilkerson, *The Warmth of Other Suns: The Epic Story of America's Great Migration* (New York: Random House, 2010); Daniel M. Johnson and Rex R. Campbell, *Black Migration in America: A Social Demographic History* (Durham: Duke University Press, 1981); and Milton C. Sernett,

Bound for the Promised Land: African American Religion and the Great Migration (Durham: Duke University Press, 1997).

40. Adam Fairclough, *Better Day Coming: Blacks and Equality, 1890–2000* (New York: Viking, 2001), 89.

41. Vincent Gordon Harding, "The Afro-American Freedom Movement and the Changing Constitution," *Journal of American History* 74, no. 3 (1987): 726.

42. Johnson and Campbell, *Black Migration in America*, 80–83.

43. Wilkerson, *Warmth of Other Suns*, 10.

44. Trotter, *Great Migration*, 1–17.

45. Wilkerson, *Warmth of Other Suns*, 11.

46. Nell Irvin Painter in Trotter, *Great Migration*, ix–x.

47. James N. Gregory, *The Southern Diaspora: How the Great Migrations of Black and White Southerners Transformed America* (Chapel Hill: University of North Carolina Press, 2005), 204.

48. Wilkerson, *Warmth of Other Suns*, 528–29.

49. Much scholarship (encompassing entire small libraries) has been devoted to the history of the blues and jazz, just to name two of the musical forms that originated with and were popularized by African-Americans. See Lawrence Cohn, *Nothing but the Blues: The Music and the Musicians* (New York: Abbeville, 1993); Alan Lomax, *The Land Where the Blues Began* (New York: Pantheon, 1993); Ted Gioia, *The History of Jazz* (New York: Oxford University Press, 1997); Alyn Shipton, *A New History of Jazz* (London: Continuum, 2001), and many, many others.

50. Likewise, numerous scholars have examined all the facets of the Harlem Renaissance from various angles, including Aberjhani and Sandra L. West, *Encyclopedia of the Harlem Renaissance* (New York: Facts on File, 2003); Cary D. Wintz and Paul Finkelman, eds., *Encyclopedia of the Harlem Renaissance* (New York: Routledge, 2004); and Janet Witalec, project ed.,

Harlem Renaissance: A Gale Critical Companion (Detroit: Thomson Gale, 2003).

51. Richard Wright, *12 Million Black Voices* (1941; repr., New York: Thunder's Mouth Press, 2002).

52. For the various facets of the story of African-Americans and their slow acceptance in the labor union movement, see Robert H. Zieger, *For Jobs and Freedom: Race and Labor in America Since 1865* (Lexington: University Press of Kentucky, 2007); Paul D. Moreno, *Black Americans and Organized Labor* (Baton Rouge: Louisiana State University Press, 2006); and William H. Harris, *The Harder We Run: Black Workers Since the Civil War* (New York: Oxford University Press, 1982), among many others. For a closer look at the integration of the United Auto Workers, see David M. Lewis-Colman, *Race Against Liberalism: Black Workers and the UAW in Detroit* (Urbana: University of Illinois Press, 2008).

53. Johnson and Campbell, *Black Migration in America*, 83.

54. W. E. B. Du Bois, "The Black Man and the Unions," *Crisis* 15, no. 5 (1918): 216–17.

55. Gunnar Myrdal, with the assistance of Richard Sterner and Arnold Rose, *An American Dilemma: The Negro Problem and Modern Democracy*, vol. 2 (New York: Harper and Brothers, 1944), 787.

56. Ibid., 789–90.

Chapter 3

The epigraphs for this chapter are drawn from John Stuart, ed., *The Education of John Reed: Selected Writings* (New York: International, 1955), 180; John L. Lewis, president of the United Mine Workers of America and of the Congress of Industrial Organizations, in *Labor Songs*, ed. and comp. Zilphia

Horton (New York: Textile Workers Union of America, 1939), 4–5; and Aunt Molly Jackson, in Henrietta Yurchenco, "Trouble in the Mines: A History in Song and Story by Women of Appalachia," *American Music* 9, no. 2 (1991): 214.

1. David King Dunaway, "Music and Politics in the United States," *Folk Music Journal* 5, no. 3 (1987): 274.

2. Clark Halker, "Jesus Was a Carpenter: Labor Song-Poets, Labor Protest, and True Religion in Gilded Age America," *Labor History* 32, no. 2 (1991): 284.

3. Philip S. Foner, *American Labor Songs of the Nineteenth Century* (Urbana: University of Illinois Press, 1975), 145, 152, 154.

4. David A. Carter, "The Industrial Workers of the World and the Rhetoric of Song," *Quarterly Journal of Speech* 66, no. 4 (1980): 365.

5. Edith Fowke and Joe Glazer, *Songs of Work and Protest* (1960; repr., New York: Dover, 1973), 9.

6. Ibid., 11, 16.

7. Pete Seeger, *The Incompleat Folksinger*, ed. Jo Metcalf-Schwartz (New York: Simon and Schuster, 1972), 74–75.

8. Ronald D. Cohen, *Work and Sing: A History of Occupational and Labor Union Songs in the United States* (Crockett, CA: Carquinez Press, 2010), 4.

9. Archie Green, David Roediger, Franklin Rosemont, and Salvatore Salerno, eds., *The Big Red Songbook* (Chicago: Charles H. Kerr, 2007), 471–72.

10. Richard Brazier, "The Story of the IWW's 'Little Red Songbook,'" *Labor History* 9, no. 1 (1968): 91–92, 96.

11. Philip Dray, *There Is Power in a Union: The Epic Story of Labor in America* (New York: Doubleday, 2010), 349.

12. Brazier, "Story of the IWW's 'Songbook,'" 94, 99.

13. Green et al., *Big Red Songbook*, 478.

14. *IWW Songs: To Fan the Flames of Discontent; Facsimile Reprint of the*

Popular Nineteenth Edition, 1923 (Chicago: Charles H. Kerr, 1989). Songs cited: "John Golden and the Lawrence Strike," 15; "Dump the Bosses," 18; "All Hell Can't Stop Us," 18; "Solidarity Forever," 25; "Remember," 34; "Industrial Unionism Speaks to Toilers of the Sea," 35; "The Preacher and the Slave," 36; "Onward 'One Big Union!'" 48; "Count Your Workers—Count Them!" 49; "There Is Power in the Union," 60; "Harvest Land," 61.

15. *Songs of the Workers: To Fan the Flames of Discontent*, 34th ed. (Chicago: Industrial Workers of the World, 1973). Religion-based songs included "Solidarity Forever" (based on "John Brown's Body"); "There Is Power in a Union" ("There Is Power in the Blood"); "Hallelujah, I'm a Bum!" ("Revive Us Again"); "Christians at War" ("Onward Christian Soldiers"); "The Boss" ("Praise God from Whom All Blessings Flow"); "Dump the Bosses Off Your Back" ("Take It to the Lord in Prayer"); "Harvest Land" ("Beulah Land"); "Hold the Fort" ("Hold the Fort"); "Stand Up! Ye Workers" ("Stand Up, Stand Up for Jesus"); "All Hell Can't Stop Us" ("Hold the Fort"); "The Lumberjack's Prayer" ("Praise God from Whom All Blessings Flow"); "Out in the Breadline" ("Throw Out the Lifeline"); and "The Preacher and the Slave" ("In the Sweet Bye and Bye").

16. Joyce L. Kornbluh, ed., *Rebel Voices: An IWW Anthology* (1964; repr., Ann Arbor: University of Michigan Press, 1972), 71–72.

17. Penelope Niven, *Carl Sandburg: A Biography* (New York: Charles Scribner's Sons, 1991), 336–40, 444–45.

18. Carl Sandburg, *The American Songbag* (New York: Harcourt Brace Jovanovich, 1927). In addition to "Hallelujah, I'm a Bum," *American Songbag*'s "labor anthems" include "John Henry," "Tramp, Tramp, Tramp," "The Dying Hogger," "ARU (American Railway Union)," and "Ever Since Uncle John

Henry Been Dead." The section titled "Road to Heaven" contains sixteen African-American sacred songs, all but a few genuine spirituals: "Jesus, Won't You Come B'm-By," "Dese Bones Gwine to Rise Again," "Two White Horses," "Way Over in the New Buryin' Groun'," "Mary Wore Three Links of Chain," "Pharaoh's Army Got Drownded," "Good-bye Brother," "God's Goin' to Set This World on Fire," "Ain' Go'n to Study War No Mo'," "Things I Used to Do," "In My Father's House," "Standin' on the Walls of Zion," "A Hundred Years Ago," "You Got to Cross It for Yourself," "I Got a Letter from Jesus," "Ezekiel, You and Me." Six additional spirituals were scattered throughout the collection: "Man Goin' Roun'," "All Night Long," "Zek'l Weep," "By'm By," and "I Know Moonlight."

19. Ibid., 478–79.

20. Ibid., 479.

21. Ibid., 478–79.

22. Kornbluh, *Rebel Voices*, 105–7.

23. Carter, "Industrial Workers of the World," 372.

24. Kornbluh, *Rebel Voices*, 132–33.

25. Dray, *Power in a Union*, 349–50.

26. Lawrence J. Epstein, *Political Folk Music in America from Its Origins to Bob Dylan* (Jefferson, NC: McFarland, 2010), 30.

27. Archie Green, *Wobblies, Pile Butts, and Other Heroes: Laborlore Explorations* (Urbana: University of Illinois Press, 1993), 92.

28. Green et al., *Big Red Songbook*, 13. Green's compilation confirms that there are numerous IWW songs through the decades set the tunes of "Hold the Fort," "John Brown's Body," and "Glory Hallelujah." Some of the songs collected by Green and his associates *not* mentioned in the earlier two collections: "Coffee An'" (set the melody of "Count Your Blessings"); "Stung Right" ("Sunlight, Sunlight"); "Nearer My Job to Thee" ("Nearer My God to Thee"); "From Slavery to Freedom" ("How

Firm a Foundation"); "The Ninety and the Nine" ("The Ninety and the Nine"); "Christians at War" ("Onward Christian Soldiers"); "Dump the Bosses Off Your Back" ("Take It to the Lord in Prayer"); "Joe Hill's Last Will" ("Abide With Me"); "Onward, One Big Union" ("Onward Christian Soldiers"); "Industrial Unionism Speaks to Toilers of the Sea" ("Sunlight, Sunlight"); "The Workers Funeral Hymn" ("Abide with Me"); "November" ("Love Divine"); "The Lumberjack's Prayer" ("Praise God from Whom All Blessings Flow"); and "The Boss" ("Praise God from Whom All Blessings Flow"). Songs with lyrics cited are on the following pages: 108, 119, 127, 149, 167, 168–69, 177, 179, 208–9, 215–16, 255, 256, 266, 267.

29. Green et al., *Big Red Songbook*, 189.

30. James Jones, *From Here to Eternity* (New York: Charles Scribner's Sons, 1951), 640.

31. Ray Stannard Baker, "The Revolutionary Strike," *American Magazine*, May 1912, 25–26.

32. Kornbluh, *Rebel Voices*, 158.

33. Baker, "Revolutionary Strike," 30A.

34. Russell Ames, *The Story of American Folk Song* (New York: Grosset and Dunlap, 1955), 166–67.

35. Green et al., *Big Red Songbook*, 109–10.

36. Cohen, *Work and Sing*, 76–77.

37. Lawrence Gellert, "Negro Songs of Protest," *New Masses*, January 1931, 17.

38. Lawrence Gellert, "Negro Songs of Protest," *New Masses*, April 1931, 6.

39. Gellert, *Negro Songs of Protest*, 46–47.

40. Steven Garabedian, "Reds, Whites, and the Blues: Lawrence Gellert, 'Negro Songs of Protest,' and the Left-Wing Folk-Song Revival of the 1930s and 1940s," *American Quarterly* 57, no. 1 (2005): 182. It is difficult to determine how much influence either the Composers' Collective or the Gellert collections had on the use and expansion of black sacred music as a vehicle for social protest. Richard A. Reuss writes that when Gellert's collection

was published in 1936, "the songs enjoyed a tremendous vogue among human rights supporters," and that Gellert believed "the songs he collected contributed in important ways to the Communist Party's belief in the revolutionary ardor of southern blacks." Richard A. Reuss and JoAnne C. Reuss, *American Folk Music and Left-Wing Politics, 1927–1957* (Lanham, MD: Scarecrow Press, 2000), 97. The Collective disbanded in 1936. Garabedian has argued forcefully for Gellert's place alongside Alan Lomax as an important, if now overlooked, archivist. See "Reds, Whites, and the Blues," 99–203.

The controversial Gellert was a white man with a passion for African-American protest music. His collection *Negro Songs of Protest* featured startlingly provocative words and music, but virtually no references or performers were listed. While many of the songs may actually be antireligious (including "Preacher's Belly" and "Sistren an' Brethren"), at least two of the twenty-four songs included in the project were probably based on spirituals, "Preacher's Belly" and "How Long, Brethren?": "How long, brethren, how long, / Mus' mah people weep an' mourn? / Too long, too long, brethren, too long" (16–17). Garabedian connects "How Long, Brethren" with "My Father, How Long?" from *Slave Songs of the United States*, and identifies it even then as a protest song ("Reds, Whites, and the Blues," 194–95). Allen, Ware, and Garrison's *Slave Songs* includes the following annotation to that effect: for singing this song, "the negroes had been put in jail in Georgetown, S.C., at the outbreak of the Rebellion. 'We'll soon be free' was too dangerous an assertion; and though the chant was an old one, it was no doubt sung with redoubled emphasis during the new events" (93).

Gellert traveled at his own expense through North Carolina,

South Carolina, and Georgia and collected more than three hundred songs. He worked diligently to see them both published and recorded. His field recordings have been reissued sporadically by Rounder and Document Records and include, amid the forceful protest songs, a number of spirituals, including "Mary Don't You Weep," "Heaven Is a Beautiful Place," "We're Going to Break Bread Together on Our Knees," and "Run Sinner and Hide Your Face (Run, Sinner, Run)." See *Negro Songs of Protest*; *Cap'n You're So Mean: Negro Songs of Protest, Volume 2* (Rounder Records, Rounder 4013, 1982); various artists, *Nobody Knows My Name: Blues from South Carolina and Georgia* (Document Records, DOCD 5599, 1984, reissued 1998); various artists, *Field Recordings, Vol. 9: Georgia, North Carolina, South Carolina, Virginia, Kentucky* (Document Records, DOCD 5599, 1998). Gellert mysteriously disappeared in 1979. See Garabedian, "Reds, Whites, and the Blues," 206.

41. Dray, *Power in a Union*, 160–63.

42. Nelson Lichtenstein, *State of the Union: A Century of American Labor* (Princeton: Princeton University Press, 2002), 40.

43. Dray, *Power in a Union*, 442–45.

44. R. Serge Denisoff, "Protest Movements: Class Consciousness and the Propaganda Song," *Sociological Quarterly* 9, no. 2 (1968): 232.

45. Lichtenstein, *State of the Union*, 147–48.

46. Michael Denning, "The Age of the CIO," in *American Studies: An Anthology*, ed. Janice A. Radway, Kevin K. Gaines, Barry Shank, and Penny Von Eschen (Chichester: Wiley-Blackwell, 2009), 166–67, 181–87.

47. Lichtenstein, *State of the Union*, 79.

48. Robin D. G. Kelley, *Race Rebels: Culture, Politics, and the Black Working Class* (New York: Free Press, 1996), 402.

49. Fowke and Glazer, *Songs of Work*, 72–73, 38–39.

50. George Korson, *Coal Dust on the Fiddle: Songs and Stories of the Bituminous Industry* (Philadelphia: University of Pennsylvania Press, 1943), 285–87, 295.

51. For "Dis What de Union Done," see ibid., 301–2; for "I Can Tell de World," 305–6; for "No Unions Down Yonder," 313–14.

52. Angus K. Gillespie, *Folklorist of the Coal Fields: George Korson's Life and Work* (University Park: Pennsylvania State University Press, 1980), 157.

53. Dave Wilson, "Record Review: Songs and Ballads of the Bituminous Miners," *The Broadside*, March 2, 1966, cited in ibid., 163.

54. Archie Green, *Only a Miner: Studies in Recorded Coal-Mining Songs* (Urbana: University of Illinois Press, 1972), 418.

55. "Kentucky Miner's Song (Written and Sung by the Kentucky Strike Executive Committee in Tazewell Jail)," *Daily Worker*, April 2, 1932, 4.

56. Alan Lomax, Woody Guthrie, and Pete Seeger, *Hard Hitting Songs for Hard-Hit People* (New York: Oak, 1967), 283.

57. Yurchenco, "Trouble in the Mines," 214–15.

58. R. Serge Denisoff, *Great Day Coming: Folk Music and the American Left* (Urbana: University of Illinois Press, 1971), 24.

59. John Greenway, "A Great Rebel Passes On," *Sing Out!*, December–January 1960–61, 31–32.

60. Julia S. Ardery, *Welcome the Traveler Home: Jim Garland's Story of the Kentucky Mountains* (Lexington: University Press of Kentucky, 1983), 23–24, 159–61.

61. Reuss and Reuss, *American Folk Music*, 104–5.

62. Pete Seeger and Bob Reiser, *Everybody Says Freedom: A History of the Civil Rights Movement in Songs and Pictures* (New York: Norton, 1989), 152–53.

63. Pete Seeger, *The Incompleat Folksinger* (1972; repr., Lincoln: University of Nebraska Press, 1992), 76. Among the titles he lists in *The Incompleat*

Folksinger are "We Shall Not Be Moved" (originally "Jesus Is My Captain, I Shall Not Be Moved"), "It's That Union Train A-Coming" (originally "The Old Ship of Zion"), and "Roll the Union On" (originally "Roll the Chariot Along").

64. Lomax, Guthrie, and Seeger, *Hard Hitting Songs for Hard-Hit People*, 272.

65. Foner, *American Labor Songs*, 212, 213.

66. "New Defense Song Gains Wide Popularity in South," *Daily Worker*, November 7, 1933, 5.

67. Harold Preece, "Folk Music of the South," *New South*, March 1938, 13–14.

68. Brenda McCallum, "Songs of Work and Songs of Worship: Sanctifying Black Unionism in the Southern City of Steel," *New York Folklore* 14, nos. 1–2 (1988): 9, 12–14, 18.

69. Herbert R. Northrup, "The Negro and Unionism in the Birmingham, Ala., Iron and Steel Industry," *Southern Economic Journal* 10, no. 1 (1943): 34–35.

70. McCallum, "Songs of Work," 20.

71. Korson, *Coal Dust*, 306.

72. Ibid., 309.

73. Doug Seroff, "On the Battlefield: Gospel Quartets in Jefferson County, Alabama," in *Repercussions: A Celebration of African-American Music*, ed. Geoffrey Haydon and Dennis Marks (London: Century, 1985), 46.

74. McCallum, "Songs of Work," 25–27.

75. Ibid., 27–28.

76. Lawrence Gellert, "Negro Songs of Protest," *New Masses*, May 1933, 15.

77. Scott Reynolds Nelson, *Steel Drivin' Man: John Henry, the Untold Story of an American Legend* (New York: Oxford University Press, 2008), 88–89, 103, 137, 140–41, 150–51, 158–59.

78. Ibid., 2, 124–25.

79. Green, *Wobblies, Pile Butts, and Other Heroes*, 52.

80. Lee Collier, "Portrait of a New Southerner: The Land of Cotton Is Ringing to Songs of Negro and White Unity and People's Dixie," *Daily Worker*, May 11, 1938, 7.

81. Ibid.

82. Michael Honey, "Industrial Unionism and Racial Justice in Memphis," in *Organized Labor in the Twentieth-Century South*, ed. Robert H. Zieger (Knoxville: University of Tennessee Press, 1991), 140–41.

83. Lucy Randolph Mason, *To Win These Rights: A Personal Story of the CIO in the South* (Westport, CT: Greenwood, 1952), 108.

84. Rose Bradley, "41–42–43!," *Labor Defender*, December 1933, 80.

85. Korson, *Coal Dust*, 315.

86. Richard Frank, "Negro Revolutionary Music," *New Masses*, May 15, 1934, 29.

87. Ibid., 29–30.

88. Ibid., 30.

89. *Richmond Planet*, cited in Richard Love, "In Defiance of Custom and Tradition: Black Tobacco Workers and Labor Unions in Richmond, Virginia, 1937–1941," *Labor History* 35, no. 1 (1994): 30.

90. Ibid., 30–31.

91. Grace Lumpkin, "A Southern Cotton Mill Rhyme," *New Masses*, May 1930, 8.

92. Stephen R. Wiley, "Songs of the Gastonia Textile Strike of 1929: Models of and for Southern Working-Class Women's Militancy," *North Carolina Folklore Journal* 30 (Fall–Winter 1982): 88–89.

93. Doug DeNatale and Glenn Hinson, "The Southern Textile Song Tradition Reconsidered," *Journal of Folklore Research* 29, nos. 2–3 (1991): 105–6.

94. Richard Randall, "Fighting Songs of the Unemployed: The Traditions of Walt Whitman and Joe Hill Live Again in 1939," *Sunday Worker/Progressive Weekly*, September 3, 1939, 2.

95. Liston Pope, *Millhands and Preachers: A Study of Gastonia* (New Haven: Yale University Press, 1942), 262–63.

96. Fred E. Beal, *Proletarian Journey: New England, Gastonia, Moscow* (1937; repr., New York: Da Capo, 1971), 159.

97. Lomax, Guthrie, and Seeger, *Hard Hitting Songs*, 186.

98. Beal, *Proletarian Journey*, 131–32.

99. Ibid., 134–35.

100. Mary Heaton Vorse, *Strike!* intro. Dee Garrison (1930; repr., Urbana: University of Illinois Press, 1991), xxi, 108.

101. DeNatale and Hinson, "Southern Textile Song Tradition," 108–14.

102. Margaret Larkin, "Ella May's Songs," *The Nation*, October 9, 1929, 382–83.

103. Margaret Larkin, "The Story of Ella May," *New Masses*, November 1929, 3–4.

104. Terese M. Volk, "Little Red Songbooks: Songs for the Labor Force of America," *Journal of Research in Music Education* 49, no. 1 (2001): 33–35.

105. Lee Hays, "'Let the Will . . .': The Deep South Is Using Its Old Hymns to Aid Farm-Worker Unionization. Here Are a Few Examples," *New Masses*, August 1, 1939, 15.

106. Denisoff, *Great Day Coming*, 28–29.

107. Hays, "Let the Will," 15.

108. Doris Willens, *Lonesome Traveler: The Life of Lee Hays* (New York: Norton, 1988), 53.

109. Ibid, 52–57.

110. Denisoff, *Great Day Coming*, 29, 82.

111. Mark Naison, "Claude and Joyce Williams: Pilgrims of Justice," *Southern Exposure* 1, nos. 3–4 (1974): 47–48.

112. Tom Tippett, *When Southern Labor Stirs* (New York: Jonathan Cape and Harrison Smith, 1931), 120–21, 124, 232–33, 246, 250.

113. Cohen, *Work and Sing*, 91.

114. Denisoff, *Great Day Coming*, 32.

115. H. L. Mitchell, *The Reminiscences of H. L. Mitchell* (Oral History Research Office, Columbia University, New York, 1957), 70.

116. Howard Kester, *Revolt Among the Sharecroppers* (1936; repr., New York: Arno Press and the *New York Times*, 1969), 78–79.

117. Denisoff, *Great Day Coming*, 35–36.

118. Fowke and Glazer, *Songs of Work*, 45.

119. Jerry Silverman, *Songs of Protest and Civil Rights* (New York: Chelsea House, 1992), 60.

120. Denisoff, *Great Day Coming*, 36–37.

121. Lomax, Guthrie, and Seeger, *Hard Hitting Songs*, 262–63, 265.

122. Ibid., 348–49.

123. Robert S. Koppelman, ed., *"Sing Out, Warning! Sing Out, Love!": The Writings of Lee Hays* (Amherst: University of Massachusetts Press, 2003), 5.

124. "'He's Goin' Free!' Cry Detroit Workers in New Song About Jas. Victory," *Daily Worker*, June 30, 1934, 7.

125. Denisoff, *Great Day Coming*, 50–51.

126. Timothy P. Lynch, *Strike Songs of the Depression* (Jackson: University Press of Mississippi, 2001), 85–86.

127. Mary Heaton Vorse, "Soldiers Everywhere in Flint; Unionists Hold the Fort," in *Rebel Pen: The Writings of Mary Heaton Vorse*, ed. Dee Garrison (New York: Monthly Review Press, 1985), 179.

128. Mary Heaton Vorse, "Women Stand by Their Men," in Garrison, *Rebel Pen*, 176.

129. Randall, "Fighting Songs," 2.

130. Lomax, Guthrie, and Seeger, *Hard Hitting Songs*, 314.

131. See Cedric Belfrage, "Cotton-Patch Moses," *Harper's Magazine*, November 1948, 94–103, and Louis Cantor, *A Prologue to the Protest Movement: The Missouri Sharecropper Roadside Demonstration of 1939* (Durham: Duke University Press, 1969), 80. This little-known sit-down demonstration is not widely recorded, although the Whitfields were eventually invited to the White House, and some relief for the nation's sharecroppers was proposed and enacted. Englishman Cedric Belfrage's account of the strike, "Cotton-Patch Moses," mentions several "hymns" and other religious songs being "vigorously" sung (to the accompaniment of banjos and violins) throughout the yearlong protest, including Isaac Watts's hymn "I Love the Lord." Belfrage also repeats a portion of one of Whitfield's sermons in the days before the sharecroppers, many of whom had been evicted, left for the impromptu highway camps: "'And Moses,' he intoned with sonorous gravity, 'got 'em to the Red Sea and they

made camp there. But here came old boss Pharaoh's ridin' bosses in their chariots. And Moses raised his hand, and the waters parted, and the children of Israel walked across on dry land. . . . We're gonna make an exodus likewise! It's history repeatin' itself in 1939!'" The reappearance of the connection between the Moses/Exodus stories and the ongoing freedom struggle of African-Americans gives further indication of the depth of that motif in the civil rights movement.

According to Cantor's *Prologue*, the *St. Louis Post-Dispatch* reported that one pastor preached at least one sermon saying that just as the Lord took care of Daniel in the lion's den, so would the Lord take care of the strikers. Hymns "were always sung following every service," and "On Jordan's Stormy Banks I Stand" was often heard in the irregular camps, late into the evenings (80). As the title of his book suggests, Cantor writes that there are direct correlations to be drawn from the Bootheel sharecropper demonstrations to the civil rights movement, now just fifteen years away.

132. Kelley, *Race Rebels*, 117–18.
133. Mike Gold, "The Negro Reds of Chicago," *Daily Worker*, September 30, 1932, 4.
134. Kelley, *Race Rebels*, 116–17, 119–20.
135. Joe Glazer, *Labor's Troubadour* (Urbana: University of Illinois Press, 2001), 30, 31, 33, 35.
136. Reuss and Reuss, *American Folk Music*, 95.

Chapter 4

The epigraphs for this chapter are drawn from Woody Guthrie, "America Singing: Author of 'Bound for Glory' Recalls What the Plain People Sing," *New York Times*, April 4, 1943, X7; John Steinbeck, from the foreword to Lomax, Guthrie, and Seeger, *Hard*

Hitting Songs, 8; and F. Brown, quoted by George Charney in *A Long Journey* (Chicago: Quadrangle, 1969), 51.

1. Gregory, *Southern Diaspora*, 239–45.
2. As mentioned in the previous chapter, almost at the same time as the emergence of gospel, one of the most volatile events of the era occurred near Scottsboro, Alabama, in 1931, when nine young African-Americans were arrested for raping two white girls on a freight train. Despite overwhelming evidence to the contrary and a lack of representation, eight of the "Scottsboro Nine" were convicted and sentenced to death. A public outcry followed and International Labor Defense desperately sought a meeting with President Franklin Roosevelt. When the Supreme Court overturned the tainted verdict, another jury convicted them again. On December 1, 1931, Langston Hughes wrote a ferocious essay on the topic:

> Daily, I watch the guards washing their hands. The world remembers for a long time a certain washing of hands. The world remembers for a long time a certain humble One born in a manger—straw, manure, and the feet of animals— standing before Power washing its hands. No proven crime. Farce of a trial. Lies. Laughter. Mob. Hundreds of years later Brown America sang: *My Lord! What a morning when the stars began to fall!*
>
> For eight brown boys in Alabama the stars have fallen. In the death house, I heard no song at all. Only a silence more ominous than song. All of Brown America locked up there. And no song.

There were more public expressions of support as well. The Apollo Theater hosted a concert benefiting the Scottsboro Boys on August 20, 1937. The show featured Blanche Calloway (Cab Calloway's talented sister) and her revue, master drummer Chick Webb and his orchestra with Ella Fitzgerald on vocals, and four of the Scottsboro Boys, who were still out on bail. The blatant injustice of the incident and events that followed helped spur African-Americans to political activism. See Nancy J. Weiss, *Farewell to the Party of Lincoln: Black Politics in the Age of FDR* (Princeton: Princeton University Press, 1983), 42; Langston Hughes, *Good Morning Revolution: Uncollected Social Protest Writings by Langston Hughes*, ed. Faith Berry (New York: Lawrence Hill, 1973), 51; and Richard Carlin and Kinshasha Holman Conwill, eds., *Ain't Nothing Like the Real Thing: How the Apollo Theater Shaped American Entertainment* (Washington, DC: Smithsonian Books, 2010), 170.

3. Guido Van Rijn, *Roosevelt's Blues: African-American Blues and Gospel Songs on FDR* (Jackson: University Press of Mississippi, 1997), 33.

4. Weiss, *Farewell to the Party of Lincoln*, 41.

5. "Sings for the President," *Chicago Defender*, June 10, 1933, 9.

6. "At the White House," *The Crisis*, July 1933, 160–61.

7. Anthony Heilbut, *The Gospel Sound: Good News and Bad Times* (1971; repr., New York: Limelight Editions, 1989), 76.

8. Seymour Martin Lipset, *Political Man: The Social Bases of Politics* (1959; repr., Baltimore: Johns Hopkins University Press, 1981), 296.

9. Weiss, *Farewell to the Party of Lincoln*, 42.

10. Arthur Raper, *Tenants of the Almighty* (1943; repr., New York: Arno Press and the *New York Times*, 1971), 376.

11. Darden, *People Get Ready*, 164–84. To date, the only significant biography of Thomas A. Dorsey is Michael W. Harris's excellent *The Rise of the Gospel Blues: The Music of Thomas Andrew Dorsey in the Urban Church* (New York: Oxford University Press, 1992).

12. Floyd, *Power of Black Music*, 63.

13. Jackson, *Singing in My Soul*, 51.

14. Guthrie P. Ramsey, Jr., *Race Music: Black Cultures from Bebop to Hip-Hop* (Berkeley: University of California Press, 2003), 121.

15. Jackson, *Singing in My Soul*, 51.

16. Joop Visser, liner notes for *Sister Rosetta Tharpe: The Original Soul Sister* (Proper Box, 51, four-CD set, 2002), 28.

17. Laurraine Goreau, *Just Mahalia, Baby* (Waco, TX: Word, 1975), 61–62.

18. See Black Americans in Congress, http://history.house.gov/people/listing/D/Dawson,-William-Levi-(d000158)/.

19. Goreau, *Just Mahalia, Baby*, 61–62.

20. Terry Teachout, *Pops: A Life of Louis Armstrong* (Boston: Mariner, 2009), 224–25.

21. William Barlow, *Voice Over: The Making of Black Radio* (Philadelphia: Temple University Press, 1999), 33–34.

22. Jonathan Kamin, "The White R&B Audience and the Music Industry, 1952–1956," *Popular Music and Society* 6, no. 2 (1978): 151.

23. Jannette L. Dates and William Barlow, eds., *Split Image: African Americans in the Mass Media*, 2nd ed. (Washington, DC: Howard University Press, 1993), 50.

24. David Riesman, "Listening to Popular Music," in *Mass Culture*, ed. Bernard Rosenberg and David Manning White (Glencoe, IL: Free Press, 1957), 415.

25. Steve Buckingham, liner notes to *From Spirituals to Swing: The Legendary 1938 and 1939 Carnegie Hall Concerts Produced by John Hammond* (Vanguard Records, 169/71-2, three-CD set, 1999), 1–3.

26. Bob Riesman, *I Feel So Good: The Life and Times of Big Bill Broonzy* (Chicago: University of Chicago Press, 2011), 92–93.

27. Buckingham, *From Spirituals to Swing* liner notes, 28–42.

28. Ibid., 1–3.

29. Studs Terkel, *And They All Sang: Adventures of an Eclectic Disc Jockey* (New York: New Press, 2005), 174.

30. Barney Josephson, with Terry Trilling-Josephson, *Café Society: The Wrong Place for the Right People* (Urbana: University of Illinois Press, 2009), 66–72.

31. Jay Warner, *The Billboard Book of American Singing Groups: A History, 1940–1990* (New York: Billboard, 1992), 35–37.

32. Josephson, *Café Society*, 48–49.

33. Allan Keiler's fine biography, *Marian Anderson: A Singer's Journey* (New York: Scribner, 2000), remains the best work on this brilliant singer. Also still available is Anderson's own *My Lord, What a Morning: An Autobiography of Marian Anderson* (New York: Viking, 1956). Most recently, Raymond Arsenault's *The Sound of Freedom: Marian Anderson, the Lincoln Memorial, and the Concert That Awakened America* (New York: Bloomsbury, 2009) has worked to reemphasize the importance of Anderson's famed concert.

34. Keiler, *Marian Anderson*, 116–17.

35. Anderson, *My Lord, What a Morning*, 188–192.

36. Mark Robert Schneider, *"We Return Fighting": The Civil Rights Movement in the Jazz Age* (Boston: Northeastern University Press, 2002), 284.

37. "Anderson Affair," *Time*, April 17, 1939, 23.

38. Anderson, *My Lord, What a Morning*, 191.

39. Arsenault, *Sound of Freedom*, 185.

40. Richard Harrington, "Facing the Music: Singing to Change the World," *Washington Post*, September 15, 2000, weekend, N40.

41. Lauren Rebecca Sklaroff, *Black Culture and the New Deal: The Quest for Civil Rights in the Roosevelt Era* (Chapel Hill: University of North Carolina Press, 2009), 15–16.

42. Harrington, "Facing the Music," N40.

43. Scott A. Sandage, "A Marble House Divided: The Lincoln Memorial, the Civil Rights Movement, and the Politics of Memory, 1939–1963," *Journal of American History* 80, no. 1 (1993): 136.

44. Several fine biographies of Robeson are available, including Martin Bauml Duberman, *Paul Robeson* (New York: Knopf, 1988); Jeffrey C. Stewart, ed., *Paul Robeson: Artist and Citizen* (New Brunswick: Rutgers University Press, 1998); Sheila Tully Boyle and Andrew Bunie, *Paul Robeson: The Years of Promise and Achievement* (Amherst: University of Massachusetts Press, 2001); and Paul Robeson, Jr., *The Undiscovered Paul Robeson: An Artist's Journey, 1898–1939* (New York: Wiley, 2001).

45. Undated *New York Times* review, cited by the editors of *Freedomways* in *Paul Robeson: The Great Forerunner* (New York: Dodd, Mead, 1978), 5.

46. Ibid., 6–9.

47. John D'Emilio, *Lost Prophet: The Life and Times of Bayard Rustin* (New York: Free Press, 2003), 31–32.

48. Editors of *Freedomways*, *Paul Robeson*, 206.

49. Lynnette Goggans Geary, "The Career and Music of Jules Bledsoe" (master's thesis, Baylor University, 1982), 77.

50. Floyd, *Power of Black Music*, 171–72.

51. Ray Funk, "Historical Gospel: Wings over Jordan," *Rejoice!* 1, no. 2 (1988): 27, 29.

52. Floyd, *Power of Black Music*, 171–72.

53. Maurine H. Beasley, Holly C. Shulman, and Henry R. Beasley, eds., *The Eleanor Roosevelt Encyclopedia* (Westport, CT: Greenwood, 2001), 89–96. See also Lois Scharf, *Eleanor Roosevelt: First Lady of American Liberalism* (Boston: Twayne, 1987), and Tamara K. Hareven, *Eleanor Roosevelt: An American Conscience* (Chicago: Quadrangle, 1968).

54. Barbara Dianne Savage, *Broadcasting Freedom: Radio, War, and the Politics of Race, 1938–1948* (Chapel Hill: University of North Carolina Press, 1999), 78, 83–84.

55. Transcript of Stephen Smith, "Radio Fights Jim Crow,"

American RadioWorks, American Public Media, February 2001, http://americanradioworks.publicradio.org/features/jim_crow/transcript.html.

56. Savage, *Broadcasting Freedom*, 36–42.
57. Ibid., 72–75, 76, 78.
58. "Radio: For Native Sons," *Time*, September 29, 1941, 59.
59. Lloyd E. Trent, "Freedom's People," *New Masses*, October 7, 1941, 30–31.
60. Savage, *Broadcasting Freedom*, 88, 85, 89.
61. Michael Denning, *The Cultural Front: The Laboring of American Culture in the Twentieth Century* (London: Verso, 1996), 91.
62. Those in attendance included the "Secretaries of War, Navy, Treasury and wives, the Chief of Staff of the Army, the Commandants of the Marine Corps and Coast Guard, Librarian of Congress Archibald MacLeish," and others. The article also noted that the Golden Gate Quartet came to Washington, D.C., for the concert in a taxi—and that the round-trip journey cost the group $100. See "Folk Songs in the White House," *Time*, March 3, 1941, 61.
63. Savage, *Broadcasting Freedom*, 168–72, 331n53.
64. Michele Hilmes, *Radio Voices: American Broadcasting, 1922–1952* (Minneapolis: University of Minnesota Press, 1997), 263.
65. Smith, "Radio Fights Jim Crow."
66. "Folk Singers in Original Revue Tonight," *Daily Worker*, May 15, 1941, 7.
67. Don Russell, "Meet the Almanac Singers: They Sing Hard-Hitting Songs That Belong to the People," *Daily Worker*, August 14, 1941, 7.
68. R. Serge Denisoff, "'Take It Easy, but Take It': The Almanac Singers," *Journal of American Folklore* 83, no. 327 (1970): 22–23.
69. Russell, "Meet the Almanac Singers," 7.
70. Fowke and Glazer, *Songs of Work*, 24.
71. Gregory, *Southern Diaspora*, 218–19.
72. Lichtenstein, *State of the Union*, 80–81.
73. Gregory, *Southern Diaspora*, 220–21.

74. Phillip McGuire, "Desegregation of the Armed Forces: Black Leadership, Protest, and World War II," *Journal of Negro History* 68, no. 2 (1983): 147–48.
75. Harvard Sitkoff, "Racial Militancy and Interracial Violence in the Second World War," *Journal of American History* 58, no. 3 (1971): 667.
76. See, for instance, Christopher Paul Moore, *Fighting for America: Black Soldiers—The Unsung Heroes of World War II* (New York: Ballantine, 2005); A. Russell Buchanan, *Black Americans in World War II* (Santa Barbara, CA: Clio, 1977); Ulysses Lee, *The Employment of Negro Troops* (Washington, DC: Center of Military History, United States Army, 1963); and Maggi M. Morehouse, *Fighting in the Jim Crow Army: Black Men and Women Remember World War II* (Lanham, MD: Rowman and Littlefield, 2000). For intensely personal reporting on the treatment of African American soldiers both during and just after the war, see Lawrence Gellert, "Jim Crow in Khaki," *New Masses*, March 19, 1946, 12–13; and Stanley Crouch, "From Spirituals to Swing," *Village Voice*, December 4, 1984, 43–44.
77. Berlin, *Making of African America*, 185–86.
78. Lichtenstein, *State of the Union*, 81.
79. Bernice Reagon, "'Uncle Sam Called Me': World War II Reflected in Black Music," *Southern Exposure* 1, nos. 3–4 (1974): 170.
80. Ibid., 173.
81. Ibid., 175, 176.
82. Ibid., 184.
83. Charney, *Long Journey*, 193.
84. Roy Hoopes, *Americans Remember the Home Front: An Oral Narrative* (New York: Hawthorne, 1977), 368.
85. William H. Chafe, "The Civil Rights Revolution, 1945–1960: The Gods Bring Threads to Webs Begun," in *Reshaping America: Society and Institutions, 1945–1960*, ed. Robert H. Bremner and Gary W. Reichard (Columbus: Ohio State University Press, 1982), 71.

86. Ibid.
87. Rebecca de Schweinitz, *If We Could Change the World: Young People and America's Long Struggle for Racial Equality* (Chapel Hill: University of North Carolina Press, 2009), 303.
88. Chafe, "Civil Rights Revolution," 72–73.
89. Hoopes, *Americans Remember*, 373.
90. Lipset, *Political Man*, 398–99.
91. T. V. Reed, *The Art of Protest: Culture and Activism from the Civil Rights Movement to the Streets of Seattle* (Minneapolis: University of Minnesota Press, 2005), 11–13.
92. *People's Songs Bulletin*, February 1946, 1–2.
93. "Keep That Line A-Moving," *People's Songs*, March 1946, 5.
94. *Songs for Wallace, 2nd Edition* (New York: People's Songs, ca. 1948), 2–10.
95. Ibid., 6.
96. "We Will Overcome," *People's Songs*, September 1948, 8.
97. Musicologist James J. Fuld rightly notes that the music in Tindley's hymn does not match what "We Shall Overcome" eventually came to sound like. He instead points to the music printed in "I'll Overcome Someday," published May 1, 1945, by Martin and Morris Music Studio of Chicago. According to the sheet music, the lyrics are by Atron Twigg, with the revised lyrics and music by well-known gospel composer and publisher Kenneth Morris. Also claiming credit is Roberta Martin. Martin and Morris Studio of Music published "I'll Be Like Him Someday," written by Martin (under her pseudonym Faye E. Brown). According to Fuld, the music of the final twelve bars of the song "appears to be the source of the comparable part of 'We Shall Overcome.'" See Fuld, *The Book of World-Famous Music: Classical, Popular, and Folk* (1966; repr., New York: Crown, 1971), 623–27.
98. "We Will Overcome," *People's Songs*, September 1948, 8.
99. "Changes," *People's Songs*, November 1948, 10.
100. Reuss and Reuss, *American Folk Music*, 201.
101. Ibid., 203–6.
102. Cohen, *Work and Sing*, 129.
103. Mitch Potter, "Father Folk Boosts Gala at Massey; Seeger: Roots Man Cometh," *Toronto Star*, February 10, 1997, E1.
104. Wilson J. Warren, Bruce Fehn, and Marianne Robinson, "They Met at the Fair: UPWA and Farmer Labor Cooperation, 1944–1952," *Labor's Heritage: Quarterly of the George Meany Memorial Archives*, Fall 2000–Winter 2001, 24–28.
105. Transcript of "Black Radio: Sounding Black," program 6 of *Black Radio . . . Telling It Like It Was*, prod. Jacquie Gale Webb, Lex Gillespie, and Sonja Williams, host Lou Rawls (Washington, DC: Smithsonian Institution, 1996), 8.
106. Transcript of "Rappers and Rhymers," program 5 of *Black Radio*, 4.
107. "Disk Jockeys: 16 Sepia Spielers Ride Kilocycle Range on 21 Stations," *Ebony*, December 7, 1947, 44.
108. John L. Landes, "WLAC, the Hossman, and Their Influence on Black Gospel," *Black Music Research Journal* 7 (1987): 68–69.
109. Ibid., 72.
110. Transcript of "WDIA," program 4 of *Black Radio*, 2.
111. Louis Cantor, *Wheelin' on Beale: How WDIA-Memphis Became the Nation's First All-Black Radio Station and Created the Sound That Changed America* (New York: Pharos, 1992), 1.
112. Transcript of "WDIA," 20.
113. Kathy M. Newman, "The Forgotten Fifteen Million: Black Radio, the 'Negro Market,' and the Civil Rights Movement," *Radical History Review* 76 (2000): 115.
114. Brian Ward, *Radio and the Struggle for Civil Rights in the South* (Gainesville: University Press of Florida, 2005), 5.
115. Henry Allen Bullock, "Consumer Motivations in Black and White—II,"

Harvard Business Review 39, no. 4 (1961): 117–18.

116. Newman, "Forgotten Fifteen Million," 132.

117. Quoted in Ward, *Radio and the Struggle for Civil Rights in the South*, 5.

118. Susan J. Douglas, *Listening In: Radio and the American Imagination* (Minneapolis: University of Minnesota Press, 1999), 3.

119. Ibid., 221–22.

120. "White Fans Hyping R&B Platter Sales," *Billboard*, May 31, 1952, 20, 41.

121. Bob Rolontz and Joel Friedman, "Teen-Agers Demand Music with a Beat, Spur Rhythm-Blues," *Billboard*, April 24, 1954, 1.

122. Douglas, *Listening In*, 223.

123. Philip H. Ennis, *The Seventh Stream: The Emergence of Rocknroll in American Popular Music* (Hanover: Wesleyan University Press, 1992), 132–33.

124. Simon Frith, *Sound Effects: Youth, Leisure, and the Politics of Rock 'n' Roll* (New York: Pantheon, 1981), 216–17.

125. Hughson F. Mooney, "Just Before Rock: Pop Music, 1950–1953, Reconsidered," *Popular Music and Society* 3 (1974): 97.

126. Kamin, "White R&B Audience," 151–52.

127. John A. Jackson, *Big Beat Heat: Alan Freed and the Early Years of Rock and Roll* (New York: Schirmer, 1991), 95.

128. Michael Lyndon, *Boogie Lightning* (New York: Dial Press, 1974), 92, interview with Ralph Bass.

129. J. Fred MacDonald, *Don't Touch That Dial!: Radio Programming in American Life, 1920–1960* (Chicago: Nelson-Hall, 1980), 368–69.

130. Pete Daniel, *Lost Revolutions: The South in the 1950s* (Chapel Hill: University of North Carolina Press, 2000), 149–50.

131. Jackson, *Big Beat Heat*, 96.

132. Wes Smith, *The Pied Pipers of Rock 'n' Roll: Radio Deejays of the 50s and 60s* (Marietta, GA: Longstreet Press, 1989), 16–17.

133. John A. Jackson, *American Bandstand: Dick Clark and the Making of a Rock 'n' Roll Empire* (New York: Oxford University Press, 1997), 148, 205. On October 30, 1956, police in Houston forcefully ended a dance featuring Fats Domino at the City Auditorium when black and white teenagers began dancing together. The show had been billed as an "all-black affair" and African-Americans were given refunds. As the white teenagers were escorted from the auditorium, they broke into a spontaneous rendition of Domino's hit "Let the Good Times Roll." See Bettye Collier-Thomas and V. P. Franklin, *My Soul Is a Witness: A Chronology of the Civil Rights Era, 1954–1965* (New York: Henry Holt, 1999), 51.

134. Tom McCourt, "Bright Lights, Big City: A Brief History of Rhythm and Blues, 1945–1957," in *American Popular Music: Readings from the Popular Press*, vol. 2, *The Age of Rock*, ed. Timothy E. Scheurer (Bowling Green: Bowling Green University Popular Press, 1989), 55.

135. "R&B Cracking Racial Barriers in Southwest Where It's Bigger'n Ever," *Variety*, July 6, 1955, 43.

136. Jackson, *Singing in My Soul*, 2–3.

137. DoVeanna S. Fulton Minor, "'Come Through the Water, Come Through the Flood': Black Women's Gospel Practices and Social Critique," *Journal of Religion and Society* 13 (2011): 3–4.

138. Goreau, *Just Mahalia, Baby*, 111.

139. Heilbut, *Gospel Sound*, 58.

140. Goreau, *Just Mahalia, Baby*, 115–16.

141. Rick Koster, *Louisiana Music: A Journey from R&B to Zydeco, Jazz to Country, Blues to Gospel, Cajun Music to Swamp Pop to Carnival Music and Beyond* (Cambridge, MA: Da Capo, 2002), 272.

142. Studs Terkel, *Talking to Myself: A Memoir of My Times* (New York: Pantheon, 1977), 259–60.

143. Heilbut, *Gospel Sound*, 98.

144. Peter Guralnick, *Last Train to Memphis: The Rise of Elvis Presley* (Boston: Back Bay, 1994), 75.

145. Bernice Johnson Reagon, ed., *We'll Understand It Better By and By:*

Pioneering African American Gospel Composers (Washington, DC: Smithsonian Institution Press, 1992), 201.

146. Anthony Heilbut, "Secularization of Black Gospel Music," in *Folk Music and Modern Sound*, ed. William Ferris and Mary L. Hart (Jackson: University Press of Mississippi, 1982), 109.

147. Heilbut, *Gospel Sound*, 97–98.

148. Anthony Heilbut, prod., *How Sweet It Was: The Sights and Sounds of Gospel's Golden Age* (Shanachie Entertainment, SHANDVCD 6901, 2010), accompanying liner notes written by Heilbut, 10.

149. Anthony Heilbut, *The Fan Who Knew Too Much: Aretha Franklin, the Rise of the Soap Opera, Children of the Gospel Church, and Other Meditations* (New York: Knopf, 2012), 97.

150. Chris Smith, "Rev. W. Herbert Brewster," *Blues and Rhythm: The Gospel Truth* 34 (January 1988): 8.

151. Heilbut, 104–5.

152. Horace Clarence Boyer, *How Sweet the Sound: The Golden Age of Gospel* (Washington, DC: Elliott and Clark, 1995), 28–29.

153. Nicholas C. Cooper-Lewter and Henry H. Mitchell, *Soul Theology: The Heart of American Black Culture* (San Francisco: Harper and Row, 1986), 45.

154. Goreau, *Just Mahalia, Baby*, 122–23.

155. Ibid., 152–53, 176–77.

156. Ron Eyerman and Andrew Jamison, *Music and Social Movements: Mobilizing Traditions in the Twentieth Century* (Cambridge: Cambridge University Press, 1998), 96.

157. Marty Jezer, *The Dark Ages: Life in the United States, 1945–1960* (Boston: South End Press, 1982), 91, 179, 205.

158. Martha Biondi, *To Stand and Fight: The Struggle for Civil Rights in Postwar New York City* (Cambridge: Harvard University Press, 2003), 54–57.

159. Chafe, "The Civil Rights Revolution," 68.

160. Heilbut, production/liner notes to *How Sweet It Was*, 7–8.

161. Guido Van Rijn, "'Climbing the Mountain Top': African American Blues and Gospel Songs from the Civil Rights Years," in *Media, Culture, and the Modern African American Freedom Struggle*, ed. Brian Ward (Gainesville: University Press of Florida, 2001), 129.

162. Louis-Charles Harvey, "Black Gospel Music and Black Theology," *Journal of Religious Thought* 43, no. 2 (1986–87): 32–33.

163. Van Rijn, "Climbing the Mountain Top," 131.

164. Riesman, *I Feel So Good*, 157–163.

165. Jezer, *Dark Ages*, 297.

166. Jervis Anderson, *A. Philip Randolph: A Biographical Portrait* (New York: Harcourt Brace Jovanovich, 1973), 320.

167. Jon Panish, *The Color of Jazz: Race and Representation in Postwar American Culture* (Jackson: University of Mississippi Press, 1997), xviii.

168. Goreau, *Just Mahalia, Baby*, 176.

169. Adam Green, *Selling the Race: Culture, Community, and Black Chicago, 1940–1955* (Chicago: University of Chicago Press, 2011), 63–64.

170. Floyd, *Power of Black Music*, 161.

171. Reed, *Art of Protest*, 7–9.

172. Ibid., 9.

173. Michael J. Klarman, *Brown v. Board of Education and the Civil Rights Movement* (New York: Oxford University Press, 2007), 57. There are numerous studies on the history, ramifications, and implications of the case, including Robert J. Cottrol, Raymond T. Diamond, and Leland B. Ware, *Brown v. Board of Education: Caste, Culture, and the Constitution* (Lawrence: University Press of Kansas, 2003); Richard Kluger, *Simple Justice: The History of Brown v. Board of Education and Black America's Struggle for Equality* (New York: Knopf, 1976); and Mark Whitman, *Brown v. Board of Education: A Documentary History; Fiftieth Anniversary Edition* (Princeton: Markus Wiener, 1993). Klarman details dozens upon dozens of specific instances of racial violence,

backlash, resistance, and repressive, often unconstitutional activities by primarily white southern congressmen, state legislators, governors, mayors, city councils, school boards, the Ku Klux Klan, and individuals spawned by *Brown v. Board of Education.*

174. Jezer, *Dark Ages*, 299.

175. Klarman, *Brown v. Board of Education*, 221.

176. Robert F. Williams, "Can Negroes Afford to Be Pacifists?" *Liberation* 4 (September 1959): 44.

177. Arna Bontemps, "Why I Returned," *Harper's Magazine*, April 1965, 182.

Chapter 5

The epigraphs for this chapter are drawn from Saint Augustine, *Sermons on the Liturgical Seasons*, trans. Sister Mary Sarah Muldowney (New York: Catholic University of America Press, 1959), 361–62; folk singer Dave Van Ronk, quoted in Gene Santoro, *Highway 61 Revisited: The Tangled Roots of American Jazz, Blues, Rock, and Country Music* (Oxford: Oxford University Press, 2004); and Walker, *"Somebody's Calling My Name,"* 181. The quotation that closes this chapter is drawn from James Baldwin, "Of the Sorrow Songs: The Cross of Redemption," *Views on Black American Music* 2 (1984–85): 12.

1. Collier-Thomas and Franklin, *My Soul Is a Witness*, 36.

2. Goreau, *Just Mahalia, Baby*, 195.

3. Ibid., 204.

4. Aldon D. Morris, "A Retrospective on the Civil Rights Movement: Political and Intellectual Landmarks," *Annual Review of Sociology* 25 (1999): 521–52.

5. Among the fine histories of Highlander are Aimee Isgrig Horton, *The Highlander Folk School: A History of Its Major Programs, 1932–1962* (Brooklyn: Carlson, 1989); John M. Glen, *Highlander: No Ordinary School* (Knoxville:

University of Tennessee Press, 1996); Thomas Bledsoe, *Or We'll All Hang Separately: The Highlander Idea* (Boston: Beacon, 1969); and Myles Horton, with Judith Kohl and Herbert Kohl, *The Long Haul: An Autobiography* (New York: Doubleday, 1990).

6. Horton, *Highlander Folk School*, 121. In addition to John L. Lewis's quote "A singing army is a winning army, and a singing labor movement cannot be defeated," Zilphia Horton's *Labor Songs* contained sixty-one songs, eight of which Horton identified as "Union Hymns" and four she termed "Spirituals": "No More Mournin'," "Somebody Knockin' at Your Door," "Strange Things Happenin' in This Land," and "We Are Building a Strong Union" (7–8). However, while listed under "hymns," "We Shall Not Be Moved" is better considered as a spiritual.

7. Horton, *Long Haul*, 77, 158.

8. Ibid., 158–59.

9. Clayborne Carson, "To Walk in Dignity: The Montgomery Bus Boycott," *OAH Magazine of History* 19, no. 1 (2005): 13.

10. Reed, *Art of Protest*, 16.

11. Potter, "Father Folk Boosts Gala," E1.

12. Bremner and Reichard, *Reshaping America*, 90–91.

13. Martin Luther King, Sr., with Clayton Riley, *Daddy King: An Autobiography* (New York: William Morrow, 1980), 98–101, 127.

14. Coretta Scott King, *My Life with Martin Luther King, Jr.* (London: Hodder and Stoughton, 1970), 51.

15. See Stewart Burns, ed., *Daybreak of Freedom: The Montgomery Bus Boycott* (Chapel Hill: University of North Carolina Press, 1997); Martin Luther King, Jr., *Stride Toward Freedom: The Montgomery Story* (New York: Harper and Brothers, 1958); Jo Ann Gibson Robinson, *The Montgomery Bus Boycott and the Women Who Started It*, ed. and foreword by David J. Garrow (Knoxville: University of Tennessee Press, 1987); and Donnie Williams

with Wayne Greenhaw, *The Thunder of Angels: The Montgomery Bus Boycott and the People Who Broke the Back of Jim Crow* (Chicago: Lawrence Hill, 2006).

16. Carson, "To Walk in Dignity," 13.

17. Ibid., 14.

18. Jim Bishop, *The Days of Martin Luther King, Jr.* (New York: G. P. Putnam's Sons, 1971), 139.

19. Carson, "To Walk in Dignity," 13.

20. Wilson Fallin, Jr., *Uplifting the People: Three Centuries of Black Baptists in Alabama* (Tuscaloosa: University of Alabama Press, 2007), 196–97.

21. King, *My Life with Martin Luther King*, 131.

22. Williams and Greenhaw, *Thunder of Angels*, 82.

23. Abernathy, *And the Walls Came Tumbling Down*, 150–51.

24. Kirt H. Wilson, "Interpreting the Discursive Field of the Montgomery Bus Boycott: Martin Luther King, Jr.'s Holt Street Address," *Rhetoric and Public Affairs* 8, no. 2 (2005): 317.

25. Williams and Greenhaw, *Thunder of Angels*, 82.

26. King, *Stride Toward Freedom*, 61.

27. Bernice Johnson Reagon, "The Civil Rights Movement," in *African American Music: An Introduction*, ed. Mellonee V. Burnim and Portia K. Maultsby (New York: Routledge, 2006), 600.

28. Williams and Greenhaw, *Thunder of Angels*, 83.

29. Abernathy, *And the Walls Came Tumbling Down*, 153.

30. Joe Azbell, quoted in Burns, *Daybreak of Freedom*, 89–92.

31. Williams and Greenhaw, *Thunder of Angels*, 109.

32. Russell Freedman, *Freedom Walkers: The Story of the Montgomery Bus Boycott* (New York: Holiday House, 2006), 45.

33. King, *Stride Toward Freedom*, 86.

34. James H. Cone, "Martin Luther King, Jr., Black Theology, Black Church," in *Martin Luther King, Jr.:*

Civil Rights Leader, Theologian, Orator, 3 vols., ed. David J. Garrow (Brooklyn: Carlson, 1989), 1:213.

35. Hortense J. Spillers, "Martin Luther King and the Style of the Black Sermon," in Garrow, *Martin Luther King*, 3:877.

36. Henry Hampton and Steve Fayer, with Sarah Flynn, *Voices of Freedom: An Oral History of the Civil Rights Movement from the 1950s through the 1980s* (New York: Bantam, 1990), 30.

37. Movement veteran Walter Fauntroy once said that one important aspect of King's leadership was that he led African Americans to take their protests to the streets of the United States to the tune of "Onward Christian Soldiers," with the marching of their feet as the musical accompaniment: "And they marched until the patter of their feet became the thunder of the marching men of Joshua, and the world rocked beneath their tread. . . . And so, the decades of the sixties, I think, will go down as a classic example of the church of God 'marching as to war, with the cross of Jesus marching on before.'" Walter Fauntroy address, "The Social Action Mission of the Church," taped at Duke University Divinity School, November 22, 1981. Cited in Jon Michael Spencer, *Re-Searching Black Music* (Knoxville: University of Tennessee Press, 1996), 27.

38. Reagon, "Civil Rights Movement," 600–601.

39. Seeger, *The Incompleat Folksinger* (1992), 171–72.

40. King, *My Life with Martin Luther King*, 142–43.

41. Howell Raines, *My Soul Is Rested: Movement Days in the Deep South Remembered* (New York: G. P. Putnam's Sons, 1977), 53–54.

42. Bayard Rustin, "Montgomery Diary," *Liberation* 1, no. 2 (1956): 8.

43. Alfred Maund, "We Will All Stand Together," *The Nation*, March 3, 1956, 168.

44. Pete Seeger, quoted in *Refuse to Stand Silently By: An Oral History of Grass Roots Social Activism in America, 1921–64*, ed. Eliot Wigginton (New York: Doubleday, 1991), 275–76.

45. Robinson, *Montgomery Bus Boycott*, 155, 157.

46. John A. Salmond, *"My Mind Set on Freedom": A History of the Civil Rights Movement, 1954–1968* (Chicago: Ivan R. Dee, 1997), 60.

47. Wayne Philips, "Negroes Pledge to Keep Boycott," *New York Times*, February 24, 1956, 8.

48. Bernice Johnson Reagon, "Songs That Moved the Movement," *Perspectives: The Civil Rights Quarterly* 15, no. 3 (1983): 28.

49. Various artists, *Sing for Freedom: The Story of the Civil Rights Movement Through Its Songs*, prod. Guy Carawan (Smithsonian Folkways, SF 40032, 1992), liner notes by Guy Carawan.

50. Burns, *Daybreak of Freedom*, 172–74.

51. Ibid., 196–99.

52. Ibid., 212–19.

53. King, *My Life with Martin Luther King*, 150.

54. Harry Belafonte with Michael Shnayerson, *My Song: A Memoir* (New York: Knopf, 2011), 148–50. Belafonte and King first met in 1953. In an interview with *The Guardian*, Belafonte said, "We talked for four hours—it was a life-changing moment. From then on, I was in his service and in his world of planning, strategy and thinking. We became very close immediately." This is significant because Wyatt Tee Walker believes that Belafonte contributed more money to the civil rights movement than any other entertainer. See Steve Howell, "'I Chose to Be a Civil Rights Warrior': Harry Belafonte Enraged Rightwingers When He Branded Bush 'the World's Greatest Terrorist.' But That's Nothing New for Him," *The Guardian*, March 14, 2007, 15; Spencer, *Protest and Praise*, 90.

55. King, *My Life with Martin Luther King*, 158–60.

56. Terkel, *And They All Sang*, 188–89.

57. Goreau, *Just Mahalia, Baby*, 221.

58. Cleopatra Kennedy, interview with the author, July 8, 2009, Birmingham, tape recording, Institute for Oral History, Baylor University, Waco, 18–19.

59. Jules Schwerin, *Got to Tell It: Mahalia Jackson, Queen of Gospel* (New York: Oxford University Press, 1992), 113.

60. Craig Werner, *A Change Is Gonna Come: Music, Race, and the Soul of America* (New York: Plume, 1999), 5–6, 8–9.

61. Goreau, *Just Mahalia, Baby*, 221.

62. "Mahalia Sings in History Wk. Concert Feb. 9," *New York Amsterdam News*, February 9, 1957, 12.

63. Reed, *Art of Protest*, 18.

64. Bremner and Reichard, *Reshaping America*, 89.

65. Collier-Thomas and Franklin, *My Soul Is a Witness*, 45.

66. Robert S. Graetz, *A White Preacher's Memoir: The Montgomery Bus Boycott* (Montgomery: Black Belt Press, 1998), 101–2.

67. Freedman, *Freedom Walkers*, 86.

68. Aldon D. Morris, "Reflections on Social Movement Theory: Criticisms and Proposals," *Contemporary Sociology* 29, no. 3 (2000): 448.

69. King, *Stride Toward Freedom*, 86.

70. Edward P. Morgan, "Rights, Power, and Equality," in *Upon These Shores: Themes in the African-American Experience, 1600 to the Present*, ed. William R. Scott and William G. Shade (New York: Routledge, 2000), 225.

71. Rev. Fred Shuttlesworth in *Eyes on the Prize*, transcript, http://www.pbs.org/wgbh/amex/eyesontheprize/about/pt.html.

72. Dave Marsh, liner notes to Bruce Springsteen, *We Shall Overcome: The Seeger Sessions* (Columbia/Sony Music, 82876 83439 1, 2006).

73. Silverman, *Songs of Protest*, 38–39.

74. Harvey, "Black Gospel Music," 36.

75. Silverman, *Songs of Protest*, 28–29.

76. Van Rijn, "Climbing the Mountain Top," 131–32.

77. James H. Cone, "Martin Luther King, Jr., and the Third World," *Journal of American History* 74, no. 2 (1987): 455.

78. Gregory, *Southern Diaspora*, 281.

79. Ennis, *Seventh Stream*, 280.

80. Donald H. Smith, "Martin Luther King, Jr.: In the Beginning in Montgomery," *Southern Speech Journal* 34, no. 1 (1968): 11.

81. Richard Harrington, "Sweet Sound of Freedom: Songs of the Civil Rights Movement Revisited," *Washington Post*, January 15, 1997, D7.

82. Reagon, "Songs That Moved the Movement," 28.

83. Johnson, quoted in Harrington, "Sweet Sound," D7.

84. King, quoted in Hampton and Fayer, *Voices of Freedom*, 30.

Selected Bibliography

Printed Sources

Abbington, James. *Let the Church Sing On! Reflections on Black Sacred Music.* Chicago: GIA, 2009.

Abbott, Lynn, and Doug Seroff. *Out of Sight: The Rise of African American Popular Music, 1889–1889.* Jackson: University Press of Mississippi, 2002.

——. *Ragged but Right: Black Traveling Shows, "Coon Songs," and the Dark Pathway to Blues and Jazz.* Jackson: University Press of Mississippi, 2007.

Aberjhani and Sharon L. West. *Encyclopedia of the Harlem Renaissance.* New York: Facts on File, 2003.

Abernathy, Ralph David. *And the Walls Came Tumbling Down: An Autobiography.* New York: Harper and Row, 1989.

Abrahams, Roger D. *Singing the Master: The Emergence of African American Culture in the Plantation South.* New York: Pantheon, 1992.

Abramowitz, Jack. "The Negro in the Populist Movement." *Journal of Negro History* 39, no. 3 (1953): 257–89.

Adams, Frank, with Myles Horton. *Unearthing Seeds of Fire: The Idea of Highlander.* Winston-Salem, NC: John F. Blair, 1975.

Allen, Ray. *Singing in the Spirit: African-American Sacred Quartets in New York City.* Philadelphia: University of Pennsylvania Press, 1991.

Allen, Richard. *The Life Experience and Gospel Labors of the Rt. Rev. Richard Allen.* 1960. Reprint, Nashville: Abingdon Press, 1983.

Allen, William F., Charles P. Ware, and Lucy McKim Garrison. *Slave Songs of the United States.* 1867. Reprint, New York: Peter Smith, 1927. Reprint, Mineola, NY: Dover, 1995.

Alter, Nora M., and Lutz Koepnick. *Sound Matters: Essays on the Acoustics of Modern German Culture.* New York: Berghahn, 2004.

American Negro Songs and Spirituals: A Comprehensive Collection of 230 Folk Songs, Religious and Secular, with a Foreword by John W. Work. 1915. Reprint, New York: Negro Universities Press, 1969.

Ames, Russell. *The Story of American Folk Song.* 1955. Reprint, New York: Grosset and Dunlap, 1960.

Anderson, Jervis. *A. Philip Randolph: A Biographical Portrait.* New York: Harcourt Brace Jovanovich, 1972.

Anderson, Marian. *My Lord, What a Morning: An Autobiography.* New York: Viking, 1956.

Anderson, Toni P. *"Tell Them We Are Singing for Jesus": The Original Fisk Jubilee Singers and Christian Reconstruction, 1871–1878.* Macon: Mercer University Press, 2010.

"Anderson Affair." *Time,* April 17, 1939, 23.

Andrews, William L., ed. *The Oxford Frederick Douglass Reader.* New York: Oxford University Press, 1996.

Appiah, Kwame Anthony, and Henry Louis Gates, Jr. *Africana: The Encyclopedia of the African and African American Experience.* 2nd ed. Vol. 3. Oxford: Oxford University Press, 2005.

Ardery, Julia S. *Welcome the Traveler Home: Jim Garland's Story of the Kentucky Mountains.* Lexington: University of Kentucky Press, 1983.

Arnesen, Eric. *Black Protest and the Great Migration: A Brief History with Documents.* Boston: Bedford/St. Martin's, 2003.

Arsenault, Raymond. *Freedom Riders: 1961 and the Struggle for Racial Justice.* Oxford: Oxford University Press, 2006.

———. *The Sound of Freedom: Marian Anderson, the Lincoln Memorial, and the Concert that Awakened America.* New York: Bloomsbury, 2009.

Arvey, Verna. "Worthwhile Music in the Movies." *Etude Music Magazine,* March 1936, 152.

Asante, Molefi Kete, and Abu S. Abarry. *African Intellectual Heritage: A Book of Sources.* Philadelphia: Temple University Press, 1996.

"At the White House." *The Crisis,* July 1933, 160–61.

Augustine. *Sermons on the Liturgical Seasons.* Translated by Sister Mary Sarah Muldowney. New York: Catholic University of America Press, 1959.

Ayers, Edward L. *The Promise of the New South: Life After Reconstruction.* New York: Oxford University Press, 1992.

Baker, Ray Stannard. "The Revolutionary Strike: A New Form of Industrial Struggle as Exemplified at Lawrence, Massachusetts." *American Magazine,* May 1912, 19–30c.

Baldwin, Davarian L. *Chicago's New Negroes: Modernity, the Great Migration, and Black Urban Life.* Chapel Hill: University of North Carolina Press, 2007.

Baldwin, James. "Of the Sorrow Songs: The Cross of Redemption." *Views on Black American Music* 2 (1984–85): 7–12.

Barlow, William. *"Looking Up at Down": The Emergence of Blues Culture.* Philadelphia: Temple University Press, 1989.

———. *Voice Over: The Making of Black Radio.* Philadelphia: Temple University Press, 1999.

Barlow, William, and Cheryl Finley. *From Swing to Soul: An Illustrated History of African American Popular Music from 1930 to 1960.* Washington, DC: Elliott and Clark, 1994.

Barnes, Sandra L. "Black Church Culture and Community Action." *Social Forces* 84, no. 2 (2005): 967–94.

Barnet, Richard D., Bruce Nemerov, and Mayo R. Taylor. *The Story Behind the Song: 150 Songs that Chronicle the Twentieth Century.* Westport, CT: Greenwood, 2004.

Barrett, George. "Jim Crow, He's Real Tired." *New York Times,* March 3, 1957, 11, 67–69, 74.

Barrett, Leonard E. *Soul-Force: African Heritage in Afro-American Religion.* Garden City, NY: Anchor/Doubleday, 1974.

Barton, William E. *Old Plantation Hymns: A Collection of Hitherto Unpublished Melodies of the Slave and the Freeman, with Historical and Descriptive Notes.* 1899. Reprint, New York: AMS, 1972.

Beal, Fred E. *Proletarian Journey: New England, Gastonia, Moscow.* 1937. Reprint, New York: Da Capo, 1971.

Beasley, Maurine H., Holly C. Shulman, and Henry R. Beasley, eds. *The Eleanor Roosevelt Encyclopedia.* Westport, CT: Greenwood, 2001.

Beckham, Albert Sidney. "The Psychology of Negro Spirituals." *Southern Workman* 60 (1931): 391–94.

Belfrage, Cedric. "Cotton-Patch Moses."
　　Harper's, November 1948, 94–103.
Benedict, Ruth. "Race Problems in Amer-
　　ica." *Annals of the American Acad-
　　emy of Political and Social Science*
　　216 (July 1941): 73–78.
Benjamin, Brawley. "The Negro Genius."
　　Southern Workman 44 (May 1915):
　　305–8.
Bennett, Lerone, Jr. "Old Illusions and
　　New Souths." *Ebony*, August 1971,
　　35–40.
———. *Wade in the Water: Great Moments
　　in Black History*. Chicago: John-
　　son, 1979.
Bergman, Peter M. *The Chronological
　　History of the Negro in America.*
　　New York: Harper and Row, 1969.
Berlin, Ira. *The Making of African Amer-
　　ica: The Four Great Migrations.*
　　New York: Viking, 2010.
Bernard, Kenneth A. *Lincoln and the Music
　　of the Civil War*. Caldwell, ID:
　　Caxton, 1966.
Berry, Mary Frances. *My Face Is Black
　　Is True: Callie House and the
　　Struggle for Ex-Slave Reparations.*
　　New York: Knopf, 2005.
Billingsley, Andrew. *Mighty Like a River:
　　The Black Church and Social
　　Reform*. New York: Oxford Univer-
　　sity Press, 1999.
Biondi, Martha. *To Stand and Fight:
　　The Struggle for Civil Rights in
　　Postwar New York City*. Cam-
　　bridge: Harvard University Press,
　　2003.
Black, Timuel D., Jr. *Bridges of Memory:
　　Chicago's First Wave of Black
　　Migration*. Evanston: Northwest-
　　ern University Press, 2003.
Blassingame, John W., ed. *Slave Testimony:
　　Two Centuries of Letters, Speeches,
　　Interviews, and Autobiographies.*
　　Baton Rouge: Louisiana State
　　University Press, 1977.
Bledsoe, Thomas. *Or We'll All Hang
　　Separately: The Highlander Idea.*
　　Boston: Beacon, 1969.

Blood-Patterson, Peter, ed. *Rise Up Singing.*
　　Bethlehem, PA: A Sing Out Publi-
　　cation, 1988.
Bogdanov, Vladimir, Chris Woodstra, and
　　Stephen Thomas Erlewine, eds.
　　All Music Guide to the Blues.
　　San Francisco: Backbeat, 2003.
Bond, Julian, and Sondra Kathryn Wil-
　　son, eds. *Lift Every Voice and Sing:
　　A Celebration of the Negro National
　　Anthem; 100 Years, 100 Voices.*
　　New York: Random House, 2000.
Bontemps, Arna. "Harlem in the Twenties."
　　The Crisis, October 1966, 431–34,
　　451.
Bontemps, Arna, and Jack Conroy. *Anyplace
　　but Here*. 1945. Reprint, New York:
　　Hill and Wang, 1966.
Boyer, Horace Clarence. *How Sweet the
　　Sound: The Golden Age of Gospel.*
　　Washington, DC: Elliott and
　　Clark, 1995.
Boyle, Sheila Tully, and Andrew Bunie. *Paul
　　Robeson: The Years of Promise and
　　Achievement*. Amherst: University
　　of Massachusetts Press, 2001.
Bradford, Perry. *Born with the Blues: Perry
　　Bradford's Own Story*. New York:
　　Oak, 1965.
Bradford, Sarah. *Harriet Tubman: The Moses
　　of Her People*. 1961. Reprint,
　　Gloucester, MA: Peter Smith, 1981.
Bradley, Rose. "41–42–43!" *Labor Defender*,
　　December 1933, 80, 93.
Branch, Taylor. *At Canaan's Edge: Amer-
　　ica in the King Years, 1965–1968.*
　　New York: Simon and Schuster,
　　2006.
———. *Parting the Waters: America in the
　　King Years, 1954–1963*. New York:
　　Simon and Schuster, 1988.
———. *Pillar of Fire: America in the King
　　Years, 1963–1965*. New York: Simon
　　and Schuster, 1998.
Brazier, Richard. "The Story of the IWW's
　　'Little Red Songbook.'" *Labor His-
　　tory* 9, no. 1 (1968): 91–105.
Bremmer, Robert H., and Gary W. Rich-
　　ard, eds. *Reshaping America:*

Society and Institutions, 1945–1960. Columbus: Ohio State University Press, 1982.

Brewster, Gurdon. *No Turning Back: My Summer with Daddy King.* Maryknoll, NY: Orbis, 2007.

Bridges, Flora Wilson. *Resurrection Song: African-American Spirituality.* Maryknoll, NY: Orbis, 2001.

Brooks, Tim. "Early Black Vaudeville on Record: Louis 'Bebe' Vasnier and the Louisiana Phonography Company." *ARSC Journal* 28, no. 2 (1997): 143–54.

Brown, Frank London. "Mahalia the Great: Queen of Gospel Music Calls Her Music the Slave's Song of Affliction." *Ebony,* March 1959, 69–72, 74, 76.

Bruce, Dickson D., Jr. *Black American Writing from the Nadir: The Evolution of a Literary Tradition, 1877–1915.* Baton Rouge: Louisiana State University Press, 1989.

Buchanan, A. Russell. *Black Americans in World War II.* Santa Barbara, CA: Clio, 1977.

Burlin, Natalie Curtis. "Negro Music at Birth." *Musical Quarterly* 5, no. 1 (1919): 86–89.

Burner, Eric. *And Gently He Shall Lead Them: Robert Parris Moses and Civil Rights in Mississippi.* New York: New York University Press, 1994.

Burnim, Mellonee V., and Portia K. Maultsby, eds. *African American Music: An Introduction.* New York: Routledge, 2006.

Burns, Stewart, ed. *Daybreak of Freedom: The Montgomery Bus Boycott.* Chapel Hill: University of North Carolina Press, 1997.

——. *To the Mountaintop: Martin Luther King Jr.'s Sacred Mission to Save America, 1955–1968.* San Francisco: HarperSanFrancisco, 2004.

Butterfield, Stephen. *Black Autobiography in America.* Amherst: University of Massachusetts Press, 1974.

Cahn, William. *A Pictorial History of American Labor.* New York: Crown, 1972.

Cantor, Louis. *A Prologue to the Protest Movement: The Missouri Sharecropper Roadside Demonstration of 1939.* Durham: Duke University Press, 1969.

——. *Wheelin' on Beale: How WDIA-Memphis Became the Nation's First All-Black Radio Station and Created the Sound That Changed America.* New York: Pharos, 1992.

Caponi, Gena Dagel. *Signifyin(g), Sanctifyin', and Slam Dunking: A Reader in African American Expressive Culture.* Amherst: University of Massachusetts Press, 1999.

Carpenter, Bill. *Uncloudy Days: The Gospel Music Encyclopedia.* San Francisco: Backbeat, 2005.

Carson, Clayborne, ed. *The Autobiography of Martin Luther King, Jr.* New York: Warner, 1998.

——, senior ed. *The Papers of Martin Luther King, Jr.* Vol. 3, *Birth of a New Age: December 1955–December 1956.* Vol. 4, *Symbol of the Movement: January 1957–December 1958.* Vol. 5, *Threshold of a New Decade: January 1959–December 1960.* Berkeley: University of California Press, 1997, 2000, 2005.

——. "To Walk in Dignity: The Montgomery Bus Boycott." *OAH Magazine of History* 19, no. 1 (2005): 13–15.

Carson, Clayborne, David J. Garrow, Gerald Gill, Vincent Harding, and Darlene Clark Hine, eds. *The Eyes on the Prize Civil Rights Reader: Documents, Speeches, and Firsthand Accounts from the Black Freedom Struggle.* New York: Penguin, 1991.

Carter, David A. "The Industrial Workers of the World and the Rhetoric of Song." *Quarterly Journal of Speech* 66, no. 4 (1980): 365–74.

Cathcart, Robert S. "New Approaches to the Study of Movements: Defining Movements Rhetorically." *Western*

Journal of Communication 35, no. 2 (1972): 82–88.

Chamberlain, Charles. "Searching for 'The Gulf Coast Circuit': Mobility and Cultural Diffusion in the Age of Jim Crow, 1900–1930." *Jazz Archivist* 14 (2000): 1–18.

"Changes." *People's Songs*, November 1948, 10.

Chappell, David L. *A Stone of Hope: Prophetic Religion and the Death of Jim Crow*. Chapel Hill: University of North Carolina Press, 2004.

Chapple, Steve, and Reebee Garofalo. *Rock 'n' Roll Is Here to Pay: The History and Politics of the Music Industry*. Chicago: Nelson-Hall, 1977.

Charles, Ray, and David Ritz. *Brother Ray: Ray Charles' Own Story*. Cambridge, MA: Da Capo, 2004.

Charney, George. *A Long Journey*. Chicago: Quadrangle, 1968.

Chavkin, Samuel. "Folk Songs of the South." *Daily Worker*, January 17, 1938, 7.

Chilton, Karen. *Hazel Scott: The Pioneering Journey of a Jazz Pianist from Café Society to Hollywood to HUAC*. Ann Arbor: University of Michigan Press, 2008.

Chong, Dennis. *Collective Action and the Civil Rights Movement*. Chicago: University of Chicago Press, 1991.

Clark, Edgar Rogie. "Negro Folk Music in America." *Journal of American Folklore* 64, no. 253 (1951): 281–87.

Clifford, James. "Further Inflections: Toward Ethnographies of the Future." *Cultural Anthropology* 9, no. 3 (1994): 302–38.

Clinton, Catherine. *Harriet Tubman: The Road to Freedom*. New York: Little, Brown, 2004.

"Clyde McPhatter Advises Kids in Dixie on 'Bias.'" *Chicago Defender*, December 9–16, 1960, 17.

Cobb, Charles E. *On the Road to Freedom: A Guided Tour of the Civil Rights Trail*. Chapel Hill, NC: Algonquin Books of Chapel Hill, 2008.

Cockrell, Dale. *Demons of Disorder: Early Blackface Minstrels and Their World*. Cambridge: Cambridge University Press, 1997.

———, ed. *Excelsior: Journals of the Hutchinson Family Singers, 1842–1846*. Stuyvesant, NY: Pendragon, 1989.

———. "Of Gospel Hymns, Minstrel Shows, and Jubilee Singers: Toward Some Black South African Musics." *American Music* 5, no. 4 (1987): 417–32.

Coffin, Tristram Potter. *Our Living Traditions: An Introduction to American Folklore*. New York: Basic, 1968.

Cohen, Ronald D., ed. *Alan Lomax: Selected Writings, 1934–1997*. New York: Routledge, 2003.

———. *Work and Sing: A History of Occupational and Labor Union Songs in the United States*. Crockett, CA: Carquinez, 2010.

Collier, Eugenia W. "James Weldon Johnson: Mirror of Change." *Phylon* 21, no. 4 (1960): 351–59.

Collier-Thomas, Bettye, and V. P. Franklin. *My Soul Is a Witness: A Chronology of the Civil Rights Era, 1954–1965*. New York: Henry Holt, 1999.

———. *Sisters in the Struggle: African American Women in the Civil Rights– Black Power Movement*. New York: New York University Press, 2001.

Cone, James H. *The Cross and the Lynching Tree*. Maryknoll, NY: Orbis, 2011.

———. *My Soul Looks Back*. Nashville: Abingdon, 1982.

———. *The Spirituals and the Blues: An Interpretation*. New York: Seabury, 1972.

Conrad, Earl. *General Harriet Tubman*. 1943. Reprint, Washington, DC: Associated, 1990.

Courlander, Harold. *Negro Folk Music, USA*. New York: Columbia University Press, 1963.

Crawford, Vicki L., Jacqueline Anne Rouse, and Barbara Woods, eds. *Women in the Civil Rights Movement:*

Trailblazers and Torchbearers, *1941–1965.* Brooklyn: Carlson, 1990.

Cripps, Thomas. *Making Movies Black: The Hollywood Message Movie from World War II to the Civil Rights Era.* New York: Oxford University Press, 1993.

Crouch, Stanley. "From Spirituals to Swing." *Village Voice,* December 4, 1984, 43–44.

Cunard, Nancy. *Negro: An Anthology.* New York: Frederick Ungar, 1970.

Curtis, Marvin V. "How to Survive in Your Native Land: A Look at the History of African-American Music in America." *Western Journal of Black Studies* 12, no. 2 (1988): 101–11.

Daniel, Pete. *Lost Revolutions: The South in the 1950s.* Chapel Hill: University of North Carolina Press, 2000.

Darden, Robert. "Laurraine Goreau and *Just Mahalia, Baby.*" *Rejoice!* Spring 1990, 20–32.

———. *People Get Ready!: A New History of Black Gospel Music.* New York: Continuum, 2004.

Dates, Jannette L., and William Barlow. *Split Image: African Americans in the Mass Media.* 2nd ed. Washington, DC: Howard University Press, 1993.

Davis, Francis. *The History of the Blues.* Cambridge, MA: Da Capo, 1995.

Davis, John P. *The American Negro Reference Book.* Englewood Cliffs, NJ: Prentice Hall, 1966.

D'Emilio, John. *Lost Prophet: The Life and Times of Bayard Rustin.* New York: Free Press, 2003.

DeNatale, Doug, and Glenn Hinson. "The Southern Textile Song Tradition Reconsidered." *Journal of Folklore Research* 28, nos. 2–3 (1991): 103–33.

Denisoff, R. Serge. "Folk Music and the American Left: A Generational-Ideological Comparison." *British Journal of Sociology* 20, no. 4 (1969): 427–42.

———. *Great Day Coming: Folk Music and the American Left.* Urbana: University of Illinois Press, 1971.

———. "The Religious Roots of the American Song of Persuasion." *Western Folklore* 29, no. 3 (1970): 175–84.

———. "'Take It Easy, but Take It': The Almanac Singers." *Journal of American Folklore Society* 83, no. 327 (1970): 21–32.

Denning, Michael. *The Cultural Front: The Laboring of American Culture in the Twentieth Century.* London: Verso, 1996.

Dennison, Sam. *Scandalize My Name: Black Imagery in American Popular Music.* New York: Garland, 1982.

Dett, R. Nathaniel, ed. *Religious Folk-Songs of the Negro as Sung at Hampton Institute.* Hampton, VA: Hampton Institute Press, 1927.

De Turk, David A., and A. Poulin, Jr., eds. *The American Folk Scene: Dimensions of the Folksong Revival.* New York: Dell, 1967.

"Disc Jockeys: 16 Sepia Spielers Ride Kilocycle Range on 21 Stations." *Ebony,* December 7, 1947, 44–49.

Dixon, Christa K. *Negro Spirituals: From Bible to Folk Song.* Philadelphia: Fortress, 1976.

Dixon, Lorraine. "Teach It, Sister! Mahalia Jackson as Theologian in Song." *Black Theology in Britain: A Journal of Contextual Praxis* 2 (April 1999): 72–89.

Douglas, Susan J. *Listening In: Radio and the American Imagination.* Minneapolis: University of Minnesota Press, 1999.

Douglass, Frederick. *Life and Times of Frederick Douglass, Written by Himself.* 1892. Reprint, New York: Collier, 1962.

———. *My Bondage and My Freedom.* Edited and with an introduction by William L. Andrews. 1855. Reprint,

Urbana: University of Illinois Press, 1987.

———. *Narrative of the Life of Frederick Douglass, an American Slave: Written by Himself.* Cambridge, MA: Belknap Press, 1960.

Drake, St. Clair, and Horace R. Cayton, Jr. *Black Metropolis: A Study of Negro Life in a Northern City.* Vol. 1. 1945. Reprint, New York: Harper Torchbooks, 1961.

Dray, Philip. *There Is Power in a Union: The Epic Story of Labor in America.* New York: Doubleday, 2010.

Drewry, William Sidney. *The Southampton Insurrection.* Washington, DC: Neale, 1900.

Duberman, Martin Bauml. *Paul Robeson.* New York: Knopf, 1988.

Du Bois, W. E. B. *The Autobiography of W. E. B. Du Bois: A Soliloquy on Viewing My Life from the Last Decade of Its First Century.* New York: International, 1968.

———. *Black Reconstruction in America, 1860–1880.* 1935. New York: Atheneum, 1962.

———. *The Souls of Black Folk: Essays and Sketches.* 1903. Reprint, McLean, VA: IndyPublish.com, 2000.

Dunaway, David King. "Charles Seeger and Carl Sands: The Composers' Collective Years." *Ethnomusicology* 24, no. 2 (1980): 159–68.

———. "Music and Politics in the United States." *Folk Music Journal* 5, no. 3 (1987): 268–94.

Dunlap, James. "Through the Eyes of Tom Joad: Patterns of American Idealism, Bob Dylan, and the Folk Protest Movement." *Popular Music and Society* 29, no. 5 (2006): 549–73.

Dunson, Josh. "Slave Songs at the 'Sing for Freedom.'" *Broadside* 46 (May 30, 1964): 9–10.

Editors of *Freedomways. Paul Robeson: The Great Forerunner.* New York: Dodd, Mead, 1978.

Ellison, Ralph. *Living with Music: Ralph Ellison's Jazz Writings.* Edited by Robert G. O'Meally. New York: Modern Library, 2001.

———. *Shadow and Act.* 1953. Reprint, New York: Random House, 1964.

Elsila, Dave. "Talking Union with Pete Seeger: Folksinger and Activist Pete Seeger Believes Workers Win When Labor Sings." *Working USA* 1, no. 6 (1998): 66.

Epstein, Dena J. *Sinful Tunes and Spirituals: Black Folk Music to the Civil War.* Urbana: University of Illinois Press, 1977.

Epstein, Lawrence J. *Political Folk Music in America from Its Origins to Bob Dylan.* Jefferson, NC: McFarland, 2010.

Eyerman, Ron, and Scott Barretta. "From the 30s to the 60s: The Folk Music Revival in the United States." *Theory and Society* 25, no. 4 (1996): 501–43.

Eyerman, Ron, and Andrew Jamison. *Music and Social Movements: Mobilizing Traditions in the Twentieth Century.* Cambridge: Cambridge University Press, 1998.

Fairclough, Adam. *Better Day Coming: Blacks and Equality, 1890–2000.* New York: Viking, 2001.

"The Faith of Soul and Slavery." *Time,* April 19, 1968, 70.

Falola, Toyin, and Amanda Warnock, eds. *Encyclopedia of the Middle Passage.* Westport, CT: Greenwood, 2007.

Feiler, Bruce. *Abraham: A Journey to the Heart of Three Faiths.* New York: William Morrow, 2002.

———. *America's Prophet: Moses and the American Story.* New York: William Morrow, 2009.

Fenner, Thomas P., Frederic G. Rathbun, and Bessie Cleveland, arr. *Cabin and Plantation Songs as Sung by the Hampton Students.* New York: G. P. Putnam's Sons, 1901.

Ferguson, Leland. *Uncommon Ground: Archaeology and Early African*

America, 1650–1800. Washington, DC: Smithsonian Institution Press, 1992.

Ferris, William, and Mary L. Hart, eds. *Folk Music and Modern Sound.* Jackson: University Press of Mississippi, 1982.

Fisher, Miles Mark. *Negro Slave Songs in the United States.* New York: Russell and Russell, 1953.

Fisher, William Arms, ed. *Seventy Negro Spirituals.* Bryn Mawr, PA: Oliver Ditson, 1926.

"Fisk Co-Ed Plans Lifetime Fight with Jim Crow." *Jet*, June 9, 1960, 46–49.

Floyd, Samuel A., Jr. *Black Music in the Harlem Renaissance: A Collection of Essays.* Knoxville: University of Tennessee Press, 1993.

———. *The Power of Black Music: Interpreting Its History from Africa to the United States.* New York: Oxford University Press, 1995.

"Folk Singers in Original Revue Tonight." *Daily Worker*, May 15, 1941, 7.

Fondation Cartier pour l'art contemporain. *Rock 'n' Roll, 39–59.* Göttingen: Steidl and Partners, 2008.

Foner, Philip S. *American Labor Songs of the Nineteenth Century.* Urbana: University of Illinois Press, 1975.

———. *Organized Labor and the Black Worker, 1619–1973.* New York: Praeger, 1974.

"For Native Sons." *Time*, September 29, 1941, 59.

Foster, Susan Leigh. "Choreographies of Protest." In "Dance," special issue, *Theatre Journal* 55, no. 3 (2003): 395–412.

Fowke, Edith, and Joe Glazier. *Songs of Work and Freedom.* 1960. Reprint, New York: Dover, 1973.

Fox, Richard G., and Orin Starn, eds. *Between Resistance and Revolution: Cultural Politics and Social Protest.* New Brunswick: Rutgers University Press, 1997.

Frank, Richard. "Negro Revolutionary Music." *New Masses*, May 15, 1934, 29–30.

Franklin, John Hope. "Civil Rights in American History." *The Progressive*, December 1962, 6–9.

Franklin, John Hope, and Alfred A. Moss, Jr. *From Slavery to Freedom: A History of Negro Americans.* 1947. Reprint, New York: Knopf, 1988.

Franklin, John Hope, and Loren Schweninger. *Runaway Slaves: Rebels on the Plantation.* New York: Oxford University Press, 1999.

Franklin, V. P. *Black Self-Determination: A Cultural History of the Faith of the Fathers.* Westport, CT: Lawrence Hill, 1984.

Franko, Mark. *The Work of Dance: Labor, Movement, and Identity in the 1930s.* Middletown: Wesleyan University Press, 2002.

Frazier, E. Franklin. *The Negro Church in America.* New York: Schocken, 1963.

Freedman, Russell. *Freedom Walkers: The Story of the Montgomery Bus Boycott.* New York: Holiday House, 2006.

Frey, Sylvia R. *Water from the Rock: Black Resistance in a Revolutionary Age.* Princeton: Princeton University Press, 1991.

Friedland, Michael B. *Lift Up Your Voice Like a Trumpet: White Clergy and the Civil Rights and Antiwar Movements, 1954–1973.* Chapel Hill: University of North Carolina Press, 1998.

Friedman, Josh Alan. *Tell the Truth Until They Bleed: Coming Clean in the Dirty World of Blues and Rock 'n' Roll.* New York: Backbeat, 2008.

Friedman, Leon, ed. *The Civil Rights Reader: Basic Documents of the Civil Rights Movement.* New York: Walker, 1967.

Frith, Simon. *Performing Rites: On the Value of Popular Music.* Oxford: Oxford University Press, 1996.

———. *Sound Effects: Youth, Leisure, and the Politics of Rock 'n' Roll.* New York: Pantheon, 1981.

Fuld, James J. *The Book of World-Famous Music: Classical, Popular, and Folk.* 1966. Reprint, New York: Crown, 1971.

Funk, Ray. "Historical Gospel: Wings over Jordan." *Rejoice!* 1, no. 2 (1988): 27–29.

Gac, Scott. *Singing for Freedom: The Hutchinson Family Singers and the Nineteenth-Century Culture of Reform.* New Haven: Yale University Press, 2007.

Garabedian, Steven. "Reds, Whites, and the Blues: Lawrence Gellert, 'Negro Songs of Protest,' and the Left-Wing Folk-Song Revival of the 1930s and 1940s." *American Quarterly* 57, no. 1 (2005): 179–206.

Garfield, John. "How Hollywood Can Better Race Relations." *Negro Digest,* November 1947, 4–8.

Garofalo, Reebee, ed. *Rockin' the Boat: Mass Music and Mass Movements.* Boston: South End Press, 1992.

Garrison, Dee, ed. *Rebel Pen: The Writings of Mary Heaton Vorse.* New York: Monthly Review Press, 1985.

Garrow, David J., ed. *Martin Luther King, Jr.: Civil Rights Leader, Theologian, Orator.* 3 vols. Brooklyn: Carlson, 1989.

Gates, Henry Louis, Jr. *The Signifying Monkey: A Theory of Afro-American Literary Criticism.* New York: Oxford University Press, 1988.

Gavins, Raymond. "The NAACP in North Carolina During the Age of Segregation." In *New Directions in Civil Rights Studies,* edited by Armstead L. Robinson and Patricia Sullivan, 105–25. Charlottesville: University Press of Virginia, 1991.

Geary, Lynnette Goggans. "The Career and Music of Jules Bledsoe." Master's thesis, Baylor University, 1982.

Gehman, Richard. "God's Singing Messengers." *Cornet* 44, no. 3 (1958): 112–16.

Gellert, Lawrence. "Four Negro Songs of Protest." *Music Vanguard* 1, no. 2 (1935): 68–70.

———. "Jim Crow in Khaki." *New Masses,* March 19, 1946, 12–13.

———. "Negro Songs of Protest." *New Masses,* November 1930, 10–11; January 1931, 16–17; April 1931, 6–8; May 1932, 22; May 1933, 15–16.

———. *Negro Songs of Protest.* New York: American Music League, 1936.

Genovese, Eugene D. *From Rebellion to Revolution: Afro-American Slave Revolts in the Making of the Modern World.* Baton Rouge: Louisiana State University Press, 1979.

———. *Roll, Jordan, Roll: The World the Slaves Made.* New York: Pantheon, 1974.

Gibson-Hunter, Claudia. *Let the Circle Be Unbroken: The Implications of African Spirituality in the Diaspora.* Lawrenceville, NJ: Red Sea Press, 1980.

Giddings, Paula. *When and Where I Enter: The Impact of Black Women on Race and Sex in America.* New York: William Morrow, 1984.

Gilkes, Cheryl Townsend. *"If It Wasn't for the Women . . .": Black Women's Experience and Womanist Culture in the Church Community.* Maryknoll, NY: Orbis, 2001.

Gillespie, Angus K. *Folklorist of the Coal Fields: George Korson's Life and Work.* University Park: Pennsylvania State University Press, 1980.

Gillespie, Dizzy, with Al Fraser. *To Be or Not . . . to Bop: Memoirs.* Garden City, NY: Doubleday, 1979.

Gillett, Charlie. *The Sound of the City: The Rise of Rock and Roll.* New York: Outerbridge and Dienstfrey, 1970.

Gilmore, Glenda Elizabeth. *Defying Dixie: The Radical Roots of Civil Rights, 1919–1950.* New York: Norton, 2008.

Gilroy, Paul. *The Black Atlantic: Modernity and Double Consciousness.* Cambridge: Harvard University Press, 1993.

Gioia, Ted. *The History of Jazz.* New York: Oxford University Press, 1997.

Glazer, Joe. *Labor's Troubadour.* Urbana: University of Illinois Press, 2001.

Glazer, Tom. *Songs of Peace, Freedom, and Protest.* New York: David McKay, 1970.

Glazier, Stephen D. *Encyclopedia of African and African American Religions.* New York: Routledge, 2001.

Glen, John M. *Highlander: No Ordinary School.* Knoxville: University of Tennessee Press, 1996.

Gloster, Hugh M. "The Van Vechten Vogue." *Phylon* 6 (1945): 310–14.

Gold, Michael. "The Negro Reds of Chicago." *Daily Worker*, September 30, 1932, 4.

"Golden Gate in Washington." *Time*, January 27, 1941, 50.

Goldfield, David R. *Black, White, and Southern: Race Relations and Southern Culture, 1940 to the Present.* Baton Rouge: Louisiana State University Press, 1990.

Goodnight, Mary Helen. "Folk Expression in Antebellum Negro Spirituals." Master's thesis, Baylor University, 1975.

Goodwin, Jeff, and James M. Jasper, eds. *The Social Movements Reader: Cases and Concepts.* Malden, MA: Blackwell, 2003.

Gordon, Robert, and Bruce Nemerov, eds. *Lost Delta Found: Rediscovering the Fisk University–Library of Congress Coahoma County Study.* Nashville: Vanderbilt University Press, 2005.

Goreau, Laurraine. *Just Mahalia, Baby: The Mahalia Jackson Story.* Waco, TX: Word, 1975.

Gorlin, Dan. *Songs of West Africa.* Forest Knolls, CA: Alokli West African Dance, 2000.

Graham, Shirley. "Spirituals to Symphonies." *Etude Music Magazine* 54 (November 1936): 691–92, 723.

Grant, Joanne. *Black Protest: History, Documents, Analyses, 1619 to the Present.* Greenwich, CT: Fawcett Premier, 1968.

Gray, Fred D. *Bus Ride to Justice: Changing the System by the System; The Life and Works of Fred D. Gray.* Montgomery: Black Belt Press, 1995.

Gray, Fred D., Willy S. Leventhal, Frank Sikora, and J. Mills Thornton. *The Children Coming On . . . : A Retrospective of the Montgomery Bus Ride.* Montgomery: Black Belt Press, 1998.

Green, Adam. *Selling the Race: Culture, Community, and Black Chicago, 1940–1955.* Chicago: University of Chicago Press, 2007.

Green, Archie. "A Great Rebel Passes On." *Sing Out!*, December–January 1960–61, 31–33.

———. "Labor Song: An Ambiguous Legacy." *Journal of Folklore Research* 28, nos. 2–3 (1991): 93–102.

———. *Only a Miner: Studies in Recorded Coal-Mining Songs.* Urbana: University of Illinois Press, 1972.

———, ed. *Songs About Work: Essays in Occupational Culture for Richard A. Reuss.* Bloomington: Indiana University, Folklore Institute, 1993.

———. *Wobblies, Pile Butts, and Other Heroes: Laborlore Explorations.* Urbana: University of Illinois Press, 1993.

Green, Archie, David Roediger, Franklin Rosemont, and Salvatore Salerno, eds. *The Big Red Songbook.* Chicago: Charles H. Kerr, 2007.

Greenway, John. *American Folksongs of Protest.* Philadelphia: University of Pennsylvania Press, 1953.

Gregory, James N. *The Southern Diaspora: How the Great Migrations of Black and White Southerners Transformed America.* Chapel Hill: University of North Carolina Press, 2005.

Griffin, Leland M. "The Rhetoric of Historical Movements." *Quarterly Journal of Speech* 38, no. 2 (1952): 184–88.

Grimshaw, William J. *Bitter Fruit: Black Politics and the Chicago Machine, 1931–1991*. Chicago: University of Chicago Press, 1992.

Grissom, Mary Allen. *The Negro Sings a New Heaven*. Chapel Hill: University of North Carolina Press, 1930.

Grossman, James R. *Land of Hope: Chicago, Black Southerners, and the Great Migration*. Chicago: University of Chicago Press, 1989.

Guralnick, Peter. *Dream Boogie: The Triumph of Sam Cooke*. New York: Back Bay, 2005.

Guthrie, Woody. "America Singing: Author of 'Bound for Glory' Recalls What the Plain People Sing." *New York Times*, April 4, 1943, X7.

——. *Pastures of Plenty: A Self-Portrait*. Edited by Dave Marsh and Harold Leventhal. New York: HarperCollins, 1990.

Haines, Herbert H. *Black Radicals and the Civil Rights Mainstream, 1954–1970*. Knoxville: University of Tennessee Press, 1988.

Hale, Grace Elizabeth. *Making Whiteness: The Culture of Segregation in the South, 1890–1940*. New York: Vintage, 1998.

Halker, Clark. "Jesus Was a Carpenter: Labor Song-Poets, Labor Protest, and True Religion in Gilded Age America." *Labor History* 32, no. 2 (1991): 273–89.

Halliwell, Martin. *American Culture in the 1950s*. Edinburgh: Edinburgh University Press, 2007.

Hamm, Charles. *Yesterdays: Popular Song in America*. New York: Norton, 1979.

Hampton, Henry, and Steve Fayer, with Sarah Flynn. *Voices of Freedom: An Oral History of the Civil Rights Movement from the 1950s through the 1980s*. New York: Bantam, 1990.

Handy, W. C. *Father of the Blues: An Autobiography*. 1941. Reprint, New York: Da Capo, 1969.

Haralambos, Michael. *Right On: From Blues to Soul in Black America*. New York: Drake, 1975.

Harding, Rachel, and Vincent Harding. "Singing to Freedom." *Sojourners* 33, no. 8 (2004): 32–35.

Harding, Vincent. *Hope and History: Why We Must Share the Story of the Movement*. Maryknoll, NY: Orbis, 1990.

——. *There Is a River: The Black Struggle for Freedom in America*. New York: Harcourt Brace Jovanovich, 1981.

——. "Wrestling Toward the Dawn: The Afro-American Freedom Movement and the Changing Constitution." *Journal of American History* 74, no. 3 (1987): 718–39.

Hareven, Tamara K. *Eleanor Roosevelt: An American Conscience*. Chicago: Quadrangle, 1968.

Harrah-Conforth, Bruce Michael. "Laughing Just to Keep from Crying: Afro-American Folksong and the Field Recordings of Lawrence Gellert." Master's thesis, Indiana University, 1980.

Harris, J. William. *Deep Souths: Delta, Piedmont, and Sea Island Society in the Age of Segregation*. Baltimore: Johns Hopkins University Press, 2001.

Harris, M. W. *The Rise of Gospel Blues: The Music of Thomas Andrew Dorsey in the Urban Church*. New York: Oxford University Press, 1992.

Harris, Michelle P. "Searching for Meaning Beyond the Spiritual." Master's thesis, University of Wisconsin, Madison, 1993.

Harris, Middleton A. *The Black Book*. New York: Random House, 1974.

Harris, William H. *The Harder We Run: Black Workers Since the Civil War*. New York: Oxford University Press, 1982.

Harrison, Alferdteen, ed. *Black Exodus: The Great Migration from the*

American South. Jackson: University Press of Mississippi, 1991.

Harrison, Daphne Duval. *Black Pearls: Blues Queens of the 1920s.* New Brunswick: Rutgers University Press, 1988.

Harvey, Mark Sumner. "New World A'Comin': Religious Perspectives on the Legacy of Duke Ellington." *Black Sacred Music: A Journal of Theomusicology* 6, no. 1 (1992): 146–54.

Harvey, Paul. *Freedom's Coming: Religious Culture and the Shaping of the South from the Civil War Through the Civil Rights Era.* Chapel Hill: University of North Carolina Press, 2005.

Haskins, Jim. *Queen of the Blues: A Biography of Dinah Washington.* New York: William Morrow, 1987.

Hay, Fred. "The Sacred/Profane Dialect in Delta Blues: The Life and Lyrics of Sonny Boy Williamson." *Phylon* 48, no. 4 (1987): 317–26.

Haydon, Geoffrey, and Dennis Marks, eds. *Repercussions: A Celebration of African-American Music.* London: Century, 1985.

Hayes, Eileen M. "Theorizing Gender, Culture, and Music." *Women and Music: A Journal of Gender and Culture* 10 (2006): 71–79.

Hayes, Eileen M., and Linda F. Williams, eds. *Black Women and Music: More Than Blues.* Urbana: University of Illinois Press, 2007.

Hayes, Roland. *My Songs: Aframerican Religious Folk Songs Arranged and Interpreted by Roland Hayes.* Boston: Little, Brown, 1948.

Hays, Lee. "Lee Hays." *People's Songs Bulletin*, February–March 1947, 11.

———. "'Let the Will . . .': The Deep South Is Using Its Old Hymns to Aid Farm-Worker Unionization; Here Are a Few Examples." *New Masses*, August 1939, 15.

Hazzard-Gordon, Katrina. *Jookin': The Rise of Social Dance Formations in African-American Culture.*

Philadelphia: Temple University Press, 1990.

Heilbut, Anthony. *The Gospel Sound: Good News and Bad Times.* 1971. Reprint, New York: Limelight Editions, 1989.

———. "'If I Fail, You Tell the World I Tried': Reverend W. Brewster on Records." *Black Music Research Journal* 7 (1987): 119–26.

Herskovits, Melville J. *The Myth of the Negro Past.* 1941. Reprint, Boston: Beacon, 1958.

Herzog, Frederick. *Liberation Theology: Liberation in the Light of the Fourth Gospel.* New York: Seabury Press, 1972.

"'He's Going Free!' Cry Detroit Workers in New Song About Jas. Victory." *Daily Worker*, June 30, 1934, 7.

Hicks, James L. "King Emerges as Top Negro Leader." *New York Amsterdam News*, June 1, 1957, 1, 36–37.

Higginson, Thomas Wentworth. "Negro Spirituals." *Atlantic Monthly*, June 7, 1867, 685–94.

Hille, Waldemar. "Freedom Songs—Compared to—Union Songs." *Et tu* 3 (December 1964): 1–3.

———. *The People's Song Book.* New York: Oak, 1948.

Hilmes, Michele. *Radio Voices: American Broadcasting, 1922–1952.* Minneapolis: University of Minnesota Press, 1997.

Hobson, Charles. "Hall Johnson: Preserver of the Negro Spiritual." *The Crisis*, November 1966, 480–85.

Hodenfield, Chris, and Tim Cahill, eds. "Mahalia Jackson Dead at 60." *Rolling Stone*, March 2, 1972, 18–19.

Hogan, Moses, ed. *The Oxford Book of Spirituals.* Oxford: Oxford University Press, 2002.

Honey, Michael Keith. *Black Workers Remember: An Oral History of Segregation, Unionism, and the Freedom Struggle.* Berkeley: University of California Press, 1999.

———. *Going Down Jericho Road: The Memphis Strike, Martin Luther King's*

Last Campaign. New York: Norton, 2007.

———. "The Popular Front in the American South: The View from Memphis." *International Labor and Working-Class History* 30 (Fall 1986): 44–58.

———. "Promoting Labor's Heritage of Solidarity: The Great Labor Arts Exchange." *International Labor and Working-Class History* 36 (Fall 1989): 90–92.

Hoopes, Roy. *Americans Remember the Home Front: An Oral Narrative.* New York: Hawthorne, 1977.

Horton, Aimee Isgrig. *The Highlander Folk School: A History of Its Major Programs, 1932–1961.* Brooklyn: Carlson, 1989.

Horton, James Oliver, and Lois E. Horton. *In Hope of Liberty: Culture, Community, and Protest Among Northern Free Blacks, 1700–1860.* New York: Oxford University Press, 1997.

Horton, Myles, with Judith Kohl and Herbert Kohl. *The Long Haul: An Autobiography.* New York: Doubleday, 1990.

Hoven, Margaret, and David Earle Anderson. "From the Church to the Union Hall: The Songs of Working People." *Sojourners* 25, no. 5 (1996): 48–52.

Huckaby, Elizabeth. *Crisis at Central High: Little Rock, 1957–58.* Baton Rouge: Louisiana State University Press, 1980.

Hughes, Langston. *Good Morning Revolution: Uncollected Social Protest Writings by Langston Hughes.* Edited by Faith Berry. New York: Lawrence Hill, 1973.

Hunter, Tera W. *To 'Joy My Freedom: Southern Black Women's Lives and Labors After the Civil War.* Cambridge: Harvard University Press, 1998.

Hurston, Zora Neale. *The Sanctified Church.* New York: Marlowe, 1981.

Hustad, Donald P. *The Worshiping Church: A Hymnal.* Carol Stream, IL: Hope, 1990.

Hutchinson, George, ed. *The Cambridge Companion to the Harlem Renaissance.* Cambridge: Cambridge University Press, 2007.

Hutter, W. H., and Ray H. Abrams. "Copperhead Newspapers and the Negro." *Journal of Negro History* 20, no. 2 (1935): 131–52.

Hyatt, Marshall, ed. *The Afro-American Cinematic Experience: An Annotated Bibliography and Filmography.* Wilmington, DE: Scholarly Resources, 1983.

IWW Songs: To Fan the Flames of Discontent; Facsimile Reprint of the Popular Nineteenth Edition, 1923. Chicago: Charles H. Kerr, 1989.

Jackson, George Pullen. *Down-East Spirituals and Others.* New York: Augustin, 1942.

———. *White and Negro Spirituals: Their Life and Kinship.* New York: Augustin, 1943.

———. *White Spirituals in the Southern Uplands: The Story of the Fasola Folk, Their Songs, Singings, and "Buckwheat Notes."* Chapel Hill: University of North Carolina Press, 1933.

Jackson, Irene V. "Afro-American Gospel Music and Its Social Setting with Special Attention to Roberta Martin." PhD diss., Wesleyan University, 1974.

———, ed. *More Than Dancing: Essays on Afro-American Music and Musicians.* Westport, CT: Greenwood, 1985.

Jackson, John A. *American Bandstand: Dick Clark and the Making of a Rock 'n' Roll Empire.* New York: Oxford University Press, 1997.

Jackson, Mahalia, as told to Alfred Duckett. "My Love Life: Why I Agreed to Write This Series." *Chicago Defender,* June 30, 1956, 8.

Jackson, Mahalia, with Evan McLeod Wylie. *Movin' On Up.* New York: Hawthorn, 1966.

Jacobs, Harriet A. *Incidents in the Life of a Slave Girl: Written by Herself.* 1987.

Reprint, Cambridge: Harvard
University Press, 2000.

Jacoway, Elizabeth. *Turn Away Thy Son: Little Rock, the Crisis That Shocked the Nation*. New York: Free Press, 2007.

Jernegan, Marcus W. "Slavery and Conversion in the American Colonies." *American Historical Review* 21 (April 1916): 504–27.

Jessye, Eva A. *My Spirituals*. New York: Robbins-Engel, 1927.

Jezer, Marty. *The Dark Ages: Life in the United States, 1945–1960*. Boston: South End Press, 1982.

Johnson, Charles, and Bob Adelman. *King: A Photobiography of Martin Luther King, Jr.* New York: Viking Studio, 2000.

Johnson, Daniel M., and Rex R. Campbell. *Black Migration in America: A Social Demographic History*. Durham: Duke University Press, 1981.

Johnson, James Weldon, and J. Rosamond Johnson, eds. *The Book of American Negro Spirituals*. New York: Viking, 1925.

Jones, James. *From Here to Eternity*. New York: Charles Scribner's Sons, 1951.

Jones, Landon Y. *Great Expectations: America and the Baby Boom Generation*. New York: Coward, McCann and Geoghegan, 1980.

Jones, LeRoi. *Black Music*. Westport, CT: Greenwood, 1980.

———. *Blues People*. 1963. Reprint, Edinburgh: Payback Press, 1995.

Jones, LeRoi, and Larry Neal, eds. *Black Fire: An Anthology of Afro-American Writing*. New York: William Morrow, 1968.

Josephson, Barney, with Terry Trilling-Josephson. *Café Society: The Wrong Place for the Right People*. Urbana: University of Illinois Press, 2009.

Joyner, Charles. *Down by the Riverside: A South Carolina Slave Community*. Urbana: University of Illinois Press, 1984.

———. *Shared Traditions: Southern History and Folk Culture*. Urbana: University of Illinois Press, 1999.

Jubilee and Plantation Songs: Characteristic Favorites, as Sung by the Hampton Students, Jubilee Singers, Fisk University Students, and Other Concert Companies; Also, a Number of New and Pleasing Selections. Boston: Oliver Ditson, 1887.

Kamin, Jonathan. "The White R&B Audience and the Music Industry, 1952–1956." *Popular Music and Society* 6, no. 2 (1978): 150–67.

Keiler, Allan. *Marian Anderson: A Singer's Journey*. New York: Scribner, 2000.

Kelley, Robin D. G. *Race Rebels: Culture, Politics, and the Black Working Class*. New York: Free Press, 1996.

"Kentucky Miner's Song (Written and Sung by the Kentucky Strike Executive Committee in Tazewell Jail)." *Daily Worker*, April 2, 1932, 4.

Kernan, Michael. "Conveying History Through Song." *Smithsonian* 29, no. 11 (1999): 32–34.

Kester, Howard. *Revolt Among the Sharecroppers*. 1936. Reprint, New York: Arno Press and the *New York Times*, 1969.

King, Coretta Scott. *My Life with Martin Luther King, Jr.* London: Hodder and Stoughton, 1970.

———, ed. *The Words of Martin Luther King, Jr.* New York: Newmarket Press, 1987.

King, Martin Luther, Jr. "Honoring Dr. Du Bois." *Freedomways* 8, no. 2 (1968): 104–11.

———. *Stride Toward Freedom: The Montgomery Story*. New York: Harper and Brothers, 1958.

King, Martin Luther, Sr., with Clayton Riley. *Daddy King: An Autobiography*. New York: William Morrow, 1980.

King, Richard H. *Civil Rights and the Idea of Freedom*. New York: Oxford University Press, 1992.

King, Richard H., and Helen Taylor. *Dixie Debates: Perspectives on Southern*

Cultures. New York: New York University Press, 1996.

"King of the Gospel Writers: Thomas A. Dorsey Gave Up Blues to Write World's Best Known Gospel Songs." *Ebony,* November 1962, 122–27.

Kirk, Elise K. *Music at the White House: A History of the American Spirit.* Urbana: University of Illinois Press, 1986.

Kirk-Duggan, Cheryl Ann. "Theodicy and the Redacted African-American Spirituals of the 1960s Civil Rights Movement." Ph.D. diss., Baylor University, 1992.

Kluger, Richard. *Simple Justice: The History of Brown v. Board of Education and Black America's Struggle for Equality.* New York: Knopf, 1976.

Koppelman, Robert S., ed. *"Sing Out, Warning! Sing Out, Love!": The Writings of Lee Hays.* Amherst: University of Massachusetts Press, 2003.

Kornbluh, Joyce L., ed. *Rebel Voices: An IWW Anthology.* 1964. Reprint, Ann Arbor: University of Michigan Press, 1972.

Korson, George. *Coal Dust on the Fiddle: Songs and Stories of the Bituminous Industry.* Philadelphia: University of Pennsylvania Press, 1943.

———. *Minstrels of the Mine Patch.* Philadelphia: University of Pennsylvania Press, 1938.

Kosokoff, Stephen, and Carl W. Carmichael. "The Rhetoric of Protest: Song, Speech, and Attitude Change." *Southern Speech Journal* 35 (Summer 1970): 295–302.

Kostelanetz, Richard, ed. *Aaron Copland: A Reader; Selected Writings, 1923–1972.* New York: Routledge, 2004.

Koster, Rick. *Louisiana Music: A Journey from R&B to Zydeco, Jazz to Country, Blues to Gospel, Cajun Music to Swamp Pop to Carnival Music and Beyond.* New York: Da Capo, 2002.

Kramer, Barbara. *Mahalia Jackson: The Voice of Gospel and Civil Rights.* Berkeley Heights, NJ: Enslow, 2003.

Kramer, Gary. "Record Firm Rule of Thumb Slips from Fickle Public Pulse." *Billboard,* December 22, 1956, 1, 22.

Larkin, Colin, ed. *The Encyclopedia of Popular Music.* New York: Oxford University Press, 2006.

Larkin, Margaret. "Ella May's Songs." *The Nation,* October 9, 1929, 382–83.

———. "The Story of Ella May." *New Masses,* November 1929, 3–4.

Lassiter, Matthew D., and Joseph Crespino, eds. *The Myth of Southern Exceptionalism.* Oxford: Oxford University Press, 2010.

Lee, Ulysses. *The Employment of Negro Troops.* Washington, DC: Center of Military History, United States Army, 1963.

Lefever, Harry G. *Undaunted by the Fight: Spelman College and the Civil Rights Movement, 1957–1967.* Macon: Mercer University Press, 2005.

Lemann, Nicholas. *The Promised Land: The Great Migration and How It Changed America.* New York: Knopf, 1991.

Levine, Lawrence W. *Black Culture and Black Consciousness: Afro-American Folk Thought from Slavery to Freedom.* New York: Oxford University Press, 1977.

Levy, Peter B. "The New Left and Labor: The Early Years, 1960–1963." *Labor History* 31, no. 3 (1990): 294–321.

Lewis, David Levering. *King: A Biography.* 3rd ed. Urbana: University of Illinois Press, 2013.

———. *King: A Critical Biography.* New York: Praeger, 1970.

———. *W. E. B. Du Bois: Biography of a Race, 1868–1919.* New York: Holt, 1993.

Lewis-Colman, David M. *Race Against Liberalism: Black Workers and the UAW in Detroit.* Urbana: University of Illinois Press, 2008.

Lhamon, W. T., Jr. *Raising Cain: Blackface Performance from Jim Crow to Hip Hop.* Cambridge: Harvard University Press, 1998.

Lichtenstein, Nelson. *State of the Union: A Century of American Labor.* Princeton: Princeton University Press, 2002.

Lieberman, Robbie. *"My Song Is My Weapon": People's Songs, American Communism, and the Politics of Culture, 1930–1950.* Urbana: University of Illinois Press, 1989.

Lincoln, C. Eric, ed. *The Black Experience in Religion.* Garden City, NY: Anchor, 1974.

Lincoln, C. Eric, and Lawrence H. Mamiya. *The Black Church in the African American Experience.* Durham: Duke University Press, 1990.

"Line of March." *Jet*, December 15, 1960, 37.

Lipsitz, George. *Midnight at the Barrelhouse: The Johnny Otis Story.* Minneapolis: University of Minnesota Press, 2010.

———. *Rainbow at Midnight: Labor and Culture in the 1940s.* Urbana: University of Illinois Press, 1981.

———. *Time Passages: Collective Memory and American Popular Culture.* Minneapolis: University of Minnesota Press, 1990.

"Little 'Little White House': FDR's Favorite Musician Builds Replica of President's Home." *Ebony*, May 1, 1948, 26–27.

Litwack, Leon F. *Been in the Storm So Long: The Aftermath of Slavery.* New York: Knopf, 1979.

———. *North of Slavery: The Negro in the Free States, 1790–1860.* Chicago: University of Chicago Press, 1961.

———. *Trouble in Mind: Black Southerners in the Age of Jim Crow.* New York: Knopf, 1999.

Locke, Alain. *The Negro and His Music: Negro Art, Past and Present.* 1936. Reprint, New York: Arno Press and the *New York Times*, 1969.

Logue, Cal M. "Rhetorical Ridicule of Reconstruction Blacks." *Quarterly Journal of Speech* 62 (December 1976): 400–409.

Lomax, Alan. *Folk Song Style and Culture.* Washington, DC: American Association for the Advancement of Science, 1968.

———. *The Land Where the Blues Began.* New York: Pantheon, 1993.

———. *Mister Jelly Roll: The Fortunes of Jelly Roll Morton, New Orleans Creole and "Inventor of Jazz."* 1950. Reprint, Berkeley: University of California Press, 1973.

Lomax, Alan, Woody Guthrie, and Pete Seeger, eds. *Hard Hitting Songs for Hard-Hit People.* New York: Oak, 1967.

Lomax, Louis. *The Negro Revolt.* 1962. Reprint, New York: Perennial Library, 1971.

Long, Richard A., and Eugenia W. Collier, eds. *Afro-American Writing: Prose and Poetry.* University Park: Pennsylvania State University Press, 1985.

Lornell, Kip. *"Happy in the Service of the Lord": Afro-American Gospel Quartets in Memphis.* Urbana: University of Illinois Press, 1988.

———. *Virginia's Blues, Country, and Gospel Records, 1902–1943.* Lexington: University Press of Kentucky, 1989.

Lott, Eric. *Love and Theft: Blackface Minstrelsy and the American Working Class.* New York: Oxford University Press, 1993.

Love, Nancy S. *Musical Democracy.* Albany: State University of New York Press, 2006.

Love, Richard. "In Defiance of Custom and Tradition: Black Tobacco Workers and Labor Unions in Richmond, Virginia, 1937–1941." *Labor History* 35, no. 1 (1994): 25–47.

Lovell, John, Jr. *Black Song: The Forge and Flame; The Story of How the Afro-American Spiritual Was Hammered Out.* 1972. Reprint, New York: Paragon House, 1986.

———. "The Social Implication of the Negro Spiritual." *Journal of Negro Education* 8, no. 4 (1939): 634–43.

Lowry, Beverly. *Harriet Tubman: Imagining a Life.* New York: Doubleday, 2007.

Lumpkin, Grace. "A Southern Cotton Mill Rhyme." *New Masses*, May 1930, 8.

Lynch, Timothy P. *Strike Songs of the Depression*. Jackson: University Press of Mississippi, 2001.

Lyon, Danny. *Memories of the Southern Civil Rights Movement*. Chapel Hill: University of North Carolina Press, 1992.

Mabee, Carleton, with Susan Mabee Newhouse. *Sojourner Truth: Slave, Prophet, Legend*. New York: New York University Press, 1993.

MacDonald, J. Fred. *Don't Touch That Dial!: Radio Programming in American Life, 1920–1960*. Chicago: Nelson-Hall, 1979.

Mackay, Forrest. "Ballads of the People's Front." *Daily Worker*, February 17, 1938, 7.

Magness, Perre. "Brewster a Father of Gospel Music." *Memphis Commercial Appeal*, June 8, 2000, CC2.

"Mahalia Jackson, Gospel Singer, Presents Sixth Annual Recital in Carnegie Hall." *New York Times*, November 19, 1956, 39.

"Mahalia Sings in History Wk. Concert Feb. 9." *New York Amsterdam News*, February 8, 1957, 12.

Malkin, John. *Sounds of Freedom: Musicians on Spirituality and Social Change*. Berkeley, CA: Parallax Press, 2005.

Marable, Manning, and Leith Mullings, eds. *Let Nobody Turn Us Around: An African American Anthology*. 2nd ed. Lanham, MD: Rowman and Littlefield, 2009.

Marsh, J. B. T. *The Story of the Jubilee Singers: With Their Songs*. 1881. Reprint, New York: Negro Universities Press, 1969.

Mason, Lucy Randolph. *To Win These Rights: A Personal Story of the CIO in the South*. Westport, CT: Greenwood, 1952.

Maund, Alfred. "We Will All Stand Together." *The Nation*, March 3, 1956, 168.

McIlhenny, E. A. *Befo' de War Spirituals: Words and Melodies*. Boston: Christopher, 1933.

McKnight, Gerald D. *The Last Crusade: Martin Luther King, Jr., the FBI, and the Poor People's Campaign*. Boulder, CO: Westview Press, 1998.

Meier, August, Elliott Rudwick, and Francis L. Broderick. *Black Protest Thought in the Twentieth Century*. 2nd ed. Indianapolis: Bobbs-Merrill, 1971.

Melton, J. Gordon. *Encyclopedia of American Religions*. 7th ed. Detroit: Thomson Gale, 2003.

Mendelsohn, Jack. *The Martyrs: Sixteen Who Gave Their Lives for Racial Justice*. New York: Harper and Row, 1966.

Merriam, Alan P. *African Music in Perspective*. New York: Garland, 1982.

———. *The Anthropology of Music*. Evanston: Northwestern University Press, 1964.

Miller, Jim, ed. *The Rolling Stone Illustrated History of Rock and Roll*. New York: Rolling Stone Press, 1980.

Miller, Karl Hagstrom. *Segregating Sound: Inventing Folk and Pop Music in the Age of Jim Crow*. Durham: Duke University Press, 2010.

Miller, Keith D. *Voice of Deliverance: The Language of Martin Luther King, Jr., and Its Sources*. New York: Free Press, 1992.

Minor, DoVeanna S. Fulton. "'Come Through the Water, Come Through the Flood': Black Women's Gospel Practices and Social Critique." *Journal of Religion and Society* 13 (2011): 1–26.

Minton, John. *78 Blues: Folksongs and Phonographs in the American South*. Jackson: University Press of Mississippi, 2008.

Mitchell, Henry H. *Black Church Beginnings: The Long-Hidden Realities of the First Years*. Grand Rapids, MI: Eerdmans, 2004.

Mitchell, Margaret. *Gone with the Wind*. 1936. Reprint, New York: Scribner, 1964.

Moore, Allan, ed. *The Cambridge Companion to Blues and Gospel Music*. Cambridge: Cambridge University Press, 2002.

Moore, Christopher Paul. *Fighting for America: Black Soldiers—The Unsung Heroes of World War II*. New York: One World/Ballantine, 2005.

Moore, LeRoy, Jr. "From Profane to Sacred America: Religion and the Cultural Revolution in the United States." *Journal of the American Academy of Religion* 39, no. 3 (1971): 321–38.

Moreno, Paul D. *Black Americans and Organized Labor: A New History*. Baton Rouge: Louisiana State University Press, 2006.

Morgenstern, Dan. "Freedom Now." *Metronome* 78 (March 1961): 51.

Morris, Aldon D. *The Origins of the Civil Rights Movement: Black Communities Organizing for Change*. New York: Free Press, 1984.

Mosher, Craig. "Ecstatic Sounds: The Influence of Pentecostalism on Rock and Roll." *Popular Music and Society* 31, no. 1 (2008): 95–112.

Moye, J. Todd. *Let the People Decide: Black Freedom and White Resistance Movements in Sunflower County, Mississippi, 1945–1986*. Chapel Hill: University of North Carolina Press, 2004.

Murphy, Larry G., ed. *Down by the Riverside: Readings in African American Religion*. New York: New York University Press, 2000.

"Musicmakers: Clara Ward and Elvis Presley." *Jet*, February 27, 1964, 36.

Myrdal, Gunnar, with the assistance of Richard Sterner and Arnold Rose. *An American Dilemma: The Negro Problem and Modern Democracy*. Vol. 2. New York: Harper and Brothers, 1944.

Neal, Larry. "The Ethos of the Blues." *Black Sacred Music: A Journal of Theomusicology* 6, no. 1 (1992): 36–46.

Neal, Mark Anthony. *What the Music Said: Black Popular Music and Black Public Culture*. New York: Routledge, 1999.

"Negro Street Songs Revived by Melody Singers on WPA." *Daily Worker*, March 29, 1938, 7.

Nelson, Mark. "Claude and Joyce Williams: Pilgrims of Justice." *Southern Exposure* 1, nos. 3–4 (1974): 38–48.

Nelson, Scott Reynolds. *The Steel-Drivin' Man: John Henry, the Untold Story of an American Legend*. New York: Oxford University Press, 2006.

"New Defense Song Gains Wide Popularity in South." *Daily Worker*, November 7, 1933, 5.

Newfield, Jack. *A Prophetic Minority*. 1966. Reprint, New York: New American Library, 1970.

Newman, Richard S. *Freedom's Prophet: Bishop Richard Allen, the AME Church, and the Black Founding Fathers*. New York: New York University Press, 2009.

———. *Go Down, Moses: A Celebration of the African-American Spiritual*. New York: Clarkson Potter, 1998.

Nichols, Charles H. *Many Thousand Gone: The Ex-Slaves' Account of Their Bondage and Freedom*. Bloomington: Indiana University Press, 1974.

Niven, Penelope. *Carl Sandburg: A Biography*. New York: Charles Scribner's Sons, 1991.

Noble, Peter. *The Negro in Films*. London: Skelton Robinson, 1948.

Noble, Phil. *Beyond the Burning Bus: The Civil Rights Revolution in a Southern Town*. Montgomery: NewSouth, 2003.

Norris, Hoke. "A Singing Man Sits Silent at His Rousing Benefit." *Chicago Sun-Times*, November 29, 1957, 57.

Northrup, Herbert R. "The Negro and Unionism in the Birmingham, Ala., Iron and Steel Industry." *Southern Economic Journal* 10, no. 1 (1943): 27–40.

Null, Gary. *Black Hollywood: The Negro in Motion Pictures.* Secaucus, NJ: Citadel Press, 1975.

Odum, Howard W., and Guy B. Johnson. *The Negro and His Songs: A Study of Typical Negro Songs in the South.* Chapel Hill: University of North Carolina Press, 1925.

Oliver, Paul. *Broadcasting the Blues: Black Blues in the Segregation Era.* New York: Routledge, 2006.

———. *Songsters and Saints: Vocal Traditions on Race Records.* Cambridge: Cambridge University Press, 1984.

Olson, Lynne. *Freedom's Daughters: The Unsung Heroines of the Civil Rights Movement.* New York: Scribner, 2001.

Panish, Jon. *The Color of Jazz: Race and Representation in Postwar American Culture.* Jackson: University Press of Mississippi, 1997.

Parrish, Lydia. *Slave Songs of the Georgia Sea Islands.* 1942. Reprint, Hatboro, PA: Folklore Associates, 1965.

"People Are Talking About." *Jet,* October 10, 1957, 43.

Peterson, Richard A. "Why 1955? Explaining the Advent of Rock Music." *Popular Music* 9, no. 1 (1990): 97–116.

Phillips, Wayne. "Negroes Pledge to Keep Boycott." *New York Times,* February 24, 1956, 8.

Phull, Hardeep. *Story Behind the Protest Song: A Reference Guide to the 50 Songs That Changed the 20th Century.* Westport, CT: Greenwood, 2008.

Pike, Gustavus D. *The Jubilee Singers, and Their Campaign for Twenty Thousand Dollars.* Boston: Lee and Shepard, 1873.

"Pilgrimage Girds for Rights Cause." *New York Times,* May 4, 1957, 15.

Pinn, Anthony B. *Why, Lord? Suffering and Evil in Black Theology.* New York: Continuum, 1995.

Pitts, George E. "Belafonte Blasts 'Parlor Liberals.'" *Pittsburgh Courier,* April 30, 1960, 23.

Pitts, Walter F. *Old Ship of Zion: The Afro-Baptist Ritual in the African Diaspora.* New York: Oxford University Press, 1993.

Polenberg, Richard. *One Nation Divisible: Class, Race, and Ethnicity in the United States Since 1938.* New York: Viking, 1980.

Pope, Liston, ed. *Labor's Relation to Church and Community: A Series of Addresses.* New York: Harper and Brothers, 1947.

———. *Millhands and Preachers: A Study of Gastonia.* New Haven: Yale University Press, 1942.

Power, J. Tracy. *I Will Not Be Silent and I Will Be Heard: Martin Luther King, Jr., the Southern Christian Leadership Conference, and Penn Center.* Columbia: South Carolina Department of Archives and History, 1993.

Pratt, Ray. *Rhythm and Resistance: Explorations in the Political Uses of Popular Music.* Westport, CT: Praeger, 1990.

Preece, Harold. "Folk Music of the South." *New South,* March 1938, 13–14.

"Presents Party Gift." *Jet,* October 29, 1959, 31.

Price, Sammy. *What Do They Want? A Jazz Autobiography.* Urbana: University of Illinois Press, 1990.

"The Private Life of Billy Eckstine." *Ebony,* March 1949, 54–60.

Raboteau, Albert J. *Canaan Land: A Religious History of African Americans.* New York: Oxford University Press, 2001.

———. *Slave Religion: The "Invisible Institution" in the Antebellum South.* New York: Oxford University Press, 1978.

Radano, Ronald. "Denoting Difference: The Writing of the Slave Spirituals." *Critical Inquiry* 22, no. 3 (1996): 506–44.

———. *Lying Up a Nation: Race and Black Music.* Chicago: University of Chicago Press, 2003.

Radway, Janice A., Kevin K. Gaines, Barry Shank, and Penny Von Eschen. *American Studies: An Anthology*. Chichester: Wiley-Blackwell, 2009.

Rampersad, Arnold. *The Life of Langston Hughes*. Vol. 2, *1941–1967: I Dream a World*. 2nd ed. 1988. Oxford: Oxford University Press, 2002.

Ramsey, Guthrie P., Jr. *Race Music: Black Cultures from Bebop to Hip-Hop*. Berkeley: University of California Press, 2003.

Randall, Richard. "Fighting Songs of the Unemployed: The Traditions of Walt Whitman and Joe Hill Live Again in 1939." *Sunday Worker/ Progressive Weekly*, September 3, 1939, 2.

"R&B Cracking Racial Barriers in Southwest Where It's Bigger'n Ever." *Variety*, July 6, 1955, 43.

Ransby, Barbara. *Ella Baker and the Black Freedom Movement*. Chapel Hill: University of North Carolina Press, 2003.

Raper, Arthur F. *Tenants of the Almighty*. 1943. Reprint, New York: Arno Press and the *New York Times*, 1971.

Ravage, John W. *Black Pioneers: Images of the Black Experience on the North American Frontier*. Salt Lake City: University of Utah Press, 1997.

Reagon, Bernice Johnson. *If You Don't Go, Don't Hinder Me: The African American Sacred Song Tradition*. Lincoln: University of Nebraska Press, 2001.

———. "In Our Hands: Thoughts on Black Music." *Sing Out!* 24 (January– February 1976): 1–5.

———. "My Black Mothers and Sisters; or, On Beginning a Cultural Autobi- ography." *Feminist Studies* 8, no. 1 (1982): 81–96.

———. "Songs of the Civil Rights Movement 1955–1965: A Study in Culture History." Ph.D. diss., Howard University, 1975.

———. "'Uncle Sam Called Me': World War II Reflected in Black Music." *Southern Exposure* 1, nos. 3–4 (1974): 170–84.

———, ed. *We'll Understand It Better By and By: Pioneering African American Gospel Composers*. Washing- ton, DC: Smithsonian Institution Press, 1992.

Reddick, L. D. "Educational Programs for the Improvement of Race Rela- tions: Motion Pictures, Radio, the Press, and Libraries." *Journal of Negro Education* 13, no. 3 (1944): 367–89.

Reed, Teresa L. *The Holy Profane: Religion in Black Popular Music*. Lexing- ton: University Press of Kentucky, 2003.

Reuss, Richard A., and JoAnne C. Reuss. *American Folk Music and Left- Wing Politics, 1927–1957*. Lan- ham, MD: Scarecrow Press, 2000.

Richards, Dona Marimba. *Let the Circle Be Unbroken: The Implications of African Spirituality in the Dias- pora*. Lawrenceville, NJ: Red Sea Press, 1980.

Richmond, Michael L. "The Music of Labor: From Movement to Culture." *Legal Studies Forum* 23, nos. 1–2 (1999): 211–46.

Ricks, George Robinson. *Some Aspects of the Religious Music of the United States Negro: An Ethnomusicological Study with Special Emphasis on the Gospel Tradition*. New York: Arno Press, 1977.

Rieder, Jonathan. *The Word of the Lord Is upon Me: The Righteous Perfor- mance of Martin Luther King, Jr.* Cambridge, MA: Belknap Press, 2008.

Riesman, Bob. *I Feel So Good: The Life and Times of Big Bill Broonzy*. Chicago: University of Chicago Press, 2011.

Rijn, Guido Van. *Roosevelt's Blues: African- American Blues and Gospel Songs on FDR*. Jackson: University Press of Mississippi, 1997.

Rivlin, Gary. *Fire on the Prairie: Chicago's Harold Washington and the Politics of Race.* New York: Henry Holt, 1992.

Roach, Hildred. *Black American Music: Past and Present.* 2nd ed. Malabar, FL: Krieger, 1992.

Roberts, John Storm. *Black Music of Two Worlds.* New York: William Morrow, 1974.

Roberts, John W. *From Trickster to Badman: The Black Folk Hero in Slavery and Freedom.* Philadelphia: University of Pennsylvania Press, 1989.

Robeson, Paul, Jr. *The Undiscovered Paul Robeson: An Artist's Journey, 1898–1939.* New York: Wiley, 2001.

Robinson, Jo Ann Gibson. *The Montgomery Bus Boycott and the Women Who Started It.* Edited and foreword by David J. Garrow. Knoxville: University of Tennessee Press, 1987.

Robnett, Belinda. *How Long? How Long?: African American Women in the Struggle for Civil Rights.* New York: Oxford University Press, 1997.

Rodnitzky, Jerome L. "The Evolution of the American Protest Song." *Journal of Popular Culture* 3, no. 1 (1969): 35–45.

———. "The New Revivalism: American Protest Songs, 1945–1968." *South Atlantic Quarterly* 70, no. 1 (1971): 13–21.

Rodriguez, Junius P., ed. *Encyclopedia of Slave Resistance and Rebellion.* Vols. 1–2. Westport, CT: Greenwood, 2007.

Rodriguez, Marc S., ed. *Repositioning North American Migration History: New Directions in Modern Continental Migration, Citizenship, and Community.* Rochester: University of Rochester Press, 2004.

Rolontz, Bob, and Joel Friedman. "Teen-Agers Demand Music with a Beat, Spur Rhythm-Blues." *Billboard*, April 24, 1954, 1, 18.

Rose, Willie Lee, ed., with commentary. *A Documentary History of Slavery in North America.* New York: Oxford University Press, 1976.

———. *Rehearsal for Reconstruction: The Port Royal Experiment.* Indianapolis: Bobbs-Merrill, 1964.

Rosenthal, David H. *Hard Bop: Jazz and Black Music, 1955–1965.* New York: Oxford University Press, 1992.

Roy, William G. *Reds, Whites, and Blues: Social Movements, Folk Music, and Race in the United States.* Princeton: Princeton University Press, 2010.

Rubman, Kerill Leslie. "From 'Jubilee' to 'Gospel' in Black Male Quartet Singing." Master's thesis, University of North Carolina, 1980.

Rudwick, Elliott M. "The Niagara Movement." *Journal of Negro History* 42, no. 3 (1957): 177–200.

Russell, Don. "Meet the Almanac Singers: They Sing Hard-Hitting Songs That Belong to the People." *Daily Worker*, August 14, 1941, 7.

Russell, Jean. *God's Lost Cause: A Study of the Church and the Racial Problem.* Valley Forge, PA: Judson Press, 1969.

Rustin, Bayard. *Down the Line: The Collected Writings of Bayard Rustin.* Chicago: Quadrangle, 1971.

———. "Montgomery Diary." *Liberation* 1, no. 2 (1956): 7–8.

Salaam, Kalamu ya. "It Didn't Jes Grew: The Social and Aesthetic Significance of African American Music." *African American Review* 29, no. 2 (1995): 351–75.

Salmond, John A. *"My Mind Set on Freedom": A History of the Civil Rights Movement, 1954–1968.* Chicago: Ivan R. Dee, 1997.

Sandage, Scott A. "A Marble House Divided: The Lincoln Memorial, the Civil Rights Movement, and the Politics of Memory." *Journal of American History* 80, no. 1 (1993): 135–67.

Sandburg, Carl. *The American Songbag.* New York: Harcourt Brace Jovanovich, 1927.

Sanger, Kerran L. "Slave Resistance and Rhetorical Self-Definition: Spirituals as a Strategy." *Western Journal of*

Communication 59 (Summer 1995): 177–92.

Savage, Barbara Dianne. *Broadcasting Freedom: Radio, War, and the Politics of Race, 1938–1948.* Chapel Hill: University of North Carolina Press, 1999.

Scarborough, Dorothy. *On the Trail of Negro Folk-Songs.* Cambridge: Harvard University Press, 1925.

Scharf, Lois. *Eleanor Roosevelt: First Lady of American Liberalism.* Boston: Twayne, 1987.

Schatz, Philip. "Songs of the Negro Worker." *New Masses,* March 1938, 6–8.

Schell, Edwin A., and Mary Chisholm Foster. *The Junior Hymnal.* New York: Eaton and Mains, 1895.

Schneider, Mark Robert. *"We Return Fighting": The Civil Rights Movement in the Jazz Age.* Boston: Northeastern University Press, 2002.

Scholes, Percy. "John Brown's Body." In *The New Oxford Companion to Music,* vol. 1, edited by Denis Arnold, 1001–2. Oxford: Oxford University Press, 1983.

Schweinitz, Rebecca de. *If We Could Change the World: Young People and America's Long Struggle for Racial Equality.* Chapel Hill: University of North Carolina Press, 2009.

Schwerin, Jules. *Got to Tell It: Mahalia Jackson, Queen of Gospel.* New York: Oxford University Press, 1992.

Scott, William R., and William G. Shade, eds. *Upon These Shores: Themes in the African-American Experience, 1600 to the Present.* New York: Routledge, 2000.

Seeger, Pete. *The Incompleat Folksinger.* Edited by Jo-Metcalf-Schwartz. New York: Simon and Schuster, 1972.

———. *The Incompleat Folksinger.* 1972. Reprint, Lincoln: University of Nebraska Press, 1992.

Seeger, Pete, and Bob Reiser. *Everybody Says Freedom: A History of the Civil Rights Movement in Songs and Pictures.* New York: Norton, 1989.

Sernett, Milton C., ed. *Afro-American Religious History: A Documentary Witness.* Durham: Duke University Press, 1985.

———. *Bound for the Promised Land: African American Religion and the Great Migration.* Durham: Duke University Press, 1997.

Shapiro, Lynn, ed. *Black People and Their Culture: Selected Writings from the African Diaspora.* Washington, DC: Smithsonian Institution, Festival of American Folklife, 1976.

Sharp, Anne Wallace. *Coretta Scott King.* Detroit: Lucent, 2008.

Shelton, Robert, and David Gahr. *The Face of Folk Music.* New York: Citadel Press, 1968.

Shipton, Alyn. *A New History of Jazz.* London: Continuum, 2001.

Silverman, Jerry. *Just Listen to This Song I'm Singing: African-American History Through Song.* Brookfield, CT: Millbrook, 1996.

———. *Slave Songs.* New York: Chelsea House, 1994.

———. *Songs of Protest and Civil Rights: Traditional Black Music.* New York: Chelsea House, 1992.

Sitkoff, Harvard. *King: Pilgrimage to the Mountaintop.* New York: Hill and Wang, 2008.

———. "Racial Militancy and Interracial Violence in the Second World War." *Journal of American History* 58, no. 3 (1971): 661–81.

Sklaroff, Lauren Rebecca. *Black Culture and the New Deal: The Quest for Civil Rights in the Roosevelt Era.* Chapel Hill: University of North Carolina Press, 2009.

Small, Christopher. *Music of the Common Tongue: Survival and Celebration in African American Music.* 1987. Reprint, Middletown: Wesleyan University Press, 1999.

Smith, Chris. "Rev. W. Herbert Brewster." *Blues and Rhythm: The Gospel Truth* 34 (January 1988): 8.

Smith, Hale. "Paul Robeson, Civil Rights Activist: An Opinion." *Black Music*

Research Bulletin 11, no. 2 (1989): 8–9.

Smith, Kenneth L., and Ira G. Zepp, Jr. *Search for the Beloved Community: The Thinking of Martin Luther King, Jr.* Valley Forge, PA: Judson Press, 1974.

Smith, R. Drew, and Frederick C. Harris. *Black Churches and Local Politics: Clergy Influence, Organizational Partnerships, and Civic Empowerment.* Oxford: Rowman and Littlefield, 2005.

Smith, Timothy L. "Slavery and Theology: The Emergence of Black Christian Consciousness in Nineteenth-Century America." *Church History* 41, no. 4 (1972): 497–512.

Smith, Wes. *The Pied Pipers of Rock 'n' Roll: Radio Dee Jays of the 50s and 60s.* Marietta, GA: Longstreet Press, 1989.

Smith, William Raymond. "Hepcats to Hipsters." *New Republic*, April 21, 1958, 18–20.

"A Song Is Born: New Danny Kaye Picture Brings Together Top Jazzmen in Single Band." *Ebony*, May 1, 1948, 41–43.

Songs for Wallace, 2nd Edition. New York: People's Songs, ca. 1948.

Songs of the Workers: To Fan the Flames of Discontent. 34th ed. Chicago: Industrial Workers of the World, 1973.

Southern, Eileen. *The Music of Black Americans: A History.* New York: Norton, 1971.

———. *Readings in Black American Music.* 2nd ed. New York: Norton, 1983.

Spencer, Jon Michael. *The New Negroes and Their Music: The Success of the Harlem Renaissance.* Knoxville: University of Tennessee Press, 1997.

———. *Protest and Praise: Sacred Music of Black Religion.* Minneapolis: Fortress Press, 1990.

———. *Re-Searching Black Music.* Knoxville: University of Tennessee Press, 1996.

Stampp, Kenneth M. *The Peculiar Institution: Slavery in the Ante-Bellum South.* New York: Knopf, 1969.

Stange, Maren. *Bronzeville: Black Chicago in Pictures, 1941–1943.* New York: New Press, 2003.

Stewart, Jeffrey C., ed. *Paul Robeson: Artist and Citizen.* New Brunswick: Rutgers University Press and the Paul Robeson Cultural Center, 1998.

Stewart, Shelley, with Nathan Hale Turner, Jr. *The Road South: A Memoir.* New York: Warner, 2002.

Stowe, David W. *How Sweet the Sound: Music in the Spiritual Lives of Americans.* Cambridge: Harvard University Press, 2004.

Stuart, John, ed. *The Education of John Reed: Selected Writings.* New York: International, 1955.

Sullivan, Patricia. "Southern Reformers, the New Deal, and the Movement's Foundation." In *New Directions in Civil Rights Studies*, edited by Armstead L. Robinson and Patricia Sullivan, 81–104. Charlottesville: University Press of Virginia, 1991.

Sunnemark, Fredrik. *Ring Out, Freedom!: The Voice of Martin Luther King, Jr., and the Making of the Civil Rights Movement.* Bloomington: Indiana University Press, 2004.

Teachout, Terry. *Pops: A Life of Louis Armstrong.* Boston: Mariner, 2009.

Terkel, Studs. *And They All Sang: Adventures of an Eclectic Disc Jockey.* New York: New Press, 2005.

———. *Talking to Myself: A Memoir of My Times.* New York: Pantheon, 1977.

———. *Will the Circle Be Unbroken? Reflections on Death, Rebirth, and a Hunger for Faith.* New York: New Press, 2001.

Thrasher, Rev. Thomas R. "Alabama's Bus Boycott." *The Reporter*, March 8, 1956, 12–16.

Thurman, Howard. *"Deep River" and "The Negro Spiritual Speaks of*

Life and Death." 1945. Reprint, Richmond, IN: Friends United Press, 1975.

Tippett, Tom. *When Southern Labor Stirs.* New York: Jonathan Cape and Harrison Smith, 1931.

Titon, Jeff Todd. *Early Downhome Blues: A Musical and Cultural Analysis.* Urbana: University of Illinois Press, 1977.

Toll, Robert C. *Blacking Up: The Minstrel Show in Nineteenth-Century America.* New York: Oxford University Press, 1974.

"Tony Bennett Tells Why He Marched with Dr. King in Selma." *Jet*, April 6, 1992, 14–16.

Travis, Dempsey J. *An Autobiography of Black Chicago.* Chicago: Urban Research Press, 1981.

———. *An Autobiography of Black Politics.* Vol. 1. Chicago: Urban Research Press, 1987.

Trent, Lloyd E. "Freedom's People." *New Masses*, October 7, 1941, 10.

Trotter, James M. *Music and Some Highly Musical People.* 1878. Reprint, New York: Johnson, 1968.

Trotter, Joe William, Jr., ed. *The Great Migration in Historical Perspective: New Dimensions of Race, Class, and Gender.* Bloomington: Indiana University Press, 1991.

Truth, Sojourner. *Narrative of Sojourner Truth; A Bondswoman of Olden Time, Emancipated by the New York Legislature in the Early Part of the Present Century; with a History of Her Labors and Correspondence, Drawn from Her "Book of Life."* 1878. Reprint, New York: Arno Press and the *New York Times*, 1968.

"Unconstitutional La. Law Nixes Satchmo's Mixed Band: Why Louis Armstrong Can't Go Home Again." *Jet*, November 25, 1959, 56–60.

UNESCO. *African Music: Meeting in Yaoundé (Cameroon), 23–27 February 1970.* Paris: La Revue Musicale, 1972.

"Union Train (for Wallace)." *People's Songs Bulletin*, November 1948, 10.

Volk, Terese M. "Little Red Songbooks: Songs for the Labor Force of America." *Journal of Research in Music Education* 49, no. 1 (2001): 33–48.

Wald, Gayle. "From Spirituals to Swing: Sister Rosetta Tharpe and Gospel Crossover." *American Quarterly* 55, no. 3 (2003): 387–416.

———. *Shout, Sister, Shout!: The Untold Story of Rock-and-Roll Trailblazer Sister Rosetta Tharpe.* Boston: Beacon, 2007.

Walker, Wyatt Tee. "Freedom's Song: The Soulful Journal of the Negro Spiritual." *Negro Digest*, July 1963, 84–95.

———. *"Somebody's Calling My Name": Black Sacred Music and Social Change.* Valley Forge, PA: Judson Press, 1979.

———. *Spirits That Dwell in Deep Woods: The Prayer and Praise Hymns of the Black Religious Experience.* Chicago: GIA, 1991.

Wallis, Jim. "America's Original Sin: The Legacy of White Racism." *Sojourners*, November 1987, 15–17.

Ward, Brian. *Just My Soul Responding: Rhythm and Blues, Black Consciousness and Race Relations.* London: UCL Press, 1998.

———, ed. *Media, Culture, and the Modern African American Freedom Experience.* Gainesville: University Press of Florida, 2001.

———. *Radio and the Struggle for Civil Rights in the South.* Gainesville: University Press of Florida, 2004.

Ward, Brian, and Tony Badger, eds. *The Making of Martin Luther King and the Civil Rights Movement.* New York: New York University Press, 1996.

Ward-Royster, Willa, as told to Toni Rose. *How I Got Over: Clara Ward and the World-Famous Ward Singers.* Philadelphia: Temple University Press, 1997.

Warner, Jay. *The Billboard Book of American Singing Groups: A History, 1940–1990.* New York: Billboard, 1992.

Warren, Gwendolin Sims. *Ev'ry Time I Feel the Spirit.* New York: Henry Holt, 1998.

Warren, Robert Penn. *Who Speaks for the Negro?* New York: Random House, 1965.

Warren, Wilson J., Bruce Fehn, and Marianne Robinson. "They Met at the Fair: UPWA and the Farmer Labor Cooperation, 1944–1952." *Labor's Heritage: Quarterly of the George Meany Memorial Archives,* Fall 2000–Winter 2001, 19–36.

Washington, Booker T. *Up from Slavery.* 1901. Reprint, New York: Penguin, 1986.

Washington, Chester L. "'No Intention of Apologizing,' Lena Horne Says." *Pittsburgh Courier,* February 27, 1960, 2.

Washington, James Melvin. *A Testament of Hope: The Essential Writings of Martin Luther King, Jr.* San Francisco: Harper and Row, 1986.

Waters, Ethel, with Charles Samuels. *His Eye Is on the Sparrow: An Autobiography.* Garden City, NY: Doubleday, 1951.

Watters, Pat. *Down to Now: Reflections on the Southern Civil Rights Movement.* New York: Pantheon, 1971.

Webb, Sheyann, and Rachel West Nelson, as told to Frank Sikora. *Selma, Lord, Selma: Girlhood Memories of the Civil-Rights Days.* Tuscaloosa: University of Alabama Press, 1980.

Webber, Charles C. "The Church at Work in the Field of Labor Relations." *Religious Education* 53, no. 4 (1958): 369–73.

Weightman, Gavin. *The Industrial Revolutionaries: The Making of the Modern World, 1776–1914.* New York: Grove Press, 2007.

Weiss, Nancy J. *Farewell to the Party of Lincoln: Black Politics in the Age of FDR.* Princeton: Princeton University Press, 1983.

Weissman, Dick. *Which Side Are You On?: An Inside History of the Folk Music Revival in America.* New York: Continuum, 2005.

Werner, Craig. *A Change Is Gonna Come: Music, Race and the Soul of America.* New York: Plume, 1998.

West, Cornel. "On Afro-American Popular Music: From Bebop to Rap." *Black Sacred Music: A Journal of Theomusicology* 6, no. 1 (1992): 282–94.

——. *Prophetic Fragments.* Grand Rapids, MI: Eerdmans, 1988.

"We Swing, Too." *The Crisis,* November 1959, 575.

Wexler, Sanford. *An Eyewitness History of the Civil Rights Movement.* New York: Checkmark, 1993.

Whalum, Wendel Phillips. "Black Hymnody." *Review and Expositor* 70, no. 3 (1973): 341–55.

"What Kind of Singing Tomorrow?" *People's Songs,* November 1948, 2.

"When Mahalia Sings: Renowned Gospel Singer Runs Gamut from Deep Religious Conviction to Unbelievable Rapture." *Ebony,* January 1954, 34–38.

White, Newman I. *American Negro Folk-Songs.* Cambridge: Harvard University Press, 1928.

Whitfield, Stephen J. *A Death in the Delta: The Story of Emmett Till.* New York: Free Press, 1988.

Wigginton, Eliot, ed. *Refuse to Stand Silently By: An Oral History of Grass Roots Social Activism in America, 1921–64.* New York: Doubleday, 1991.

Wiley, Stephen R. "Songs of the Gastonia Textile Strike of 1929: Models of and for Southern Working-Class Women's Militancy." *North Carolina Folklore Journal* 30 (Fall–Winter 1982): 87–98.

Wilkerson, Isabel. *The Warmth of Other Suns: The Epic Story of America's Greatest Migration.* New York: Random House, 2010.

Willens, Doris. *Lonesome Traveler: The Life of Lee Hays.* New York: Norton, 1988.

Williams, Donnie, with Wayne Greenhaw. *The Thunder of Angels: The Montgomery Bus Boycott and the People Who Broke the Back of Jim Crow.* Chicago: Lawrence Hill, 2006.

Williams, Juan. *My Soul Looks Back in Wonder: Voices of the Civil Rights Experience.* New York: AARP/Sterling, 2004.

Williams, Julian. "Black Radio and Civil Rights: Birmingham, 1956–1963." *Journal of Radio Studies* 12, no. 1 (2005): 47–60.

Wilson, Jack S. "Newport: The Music." *down beat*, August 18, 1960, 18–19.

Wilson, Kirt H. "Interpreting the Discursive Field of the Montgomery Bus Boycott: Martin Luther King's Holt Street Address." *Rhetoric and Public Affairs* 8, no. 2 (2005): 299–326.

Wintz, Cary D., and Paul Finkelman, eds. *Encyclopedia of the Harlem Renaissance.* New York: Routledge, 2004.

Witalec, Janet, project ed. *Harlem Renaissance: A Gale Critical Companion.* Detroit: Thomson Gale, 2003.

Wolff, Daniel, S. R. Crain, Clifton White, and David Tenenbaum. *You Send Me: The Life and Times of Sam Cooke.* New York: Quill, 1996.

Wolff, William. "Songs That Express the Soul of a People." *People's (Daily) World*, November 24, 1939, 5.

———. "Use Traditional Tunes for New Union Songs." *Daily Worker*, November 16, 1939, 7.

Work, John W. *Folk Song of the American Negro.* 1915. Reprint, New York: Negro Universities Press, 1969.

Wright, Richard. *12 Million Black Voices.* 1941. Reprint, New York: Thunder's Mouth Press, 2002.

Writer's Congress: The Proceedings of the Conference Held in October 1943 Under the Sponsorship of the Hollywood Writer's Mobilization and the University of California. Berkeley: University of California Press, 1944.

Yurchenco, Henrietta. "Trouble in the Mines: A History in Song and Story by Women of Appalachia." *American Music* 9, no. 2 (1991): 209–24.

Zak, Albin J., III. *I Don't Sound Like Nobody: Remaking Music in 1950s America.* Ann Arbor: University of Michigan Press, 2010.

Zieger, Robert H. *For Jobs and Freedom: Race and Labor in America Since 1865.* Lexington: University Press of Kentucky, 2007.

———, ed. *Organized Labor in the Twentieth-Century South.* Knoxville: University of Tennessee Press, 1991.

Interviews and Oral History Transcriptions

Black Radio . . . Telling It Like It Was. Produced by Jacquie Gale Webb, Lex Gillespie, and Sonja Williams. Hosted by Lou Rawls. Programs 1–6, 9. Radio Smithsonian Transcript. Washington, DC: Smithsonian Institution, 1996.

Kennedy, Cleopatra. Interview by author. July 8, 2009, Birmingham. Tape recording, Institute for Oral History, Baylor University, Waco.

Lewis, John. Interview by author. May 20, 2009, Waco, TX. Tape recording, Institute for Oral History, Baylor University, Waco.

Smith, Stephen. "Radio Fights Jim Crow." *American RadioWorks*. American Public Media. February 2001. Transcript at http://americanradioworks .publicradio.org/features/jim _crow/transcript.html.

Online Sources

Black Americans in Congress. http:// history.house.gov/people/listing /D/Dawson,-William-Levi -(d000158)/.

Blake, John. "Freedom Riders Inspire New Generation of Arab Protest Leaders." CNN, May 15, 2011. http://www.cnn.com/2011/US/05/15/freedom.riders.arab/index.html.

Highlander Research and Education Center. http://highlandercenter.org/.

Newport Jazz Festival Index. http://newportjazzfest.org/index.php?pID=51.

Walking Montgomery: The 50th Anniversary of the Montgomery Bus Boycott and Annual Celebration of the Birthday of Martin Luther King, Jr. http://americanhistory.si.edu/.

Recordings

Alabama Christian Movement for Human Rights Choir. *We've Got a Job.* CM-1001. Dir. Carlton Reese. Released 1963. Recording of a live concert presented August 30, 1963, at L. R. Hall Auditorium. CD copy of original LP.

Anderson, Marian. *Spirituals.* RCA Victor Red Seal, LSC-2592 (M2RY-3539). Released 1962. Liner notes by Edward R. Murrow.

Leadbelly. *Negro Sinful Songs Sung by Lead Belly, Accompanying Himself on the Twelve-String Guitar.* Musicraft, 31. Released 1939. Liner notes by Alan Lomax.

Tharpe, Sister Rosetta. *The Original Soul Sister.* Proper Box, 51. Four-CD set. Recorded 1930s–40s. Released 2002. Liner notes by Joop Visser.

Various artists. *A Capella Gospel Singing.* Folklyric Records, FL-9045. Recorded 1937–52. Released ca. 1986. Liner notes by Ray Funk.

Various artists. *Folk Music of the United States: Afro-American Blues and Game Songs, and Ballads from the Archive of American Folk Song.* Edited by Alan Lomax. The Library of Congress Division of Music Recording Laboratory, Album 4. Released 1942. Liner notes.

Various artists. *Folk Music of the United States: Afro-American Spirituals, Work Songs, and Ballads from the Archive of American Folk Song.* Edited by Alan Lomax. The Library of Congress Division of Music Recording Laboratory, Album 8. Released 1942. Liner notes.

Various artists. *Folk Music of the United States: Negro Religious Songs and Services from the Archive of American Folk Song.* Edited by B. A. Botkin. The Library of Congress Division of Music Recording Laboratory, Album 10. Released 1943. Liner notes.

Various artists. *Folk Music of the United States: Negro Work Songs and Calls from the Archive of American Folk Song.* Edited by B. A. Botkin. The Library of Congress Division of Music Recording Laboratory, Album 8. Released 1943. Liner notes.

Various artists. *From Slavery 'Til Now: An Anthology of Negro Gospel and Spiritual Music.* Vee-Jay Records, VJS-8505. Released 1964.

Various artists. *From Spirituals to Swing: The Legendary 1938 and 1939 Carnegie Hall Concerts Produced by John Hammond.* Vanguard Records, 169/71-2. Three-CD set. Released 1999. Liner notes by Steve Buckingham, and reproduction of the original program.

Index